Further
From the Farm

By
Philip Potempa

With love, admiration and appreciation to my dear friend Irene Jakubowski, who was always at my side to lend a helping hand and support. Irene would always say: "Phil, you live a charmed life. Always have fun every chance you get, kiddo!" Here's to you, Irene . . . Cheers!

May 2007 - The author with dear friend Irene Jakubowski (1922-2008) at her home in Monticello, Ind. toasting good memories.

(Photo by Michael Berkos)

Copyright© 2010 ● ISBN: 978-1-59725-256-0

Published by Pediment Publishing, a division of The Pediment Group, Inc. www.pediment.com Printed in Canada

Contents

A Note From My Editor

Reading and editing Phil's weekly From the Farm column transports me to my childhood.

I spent a lot of time growing up in the kitchen with my grandma, Geneva Bridges, and I owe her a lot for teaching me the culinary ropes. From the basics like veggie pizza to the most amazing cream pies to Thanksgiving stuffing I still long for today, my grandma knew her way around a stove.

As a professional cook for a state park restaurant, she regularly spent hours on her feet in a hot kitchen. When she got home from work, she would toil in her own kitchen to cook a hot meal for her family. Not once did she complain. In fact, she loved taking care of her family.

And just like Phil's family gathered at Grandma Green's on Sundays, my family also gathered to share a meal and spend time together.

(Photo by Natalie Battaglia)

Unfortunately, most of my grandma's recipes left the earth with her because they were never written down.

But the recipes in Phil's From the Farm column help me re-create some of those mouth-watering, oh-so-familiar, comforting tastes. His passion for cooking runs deep, and he tells each tale with a familiar, friendly voice.

I often find myself smiling after reading From the Farm because it takes me to those days long gone, but never forgotten. I hope you use some of these creations to start your own family traditions.

Thanks, Phil.

Karin Saltanovitz

Features and Food Editor, The Times

March 8, 2010

Foreword

Philip's writings, including those about me, and especially my visits back home to Indiana, are always such a delight. What a talent with words he has — both in his columns in The Times and in his wonderful books. It's always such a pleasure spending time with Philip and his dear parents. Even while away, I get to enjoy that same company page after page in his warm and inviting books, both which I cherish and keep close at hand on a small shelf in my kitchen. These cooking-life-remembrance books are a joy! They always remind me of my friends and memories of my Indiana home.

Phil's April 2005 "welcome home" hug for Betsy at a party in her honor.

Betsy Palmer

March 17, 2010

Introduction

When I think of my many memories while growing up on our family farm, it's easy to realize just how some of the most basic everyday moments are so simple and satisfying.

While working in the yard in the summer heat, whether mowing grass, weeding or in the garden, nothing tastes quite as heavenly as a glass of cold well water in a Mason canning jar, poured by way of a hand-pitcher pump.

To this day, when I close my eyes at any water fountain, every sip transports me back to those summer days and to the best well water to ever flow from the ground.

In fact, when my aunts and uncles would drive out to the farm from Chicago for the weekends, they'd often take big glass jugs of water back with them to the city.

It's an easy-going approach, when you follow the lead of Paula Deen, shown here in March 2010.

These are memories that make writing my weekly From the Farm recipe column so enjoyable for me.

When I leave the newsroom and drive home to the farm, the minute my car turns from the road and down our long and winding gravel lane leading to the house and other buildings, there's a wonderful feeling of comfort, quiet and peace.

Of the many nice compliments I receive from my readers, I feel most grateful when someone tells me how my writings and memories help them and others recall their own personal stories with the same importance and meeting.

When you think of it, it's really not been that long since telephones had rotary dials and everyone shared the same telephone party line.

And somehow, we managed without cell phones, cable television, the Internet, personal computers, answering machines and

In April 2004, Phil serving up conversation and "Hummingbird Cakes" with Art Smith, chef to Oprah Winfrey.

Phil's first introduction to the great lady, herself, Julia Child, September 1993 in Deerfield, Ill.

microwaves.

It's hard to believe my From the Farm column only has been a weekly feature in The Times for just eight years.

Doesn't it seem so much longer than that?

But it first launched on the pages of The Times food section on April 27, 2002.

Time really does slip away. Now, here we are with a third "From the Farm" cookbook as a page-by-page companion to the original book, which published in 2004 and compiled the first two years of columns and recipes, followed by the second edition, released in 2007, providing readers with the next three years of material and musings.

That brings us to this book, which covers all of my treasured columns and recipes from May 2007 to May 2010, along with a few new recipes, stories and other familiar and famous faces included for fun.

I've always modeled my breezy, conversational style for sharing recipes and stories in similar style to the food great Julia Child, whom I feel so privileged and honored to have met and interviewed on a few occasions. She made everyone always feel at home with her smile and the warm tone of her voice.

Martha Stewart, Paula Deen and so many others follow this same folksy format, and it's always a welcoming atmosphere.

That's the reason the faces, names and memories served up in this book are truly an inviting reunion of sorts, with you the reader as the guest of honor.

But don't worry about not having brought a covered dish to share.

Just find a shady spot and sit back, relax and savor the return to good times you'll find with "Further From the Farm: Family Recipes and Memories of a Lifetime."

Philip Potempa
March 15, 2010

It's a relaxing and inviting scene: family conversation at the farm under the canopy of shade trees, setting the perfect tone to turn the page and enjoy the wonderful recipes, photos and memories that await.

Book launch party honors featured readers

May 2, 2007

Thank you to the many readers who called to congratulate me about the fifth anniversary of this farm column and the arrival of my second cookbook "More From the Farm."

A number of readers have already called in for the free Mother's Day weekend book-launch party May 12 from 1 to 3 p.m. at Borders Books and Music in Merrillville.

I received a nice letter recently from actress Betsy Palmer, who lives in New York City, thanking me for including her in my second cookbook.

As for Betsy Palmer, this game show claim-to-fame, who originally hails from East Chicago, Ind., likes to kid me about having included an old recipe from my file for her "Steak au Poivre," since she's been a vegetarian now for three decades. To balance things out, she gave me her favorite garlic bread recipe, to be included in my third cookbook, along with this note:

"Philip: This note is such a long time in coming. I so enjoy your cook and story book(s). And mostly because they mark a return trip to the region for my mind, heart and soul. Once a Hoosier, always a Hoosier, and then some! Your words, photos and family memories from the Midwest bring me great joy. Thank you and sweet love to your parents.

Lovingly, Betsy"

Betsy Palmer's Easy Garlic Bread

- Mix mayonnaise, garlic and Parmesan cheese together.

- Spread a thin layer of mayonnaise mixture on sliced French bread.

- Arrange bread slices on a baking sheet and then sprinkle each slice with a generous shake of black pepper.

- Bake in 350-degree oven for 3 to 4 minutes until brown. (Watch carefully, so bread doesn't burn.)

- Makes 6 slices.

INGREDIENTS:

3 tablespoons mayonnaise

2 teaspoons chopped and mashed fresh garlic

1 tablespoon Parmesan grated cheese

6 slices French bread, each 1-inch thick

Sprinkle black pepper

Blueberry muffin recipe's a century old

July 11, 2007

Even though it's been an early season for blueberries, the extreme hot and dry weather hasn't been kind for blueberry picking.

(Although my parents do have an extra-large bounty of wild raspberries and blackberries this season and my mom has been making lots of jam.)

Growing up, during the summer months, I used to pick blueberries for 22 cents a pound to earn money for back-to-school clothes (my mom's idea, I wanted to buy Batman and Archie comic books) at our neighbors' farm.

Last week, my parents went to my older sister Carol's family blueberry patch near Culver, Ind. for "the first pickings" and reported back about how "few and far between" the berries are. I was glad I wasn't still working my summers for Jerry and Dee Spenner at their fruit and produce farm in North Judson. Along the edge of our woods at the farm, we also still have lots of low-growing wild blueberries, which are very tiny, yet very sweet.

Whether from planted or wild bushes, either way, there are enough blueberries to use in today's recipe for a true blueberry muffin.

I always wanted this recipe and it was mailed to me last week from our family friend Irene Jakubowski, who turns 85 for her August birthday next month.

Irene, born and raised in LaPorte, Ind. before becoming a 40-year resident of Valparaiso. Ind. and then retiring to Monticello, Ind. in 1996, received this recipe from one of her good friends from Merrillville, Ind.

Margaret Massa, who I also have had the pleasure of meeting and spending time with over the years, is now retired and a resident at Lifecare Center at the Willows in Valparaiso. She will be 101 next month.

When I think of Margaret, I think of her bright red hair, just like the late Lucille Ball's and this delicious muffin recipe, which she says is more than 100 years old.

Margaret Massa's Blueberry Muffins

- Heat oven to 400 degrees. In a large bowl, mix together sugar, egg and oil.

- Slowly add in flour and baking powder, ending with milk. Mix until smooth, but do not over-mix.

- Fold in blueberries.

- Pour batter into greased muffin tins or tins lined with paper or foil cups.

- Bake for 20 to 25 minutes.

- Makes 1 dozen.

INGREDIENTS:

1/2 cup sugar

1 egg

1/2 cup oil

1-1/2 cups flour

2 teaspoons baking powder

1/2 cup milk

1 cup blueberries, rinsed and patted dry

Flat bread ideal for chili cook-off

February 6, 2008

It's once again time for the Lupus Foundation of Northwest Indiana's annual Chili Cook-Off and Tasting Event.

Each year, it's my pleasure to print the winning recipes in this column. Last year, I judged more than 20 entries from eager cooks helping to raise money for this good cause. In 2007, $4,100 was collected.

This year's event is from 4 to 6 p.m. March 1 at Merrillville High School.

Lupus is a debilitating, chronic autoimmune disease that causes inflammation and tissue damage to any organ system in the body. It can cause significant disability as well as death.

Approximately 1.5 million Americans have a form of lupus. Nine of 10 people with lupus are females. Lupus strikes most often during the prime of life, between ages 15 and 45.

Rather than share one of my own, or a family member's or friend's chili recipe in this space for today's column, I've learned in recent years as one of the event judges it's best not to let possible contestants sneak a peek at my personal chili favorites.

So instead, here's a wonderful complement for soup or chili, as well as the ideal companion for dips and spreads.

At an office event last month, I scored a big hit when I served today's featured recipe for Armenian Flat Cracker Bread with the roasted eggplant and sun-dried tomato spread recipe, which appeared in my second cookbook, "More From the Farm."

This recipe is from our farm-wife friend Joann Scamerhorn, and it stores well for weeks in an air-tight container.

Grandma Potempa looks intent scanning her garden in 1968 for hiding melons amidst the tall grass, as Uncle Joe, Uncle John, her niece, Sister Ephrem and Uncle Wally observe.

Easy Armenian Flat Cracker Bread

● Pour warm water into a large mixing bowl and sprinkle in yeast, allowing it to proof (dissolve and slightly foam).

● Add to the yeast and water, the melted butter, salt, sugar and 2 cups of flour and combine, adding enough additional flour to create a stiff dough. Work dough thoroughly (adding a dusting of flour if too sticky or a few drops of water if too dry) until it has a pliable consistency.

● Move the dough to a lightly floured board and knead it for 8-10 minutes.

● Butter the inside of a bowl and place the kneaded ball of dough inside, turning it to coat all sides with butter, cover with a towel or cloth, and place in a warm area and allow to set for 30 minutes or slightly more, until dough almost doubles in size.

● Preheat oven to 350 degrees.

● Punch dough down, and turn out onto a lightly floured board or surface and divide it into four equal parts.

● Roll out pieces of dough until flat. Place on ungreased cookie sheets or pizza pans or jelly roll pans and brush lightly with a little melted butter or olive oil.

INGREDIENTS:

1 cup warm water

1 envelope/package (1/4 ounce) active dry yeast

1/2 stick butter, melted, cooled

1-1/2 teaspoons salt

1 teaspoon granulated sugar

3-1/4 to 3-3/4 cups all-purpose flour

Parmesan cheese, garlic powder, dried parsley flakes, sea salt (if desired)

● If desired, lightly sprinkle the pieces of dough before baked, with a garnish of choice, like a little garlic powder and Parmesan cheese, dried parsley flakes or even just a little black pepper or salt.

● Bake 20 minutes, baking slightly longer for a crisper cracker or slightly less time for a softer, pita-bread consistency.

● After first batch is removed from the oven, immediately transfer while still warm to a cutting surface and cut into strips, or squares, or triangles, or just assorted odd sizes and shapes as desired, as the next batch is baking.

● Makes 20 servings.

Join me Sunday for free Thanksgiving program

November 12, 2008

DATELINE - - **Alberta** - - Philip Potempa is reporting from Canada this week while traveling.

Even though I'm in Canada this week for the 20th anniversary of Christmas in November event talking about holiday entertaining and recipe ideas, I'm also busy planning for a special event Sunday at the Hammond Public Library.

You're invited to a free program "Thanksgiving From the Farm" at 2:30 p.m. sponsored by The Times and the Hammond Historical Society and Friends of the Library which will feature some of our favorite ideas and traditions for November's holiday gatherings.

I'll be joined by my parents and my mother will help me with a food demonstration featuring a fresh baked batch of today's featured recipe for Chef Michael's Easy Cheddar and Chive Biscuits, which was given to me by Chef Michael Smith, one of the stars on the Food Network in Canada and also a guest presenter at this week's conference.

Despite the frost, we still have lots of fresh chives at the farm and there will be samples on Sunday for guests to enjoy. I know I'll be making these to have with our Thanksgiving dinner this year at the farm.

Plan to enjoy a nice, fun and relaxing afternoon of pleasant farm memories and good food in warm and inviting surroundings on a cold and gray Sunday afternoon.

Chef Michael's Easy Cheddar and Chive Biscuits

- Preheat oven to 450 degrees.

- In a medium-size bowl, whisk together flour, baking powder and salt.

- Add the cheddar and chives and stir to evenly combine.

- Add the cream and stir until the mixture just comes together.

- Knead the dough a few times and pat dough into a flat round about 1 inch thick and cut into 8 wedges.

- Place them on a baking sheet and bake for 12 to 15 minutes, until the tops are golden brown.

- Makes 10 large biscuits.

INGREDIENTS:

2 cups flour
1 tablespoon baking powder
1/2 teaspoon salt
1 cup cheddar cheese, grated
1/4 cup chives, minced
1 1/2 cups heavy whipping cream

Chili winners give new twists to old recipe favorite

March 14, 2007

It's always nice to know readers are really reading this column very closely.

Online reader Sharon Craig, of Noblesville, e-mailed me last week to assure that I would be printing the winning recipes, as promised, in this week's column.

Once again, I served on the judging panel for the annual Northwest Indiana Lupus Foundation's Chili Cook-Off at Merrillville High School March 3, 2007.

So, for Sharon and everyone else who has asked, here are two of the top recipes.

Christina Haverty of Merrillville, Ind. created the clever cactus chili, which makes 20 servings, but can easily be whittled down.

Kelly and Sean Hayes of Munster, Ind. won with a yummy chicken chili with buffalo wing seasoning accents.

Ranch Hands' Cactus Chili

- In a heavy frying pan, cook meat and onions until meat is lightly brown, stirring often.

- Rinse cactus and chop very fine.

- In a large stock pot, add meat mixture and cactus to all remaining ingredients.

- Heat chili to boiling, then reduce to a slow boil for 6 hours.

- Makes 20 servings.

CACTUS CHILI INGREDIENTS:

5 pounds lean ground beef

1-1/2 pounds ground pork

3 large onions, chopped

1 (16-ounce) jar cactus, drained with all added ingredients removed

1 (30-ounce) can hot chili beans, undrained

1 (30-ounce) can mild chili beans, undrained

2 (20-ounce) cans dark red kidney beans, undrained

1 (20-ounce) can light red kidney beans, undrained

2 (49-ounce) cans diced tomatoes

6 fresh jalapeño peppers, diced, seeds removed (handle with gloves)

2 fresh serrano peppers, diced, seeds removed (handle with gloves)

Chili powder to taste

Salt to taste

Pepper to taste

Crushed garlic to taste

GAME DAY CHILI INGREDIENTS:

2 pounds ground chicken

1/4 cup salad oil

1/4 cup margarine

3 ounces "spicy wings" seasoned coating mix

1 onion, chopped

16 ounces "buffalo wings" sauce

8 ounces tomato paste

2 tomatoes, diced

6 vine sweet mini peppers, diced

16 ounces kidney beans, drained

16 ounces pinto beans, drained

16 ounces water

1-1/2 tablespoons chili powder

1 teaspoon paprika

1 teaspoon sugar

1 teaspoon ginger

3 cloves garlic

Celery sticks for garnish

Game Day Buffalo Wings Chicken Chili

● Brown ground chicken in salad oil.

● Add margarine (for moisture) and spicy wings seasoned coating mix to meat and continue to cook a few minutes longer. Drain off drippings.

● Add onion and continue to cook until soft, adding a little water if necessary for even cooking.

● Transfer meat to slow cooker and add all remaining ingredients.

● Cook chili on low setting for 8 hours, stirring occasionally.

● Makes 10 servings.

Just the right blend of fresh ingredients and balance of seasonings result in an award-winning chili recipe.

(Photo by Michael Berkos)

Column's fifth anniversary celebrated with new book

March 21, 2007

May 2007 marks the fifth anniversary of my weekly "From the Farm" column.

April 27 is the actual anniversary date marking when the first column appeared on our Food cover.

I often say this column premiered at a time when our country needed a reminder to appreciate the simple gifts of everyday life.

When "From the Farm" launched on April 27, 2002, it was just six months after the devastation of Sept. 11, 2001, when our world and lives changed forever.

We're celebrating this fifth anniversary of "From the Farm" with a second cookbook -- "More Recipes From the Farm: Family Recipes and Memories of a Lifetime" (Pediment Press, 2007, $29.95).

While the dedication in my first book was to my parents, Chester and Peggy, I've made the dedication in this new cookbook to the faithful readers of this column each week.

The book will debut Mother's Day weekend, May 12.

Today's recipe is one I've been saving since I first sampled it last fall at the honors luncheon at Westville Correctional Center, where I teach a public speaking course on Friday mornings for Purdue North Central. This soup was prepared by Ron Edwards and his culinary arts class as part of the menu served at the event to recognize students/inmates with high grades. Created by 27-year-old Timothy Craft No. 123355, of Anderson, Ind., who is serving six years for burglary, this soup is simple, sinless and ideal for the Lenten season because you'll notice it doesn't contain any meat or even a broth base.

Cell Block Cream of Celery Soup #123355

- Melt butter in skillet and add onion, carrot and celery and heat until soft.

- Gently sprinkle flour and seasonings over mixture as it is heating and blend to combine, eliminating any lumps of flour.

- Transfer skillet mixture to a small soup pot, using a little water to rinse pan to assure all ingredients and seasoning have been transferred into soup pot.

- Add both the canned and whole milk and simmer 25 to 30 minutes to thicken, adjusting soup consistency as desired by adding more flour and water as needed.

- Adjust seasonings as desired.

- Serve hot with fresh bread or crackers.

- Makes 6 generous servings.

INGREDIENTS:

1 tablespoon butter

1 small onion, finely chopped

1 large carrot, diced

1 stalk of celery (about 6 or 7 ribs)

1 tablespoon all-purpose flour

2 teaspoons salt

Pinch white pepper

2 (12-ounce) cans evaporated milk

3 cups whole milk

Avocado an unusual chili garnish

September 19, 2007

Don't let the midweek sudden weather warm-up fool you.

It's still ideal chili weather.

Last weekend, I served as one of the judges at the chili cook-off at the annual fall festival in the village of Homewood, Ill.

As promised, today I'm sharing the grand prize winner's recipe.

It's the masterpiece of Jennifer Eick-Magan, 38, of Homewood, who teaches English as a second language at Prairie State College in Chicago Heights, Ill.

Jennifer was very proud that many of the ingredients she used came from her own garden. Her husband Jose and their daughter Sofia, 3, were equally excited about the contest win.

Although this recipe yields a large number of servings, it can be scaled down. As is, it's perfect for tailgating, bonfires and fall gatherings. And Jennifer says with her "good, heavy cooking pot" her chili never burned or stuck, despite the lengthy cooking time.

The name of the recipe includes the words "El Grito," which means "the yell or cry," as is the tradition to proclaim "Viva Mexico!" in honor of this week's Mexico's Independence Day.

Home-grown ingredients, as used by Jennifer Eick-Magan, of Homewood, Ill., help "better-than-all-the-rest" chili recipes (like hers) earn top honors.

(Photo by Michael Berkos)

INGREDIENTS:

1-1/2 pounds sweet/mild sausage

1-1/2 pounds hot sausage (such as chorizo)

6 tablespoons olive oil

4 chopped onions

6 to 8 cloves garlic

4 multicolored peppers (red, yellow, green), chopped

3 minced jalapenos

6 tablespoons chili powder

4 tablespoons ground cumin

3 tablespoons dried basil

3 tablespoons dried oregano

3 tablespoons paprika

Plenty of black pepper, to taste

Salt to taste

6 (28-ounce) cans crushed tomatoes

1 (8-ounce) can tomato paste

1 quart tomato juice

4 fresh garden tomatoes, peeled and diced

12 sun-dried tomatoes, diced

1 (7-ounce) can chipotle chilies, minced

1/4 cup blackstrap molasses

2 pounds dried beans, at least three varieties, like red, pinto and black, soaked and cooked till soft

1 cup tequila

2 (12-ounce) bottles flavorful beer, like Bohemia Beer

Jennifer's Chili "El Grito" ("the Yell or Cry")

● Saute sausages in olive oil with onions; do not drain. Mix all of these ingredients together in a large, heavy cooking pot or soup kettle.

● Simmer chili over a very low flame for three days, stirring occasionally.

● Serve this chili topped with fresh diced avocado, cilantro and scallions, just before serving.

● Makes 25 servings.

Praying friend is on the mend

November 7, 2007

One of the names that appears in this column so often, and someone who usually attends the programs I speak at, is our good family friend Irene Jakubowski.

If you own either of my first two cookbooks, you know they are filled with many of Irene's great recipes, as well as plenty of photos.

Irene's been in the hospital for the past two weeks and she's awaiting a possible surgery in Indianapolis, very similar to the one my own father had last spring, for her heart valve.

I drove down for a nice visit with her Sunday and she was smiling.

She hasn't felt much like eating, so today, I'm sending my parents down to see her with something I know she will enjoy.

Broadway star Carol Lawrence, 75, the ex-wife of Robert Goulet, who died last week at age 73, gave me her family's fantastic recipe for her grandmother's old-fashioned Italian chicken soup when I interviewed her in 2001. She was in the region to perform a Mother's Day concert with son Michael Goulet with the NWI Symphony.

Here's what Carol Channing had to say about this extraordinary chicken soup recipe: "When I had a bad cold, Carol Lawrence brought me the most deliciously healing and soothing Italian chicken soup I've ever eaten. I couldn't pronounce it, but I loved every drop and felt better immediately. It should be a prescription!"

I've had the pleasure of interviewing not only Lawrence, but also the late Goulet, who performed in South Bend in 1998. I love the way Lawrence describes her grandmother's soup: "It's so tasty, light and easy to digest, full of healing and nourishing substance. My Nana's sunny spirit is contained in the broth, and I'm convinced it's the magic ingredient and a true homeopathic remedy."

Carol Channing greets Chicago Sun-Times gossip columnist great Irv Kupcinet, 92, at a May 2003 party honoring his column's 60th anniversary.

Carol Lawrence's Homemade Chicken Soup aka Stracciatelli or Italian Penicillin (as Ms. Lawrence calls it)

- Fill a large stock pot 3/4 with water, sprinkled with salt and bring to a boil.

- Add chicken pieces, including neck and innards. Simmer for 20 minutes or until chicken tests done.

- Remove chicken from water to cool and add carrots, celery, onions, parsley, scallions, bouillon, basil and salt and pepper. Simmer about 15 minutes or until carrots are tender.

- Remove chicken meat from bone, cut into small pieces and return to simmering pot.

- In a small bowl, whisk together eggs, cream and Parmesan cheese. Increase flame and bring soup to a fast boil and pour in egg mixture all at once and stir for 2 minutes.

INGREDIENTS:

1 large chicken, cut into pieces

8 medium carrots, sliced into nickel-sized rounds

6 large ribs of celery with leaves, sliced into thick pieces

3 large onions, chopped

1 bunch fresh parsley, chopped

1 bunch scallions with some of the green, chopped

5 bouillon cubes

4 tablespoons dried basil or 4 fresh leaves torn

Salt and black pepper to taste

4 eggs

1/4 cup cream

1 cup Parmesan cheese, grated

- Simmer a few minutes longer and serve. This soup has soft and delicate flecks in the broth that lend a flavor that's out of this world!

- Makes 8 servings.

Swapping family recipes with the legendary Carol Lawrence in May 2001. Lawrence, shown in inset photo during her honeymoon in 1964, was married to stage leading man Robert Goulet.

This 'Green' split pea soup is just like Mom's maiden name

February 27, 2008

I had a number of readers smiling and chuckling a couple years ago when I wrote a column that mentioned: "Sometimes the tools of the kitchen include the tools of the wood shop."

That column detailed how I had heard my mom ask my dad over breakfast to take the leftover ham bone from our Easter dinner out to his wood shop at the farm to saw it in half so she could make two separate meals of homemade ham and beans and old-fashioned split pea soup.

This year, it was the large bone from our Christmas dinner 17-pound ham that had my dad happily sawing away for our supper.

We already had ham and bean soup made with one half of the bone last month and this month, the other half of the bone is being dedicated to my mom's homemade Split Green Pea Soup.

We always see a batch of this delicious emerald shade soup this time of year, not only because St. Patrick's Day is just around the corner, but since my mom's maiden name is Green, she considers it one of her specialties.

And after I mentioned this soup in passing in that 2006 column, I've had a number of readers request the recipe, which I've included this week.

Peggy's Green Split Pea Soup

● Soak dry split peas 2 to 3 hours, drain, sort and remove any less than perfect peas and rinse.

● Place peas in a large soup kettle, along with ham bone or diced ham pieces and 10 cups water.

● Cook soup over medium flame for 1 hour.

● Remove ham bone, and allow to cool enough to remove meat from the bone and return the meat to the soup pot. (Give the ham bone to a grateful farm dog, if possible.)

● Add all remaining ingredients and simmer for 2 hours until peas are soft enough to test done. Soup thickens on its own, without adding any additional thickening agents.

● Makes 10 to 12 servings.

INGREDIENTS:

1 pound dried split peas

1 large ham bone (with some meat intact) or 5 cups chopped ham pieces

2 cups sliced carrots

1 cup chopped celery

1 large onion chopped

1/2 of (1.35-ounce) envelope dry onion soup mix

Salt and pepper to taste

Winning white chili hits home run

March 5, 2008

I received an e-mail request this week looking for a treasured tried and true recipe from one of my earlier "From the Farm" columns, which the reader has misplaced.

Hello Phil,

My father had been using a chili recipe he found in your column several years ago. Recently, the recipe was misplaced and he asked me to e-mail you in hopes of you finding it in your archives. He believes the recipe may have come from Whiting, Indiana. Here are the main ingredients he recalls: Bush brand beans in chili sauce, ground beef or sirloin, Goya brand seasoning mix, tomatoes (canned), onions, salt and pepper

I hope you will be able to find the recipe. He hasn't made chili all winter, as this is the only recipe he craves!

Thank you in advance for looking for it. If you find it, please send it to me or to my father, William Burley of Munster.

Christina Burley

I believe I've found just the recipe you've been looking for Christina and there's still a couple "official" weeks of winter left for your father to whip up this easy recipe. It's the 2005 creation of chili cook-off contest winner Robin Hartman, 39, of Valparaiso, and it's featured in my second cookbook "More From the Farm" (Pediment Publishing 2007).

On the subject of the Lupus Foundation of Northwest Indiana's annual Chili Cook-Off and Tasting, this year's grand prize winning recipe was a healthy and unique thick and delicious white bean chicken chili, dreamed-up by soon-to-be mother Alina Kilarski, of Crown Point, and her cooking counterpart Noreen Castor of Chicago. Congratulations!

Mean Jean and Pregnant Bean's White Bean Chicken Chili

- Heat a large crock pot on low setting or prepare a large soup pot to heat over a low flame.

- Add olive oil to a saute pan and cook onions until soft and clear.

- Add cooked onions and prepared chicken to slow cooker or soup pot, along with both bean varieties and chilies and mix well.

- Add cumin, cayenne pepper, garlic and chicken stock to chili and salt and pepper according to taste.

- Allow chili to simmer on low setting or over low flame for 3 to 5 hours, stirring and checking seasoning occasionally.

INGREDIENTS:

1 pound cooked, cubed white chicken

1 tablespoon olive oil

1 medium Spanish yellow onion, chopped

2 to 3 large cloves garlic, minced

2 (16 ounce) cans great northern beans, undrained

2 (16 ounce) cans cannellini beans, undrained

1 (4.5 ounce) can chopped green chilies

Ground cumin to taste

Cayenne pepper to taste

Salt and black pepper to taste

2 cups chicken broth

4 tablespoons butter

4 tablespoons flour

- Just before serving, make a simple roux to thicken chili by melting 4 tablespoons of butter in a saucepan and slowly adding 4 tablespoons of flour to make a smooth paste.

- Slowly add the thickening mixture to the chili, stirring well to blend for proper consistency.

- Makes 16 to 20 servings.

Soon-to-be mother Alina Kilarski, of Crown Point, and her cooking counterpart Noreen Castor of Chicago, created a delicious "white" chili recipe that landed them three trophies at the 2008 Lupus Foundation Indiana Chapter Chili Cook-Off on March 1, 2008.

(Photo by Michael Berkos)

Vanderbilt's chili recipe a wealth of flavor

December 31, 2008

Editor's note: Columnist Philip Potempa is reporting while traveling by train to New York City for New Year's Eve in Times Square.

All-around good guy newsman Anderson Cooper is back hosting for CNN.

Cooper is the son of legendary fashion designer and "poor little rich girl" heiress Gloria Vanderbilt, who will celebrate her 85th birthday in February.

And even though many might think of Vanderbilt more for her trademark "swan" logo designer jeans and perfume, she also enjoys painting and cooking.

In fact, while traveling by private railcar to New York on this trip, I've thought about how the Vanderbilt family's early American fortune, $80 million amassed as early as 1930 by Gloria's grandfather Cornelius Vanderbilt, came from the ownership of the country's trains and railway system.

I decided to share Gloria Vanderbilt's recipe for what she calls her Manhattan Chili. In today's tough economic times, it reflects Gloria's simple and refined good taste.

INGREDIENTS:

3 tablespoons olive oil

1 large onion, minced

2 cloves garlic, minced

1 pound lean ground beef

3 cups water

1-1/3 cups canned chopped tomatoes

1 green pepper, seeded and minced

1/2 teaspoon celery seed

1/4 teaspoon cayenne pepper

1 teaspoon cumin

1 small bay leaf

1 to 2 tablespoons chili powder (desired taste)

1/8 teaspoon dried basil

1-1/2 teaspoons salt

1 (15 ounce) can of red kidney beans, undrained

Gloria Vanderbilt's Manhattan Chili

- In a skillet, heat oil and add onion and garlic and saute until golden. Add meat and brown lightly.

- Transfer meat mixture to a soup pot and add 1/2 cup water to the empty skillet and bring to a boil and pour into soup pot, scraping any browned bits of flavor to the pot.

- Add all remaining water and ingredients to soup pot and bring chili to a boil, then reduce heat and allow to simmer gently, uncovered until it thickens slightly, about three hours.

- Makes 10 generous servings.

Woolworth's luncheon to feature 'Babs' ring

January 28, 2008

When Dennis Zelenke of Highland, Ind. called to make a reservation for my Feb. 15 Valentine's Day luncheon at Teibel's benefiting The Caring Place Shelter for victims of domestic violence, he was intrigued by the event's theme, the life of eccentric five-and-dime heiress Barbara Woolworth Hutton.

He said one of the reasons he decided to surprise his wife and fellow teacher with tickets for the lunch is because she grew up working at the old Woolworth's in Hammond.

Reader Karen Kil of Cedar Lake has an excellent memory, which she displayed when she made her reservation. She recalled an afternoon tea I hosted in September 2004 at the Hotel Florence in Chicago's Pullman neighborhood, which she attended and remembered I have a rare collectors' piece based on the life of "Babs" that I displayed.

Hutton, whose passions included collecting husbands and jewelry, owned the enormous 39-carat Pasha of Egypt diamond ring. I have the glass replica, bought at an auction, designed to be used in the 1987 made-for-TV miniseries about Hutton's life, "Poor Little Rich Girl: The Barbara Hutton Story," starring Farrah Fawcett as the heiress.

Millionaire "Five and Dime" Heiress Barbara Woolworth Hutton insisted on only the very best, from her jewelry and pets to her homes and husbands, with the latter (expensive) collection of nuptials numbering seven!

I'll bring the ring to pass around for guests to examine and try on.

Today's recipe comes from Hutton's cousin, actress Dina Merrill, who is now 83 and the daughter of cereal heiress Marjorie Meriwether Post and financial wiz E.F. Hutton.

Merrill, who starred in "Butterfield 8" with Elizabeth Taylor, has been married five times, including to actor Cliff Robertson, famed banker Richard Merrill and Colgate toothpaste heir Stanley Rumbough Jr. Today, she is married to actor Ted Hartley, who starred in the TV series "Peyton Place."

Dina Merrill's Cream of Zucchini and Curry Soup

- Saute onion and celery in butter until soft and add to soup pot.

- Stir curry powder into sauteed mixture at bottom of pot and cook over low heat for 3 minutes.

- Add zucchini and cool for another 5 minutes or until it begins to soften.

- Pour chicken broth over mixture and bring soup to a boil, stirring, then reduce heat and simmer for 15 minutes or until zucchini is soft.

- Add parsley, lime juice and salt and pepper to soup, and continue to simmer another 5 minutes.

- Using a portion of the soup at a time, puree soup in blender, returning soup to pot to add buttermilk.

- Simmer and adjust seasoning, but do not boil.

- Makes 8 servings.

INGREDIENTS:

2 medium-sized onions, chopped
1 large celery rib, chopped
3 tablespoons butter
1 teaspoon curry powder (or to taste)
6 medium zucchini, diced (about 6 cups)
4 cups chicken broth
3 tablespoons chopped parsley
Juice of 1/2 lime (optional)
Salt and black pepper to taste
1 cup buttermilk

After wealthy, already much-married, heiress Barbara Woolworth Hutton married actor Cary Grant in 1942, the press dubbed the couple as "Cash and Cary" in newspaper headlines. By 1945, the marriage (her third) had ended in divorce.

Making the most with the least

While having breakfast with my parents at the farm over the weekend, we began talking about how it's often the simple everyday gifts of life that mean the most.

My dad's mother, my Grandma Potempa, was especially gifted at making the most from the least.

For example, when Grandma Potempa first came to Chicago on the "big ship" from Poland for her new life, she was just a teenage girl traveling with two best girlfriends.

Even after Grandma and Grandpa Potempa married and bought our small family farm in Indiana, she still stayed in close contact with her two girlfriends, Mary Podlasek and Ann Czuba.

The Czuba Family opened a bakery in Chicago, and once a month, my dad said their family would make a pilgrimage to our farm bringing all the day-old bread and pastry for Grandma and Grandpa Potempa and their nine children, the youngest who is my dad.

He said he and his siblings, my aunts and uncles, would dig through all the donuts to find and eat the jelly bismarks first, which were their favorite treat.

And then for coffeecakes and loaves of rye bread, Grandma Potempa would dampen a clean linen cloth and place it over these baked goods and gently "rebake" them and restore them to freshness.

Today's soup recipe comes from Keith Peffers, director of food services for Purdue North Central's Cafeteria in Westville, where I teach part-time.

Boilermaker Cheddar Ale Soup

- Put onion and carrot in food processor or electric blender and coarsely chop about 3 seconds.

- Melt margarine or butter in slow cooker or stock pot on a medium heat.

- Add onion, carrot and diced red pepper, sauté until soft.

- Add flour, dry mustard, stir to make pasty roux.

- Add beer (drink other half of beer while cooking) and half and half, stir until mixture just begins to thicken.

- Immediately add hot chicken stock, stir until smooth and creamy.

- Add shredded cheese, stir until smooth.

- Salt and pepper to taste.

- Makes 12 servings.

INGREDIENTS:

1 small onion

1 peeled carrot

1/2 cup diced red bell pepper

1 stick of margarine or butter

1/2 teaspoon dry mustard

2/3 cup flour

1 quart hot chicken stock

1 pint half and half

1/2 bottle (6 ounce) English ale (Bass Beer works well)

2 pounds aged sharp Cheddar, shredded

Salt and pepper to taste

Chili event
extra special this year

February 25, 2009

It's Ash Wednesday and that means Lent and sacrifice for the next 40 days.

Over the weekend, my mom made her homemade ham and bean soup, which is featured in my second cookbook.

This is also the time of year I remind readers that this year's Lupus Foundation of Northwest Indiana's annual Chili Cook-Off and Tasting Event is just around the corner.

This year's event is from 3 to 6 p.m. this Saturday, March 7, at Merrillville High School. It is a special year, since earlier this month, the event and foundation's founder Phyllis Simko lost her beloved husband Richard to Lupus.

For Ash Wednesday, Valparaiso readers Ed and Karin Seykowski shared their wonderful Creamy Salmon Chowder recipe, which I tested and served to family and friends on Sunday during the Oscar telecast.

INGREDIENTS:

2 onions, finely chopped

2 cups finely chopped celery

1 green pepper, finely chopped

2 cloves of garlic, minced

4 tablespoons butter or margarine

3 cups peeled and cubed potatoes

2-1/2 cups thinly sliced carrots

1 cup water

2 (14-1/2 ounce) cans of vegetable or chicken broth

1 teaspoon ground dill

1/2 teaspoon rosemary

1 teaspoon salt

1 teaspoon pepper

2 (12-1/2 ounce) cans evaporated milk or 2 cups half and half or whipping cream (depending on desired consistency)

2 (15-ounce) cans cream-style corn

1 (14.75-ounce) can red salmon, undrained, boned and flaked into large pieces

Ed and Karin's Creamy Salmon Chowder

● Cook onion, celery, green pepper, garlic, potatoes and carrots in butter in the bottom of a large soup pot until they soften, gradually adding the one cup of water.

● Add broth and seasonings and continue to cook covered, occasionally stirring and bringing to a slow boil for 20 minutes or until carrots and potatoes test tender.

● Add salmon with liquid and cream-style corn and stir to blend, while reducing heat to a simmer. Add milk (or cream) and taste to adjust seasonings, adding more dill and rosemary and if desired, some seasoning salt for added flavor.

● Simmer for another 20 minutes.

● Makes 10 servings.

Cubs, chili and memories go together

March 18, 2009

This year's Lupus Foundation Chili Cook-off resulted in an array of new winning faces and recipes.

The judging panel, which included me, our restaurant columnist Eloise Valadez (whose weekly feature Restaurant Scene is now found on Saturdays) and Keith Peffers, director of dining services at Purdue North Central, selected a Cubs inspired chili recipe called "Hey! Hey! What Do You Say?! Chili" by Nick Petralla and Alison Roumbos of Crown Point, Ind.. The recipe honors the late, great Wrigley Field broadcaster Jack Brickhouse.

Who says that nothing connected to the Cubs has to do with winning?

And notice the recipe does NOT call for any goat or lamb meat, as a way to break the infamous Cubs Billy Goat Curse.

Restaurateur Ken Varnes, of Schererville, who owned blue restaurant in Valparaiso with wife Julie, is one of the other many local notables to help me during the past decade to judge this chili contest.

I'm sorry to report that Ken's 81-year-old mother, Violette Straka, of Lansing, passed away on Friday, March 13.

I hope that readers will keep Ken and his mother in thoughts and prayers.

I know Ken mentioned one of her best Mother's Days was in 2007 when she saw Ken featured in my second cookbook, "More From The Farm" photographed judging the Lupus Chili Cook-Off.

I was joined by our newspaper's restaurant columnist (and my good friend) Eloise Valadez, along with Keith Peffers, director of dining services for Purdue University North Central, to serve on my celebrity judging panel for the seventh annual Lupus Foundation of Northwest Indiana Chili Cook-Off.

Further From the Farm

Hey! Hey! What Do You Say?! Chili

- Preheat oven to 450 degrees.

- Rinse poblano and Anaheim peppers and arrange evenly on a cookie sheet. Roast in the oven for 4-5 minutes on each side. Pepper skin will blister. Do not let them burn. But the more they blister, the easier it will be to peel the skin off later.

- Immediately after removing from oven, place roasted peppers in a plastic bag and seal it. Allow peppers to sweat in bag for 30 minutes. Dump peppers from the bag into a colander and rinse with cool water.

- Using gloves (and not touching your eyes!!!), seed and peel off pepper skin. Finely chop peppers and set aside.

- Chop remaining peppers and onion. Set aside.

- Chop garlic. Set aside.

- Trim and cut chuck steak. Crumble sausage. Preheat large pot over medium heat. Add butter and canola oil. Allow butter to melt. Add all peppers and onions. Cook until softened.

- Add garlic and stir. Add chuck steak and allow to cook through.

- Add ground beef and sausage. Allow to cook through, sautéing up to 10 minutes.

- Stir in all spices.

- Stir in tomato sauce and paste.

- Stir in beer and chicken stock.

- Stir in beans. Reduce heat to low and simmer a minimum of 3 hours.

- Makes 20 servings.

INGREDIENTS:

3 poblano peppers, chopped

3 Anaheim peppers, chopped

2 orange, red, or yellow bell peppers, chopped

2 jalapeno peppers, seeded and chopped

2 yellow onions, chopped

1 head garlic, chopped

1 pound boneless chuck steak, fat trimmed and cut into small pieces

2 pounds ground beef

1/3 pound spicy Italian sausage, crumbled

2/3 pound mild Italian sausage, crumbled

2 tablespoons butter

3 tablespoons canola oil

1 teaspoon onion powder

1 teaspoon garlic powder

2 tablespoons chili powder

2 teaspoons paprika

2 teaspoons ground cumin

2 teaspoons ground coriander

1 teaspoons ground red pepper

2 teaspoons kosher salt

2 teaspoons freshly ground black pepper

2 cups tomato sauce

1 cup tomato paste

1 (12 ounce) Harp Lager beer

1 cup chicken stock

2 (15-1/2 ounce) cans pinto beans, undrained

2 (15-1/2 ounce) cans dark red kidney beans, undrained

Walt Disney and family enjoyed classic, traditional every day

November 11, 2009

DATELINE - - Orlando - - Columnist Philip Potempa is reporting from Florida this week while traveling.

I was rather surprised last month when I read a story about the childhood home on Chicago's Northwest side childhood being up for sale, where Walt Disney was born in 1901 and spent his early.

Besides the fact that the privately-owned four-bedroom frame house at 2156 N. Tripp Ave. has been on the market for more than three years and the asking price is only $200,000, what really surprised me was just how modest his family home and roots really were, especially by today's standards.

But it certainly makes sense and helps explain the basic honest hardworking faith and values held by Disney throughout his life, right until his death on Dec. 15, 1966, just a few years before the opening of his dream amusement park landscape in Florida.

And like his wonderful everyday approach to life and business, Walt's dining tastes were equally simple and satisfying.

Dining at Walt Disney World Resorts is vast and expansive. My favorite option, and I've written about it often over the years, is the recreated Brown Derby restaurant at Disney's Hollywood Studios theme park.

My last visit to Walt Disney World was just a quick afternoon visit in March 2006 while covering the Pillsbury Bake-Off competition held in Orlando that year. It was then I had the good fortune to meet author Pam Brandon, who is a wiz when it comes to writing about everything Disney, especially when it comes to the culinary category.

I've always hung on to a copy of her "Cooking with Mickey and the Disney Chefs" (2004 Disney Enterprises $19.95) which she gave me during our last visit.

While chatting with Pam during this visit, I'm amazed by the many changes here at the Disney properties during my few years of absence. But one thing that remains the same are some of Walt Disney's favorite recipes, which Pam managed to unearth and share in her wonderful book. She was equally kind enough to allow me to share

Further From the Farm

them both with readers. They are certainly rare culinary conversation starters. She tells me Walt's favorite chili recipe is still served at a few select locations at the Disneyland property in California.

Walt Disney's Own Favorite Chili with Beans

- Wash and sort beans and soak overnight in cold water.

- Drain beans and place in a 2-quart saucepan.

- Add fresh water and cover by 2 inches.

- Add sliced onion and simmer, covered, for 2 hours, until tender.

- Heat oil in a large pan and saute garlic.

- Add beef and celery and cook until lightly browned.

- Add chili powder, paprika and thyme.

- Mix in chopped tomatoes. Cover and simmer for 1 hour.

- When beans are tender, combine with meat, stirring gently.

- Add salt and pepper to taste.

- Makes 4 servings.

- Published courtesy of author Pam Brandon and "Cooking with Mickey and the Disney Chefs" (2004 Disney Enterprises $19.95)

INGREDIENTS:

2 pounds pinto beans, dry
2 medium onions, sliced
1/4 cup vegetable oil
2 garlic cloves, divided
2 pounds lean ground beef
1 cup chopped celery
1 teaspoon chili powder
1 teaspoon paprika
1 teaspoon dried thyme
1 (28 ounce) can chopped tomatoes, undrained
Salt and pepper to taste

My mom and Minnie Mouse make a delightful pair, exchanging morning greetings, following breakfast at Walt Disney World in Florida in this December 2000 photo.

Weight-conscious aunt loved soups, hearty cooking

February 3, 2010

While my dad's oldest brother, my Uncle Joe, was always a very picky eater, his wife, my Aunt Rose loved cooking and eating a variety of recipe specialties.

Uncle Joe, who particularly did not like onions and lamb, was often difficult to cook for, as Aunt Rose would often remind.

But both loved to eat, whether home-cooked meals or when selecting favorites from expansive restaurant menus from the great eatery choices along Archer Avenue on Chicago's Southwest Side, near their traditional brick "raised ranch" home. The formal dining room of their home was always filled with entertaining finery, and my Auntie Lottie, still says what a great gourmet cook Aunt Rose was and how she loved to invite her and Uncle Swede for great dinner parties.

In later years, Uncle Joe and Aunt Rose had a series of housekeepers, live-in Polish cooks and caregivers who did most of the cooking.

In particular, a couple of these Polish cook-housekeepers, were really quite wonderful in the kitchen, whipping up many feasts that Aunt Rose particularly enjoyed during the last five years before her death at age 85 in March 2000. Uncle Joe, preceded her, at age 78, in November 1995.

Throughout her life, Aunt Rose, who worked for many years as a bookkeeper for Goldblatt's Department Store, also was always on "the perpetual diet" and her weight would often yo-yo. Through the years, her weight could range from 165 to 230. She was always trying diets, with one of her favorites being "a vinegar diet," since she loved anything or everything to do with cooking with vinegar.

But she also loved roast duck, spiral honey-basted ham, Polish sausage, dumplings and beef-cabbage beet borscht soup, in addition to an array of sweets.

I wasn't fond of the soups she enjoyed, which her Polish cooks loved to make, especially "cow stomach soup" called Flaki and "duck blood soup," called Czernina.

However, Aunt Rose did introduce me to a variation of traditional beet borscht soup, which I still love today.

My good friend Mary Beth Schultz helped me create an easier and more convenient version of Aunt Rose's favorite borscht soup.

Aunt Rose would have loved this recipe.

As for Uncle Joe?

Probably not.

Mary Beth's Slow Cooker Beef Borscht Soup

- Mix stew meat with flour until all pieces are completely covered.

- Sauté in olive oil in a large frying pan until meat is evenly browned.

- Place meat in crock pot first.

- Add the vegetables in the following order: tomatoes, beets, and carrots, then onions and cabbage on top of the meat.

- Whisk together beef broth, tomato paste, cider vinegar, brown sugar, garlic salt and pepper and pour over meat and vegetables.

- Add bay leaves and cook in large Crock-Pot covered on low heat 9-10 hours.

- Remove bay leaves before serving.

- If desired, garnish each hot bowl served with a generous dollop of sour cream.

- Makes 10 servings.

INGREDIENTS:

1-1/2 pounds beef stew meat, cut into 1/2-inch pieces

1/3 cup flour

3 tablespoons olive oil

1 (14.5 ounce) can diced tomatoes, undrained

4 whole carrots cut into 1/2-inch pieces

1 onion, chopped

1 small head cabbage sliced lengthwise into 1/2-inch wide strips (enough to make about 4 to 5 cups)

1 (14.5 ounce) can sliced beets drained and diced into 1/2-inch pieces

4 cups beef broth

1/3 cup cider vinegar

1 small (6-ounce) can tomato paste

1/3 cup brown sugar

2 teaspoons garlic salt

1 teaspoon ground black pepper

2 bay leaves

1 cup sour cream, for garnish, if desired

Here's my Aunt Rose, just as a I remember her, at the head of the table seated in the formal dining room of the Chicago home she shared with Uncle Joe for more than half a century.

My original 'Farm' cookbook a rare find

May 23, 2007

Thank you to the more than 150 people who attended last night's "An Evening From the Farm" party and recipe sampling hosted by the ladies at Griffith Lutheran Church.

What a great time and great way to meet so many new faces while also visiting with so many familiar faces.

I know my mom and dad also had a great time.

One of the questions I have been asked the most since my second cookbook "More From the Farm: Family Recipes and Memories of a Lifetime" (2007 Pediment Press $29.95) was released in May 2007 is whether there are still copies of my original/first "From the Farm" book from 2004 still available.

On the Internet right now, www.amazon.com is selling it for $100 a copy! So, if you're someone who bought one of the 1,800 books originally published, hang on to your copies!

As for today's recipe, it was provided to me by Sandra Ruban of Griffith at last night's event. Sandra is one of the dedicated members of Griffith Lutheran Church. I'm always getting requests for lowfat and sugar-free recipes, and this strawberry pie is a real winner.

Sandra's Fresh Strawberry Dieter's Delite Pie

- Slice 4 cups fresh strawberries and set aside.

- Mix 2 cups water with box of sugar-free pudding and microwave for 3 minutes. Stir pudding and microwave for an additional 3 minutes.

- Add the dry sugar-free gelatin to the pudding mixture and allow to cool for 10 minutes.

- Fold in sliced strawberries to the pudding and gelatin mixture and pour into pie pan (there's no crust to this pie, but it firms up nicely to serve.)

- Refrigerate for at least one hour and top with thawed frozen fat-free nondairy topping.

- Makes 8 serving slices.

INGREDIENTS:

4 cups fresh strawberries, sliced

1 small (.9 ounce) package sugar-free cook-and-serve vanilla pudding

2 cups water

1 small (.9 ounce) package sugar-free and fat-free strawberry gelatin

1 carton fat-free thawed frozen nondairy topping

Happy birthday cake for Dear Abby

July 4, 2007

Happy Fourth of July!

Today is a special day for many reasons.

It's not only Independence Day, but July 4, 2007 is also the 89th birthday of a very special lady whose name and newspaper column have been cherished for more than half a century.

The name Pauline Ester Friedman Phillips may not sound very familiar to most, but I know the pen name Abigail Van Buren aka "Dear Abby" must ring a bell.

Abby, known to her friends as "Popo," founded her advice column in 1956 at The Los Angeles Times, just one year after her identical twin sister "Eppie" Lederer took over the Ann Landers column at The Chicago Sun-Times.

I had the pleasure of meeting both of these advice column legends a few times during my writing career. My favorite photo on my desk at work is one of me standing with both sisters at a party in Chicago in 1996.

We lost Eppie aka Ann Landers much too soon in June 2002, just a few weeks before her 84th birthday.

In my second cookbook, I shared Ann Landers' recipe for her famous meat loaf. Today, I'm going to share a recipe from her sister for her famous Coconut Custard Cake that I was given by Abby when we met.

For today, we can consider it her birthday cake, as she continues her quiet life in retirement in Minneapolis, Minn.. happy to know her daughter Jeanne Phillips has taken over her advice column, continuing the family tradition.

Abigail Van Buren is better known to the world as advice columnist "Dear Abby" and twin sister of rival newspaper advice columnist Ann Landers. Here she is having fun in 1980 on Dinah Shore's talk show, with fellow guest Zsa Zsa Gabor.

Dear Abby's Coconut Cake with Custard Frosting

- Heat oven to 325 degrees.

- Beat egg yolks until pale.

- Combine 3/4 cup sugar with water and mix with egg yolks.

- Add flour and mix well.

- In another bowl, combine egg whites and salt, beating until foamy. Add cream of tartar, vanilla and remaining sugar and beat until stiff peaks form.

- Gently fold yolk mixture into whites mixture and pour the batter into a 10-inch ungreased tube pan.

- Bake at 325 degrees for 60 to 65 minutes or until toothpick inserted comes out clean. Remove from oven and invert to cook before removing from pan, first loosening the edges with spatula.

- When cool, cut cake in half horizontally before frosting.

- To make frosting, soften gelatin in 1/2 cup cold water.

- Combine egg yolks and sugar and beat until pale.

- Add milk, gelatin, flour and vanilla and cook in top of a double boiler over gently boiling water 12 to 15 minutes, stirring occasionally, until mixture coats a metal spoon.

- Remove from heat and allow to cool and then refrigerate for several hours so custard is very cold.

- Using an electric mixer, beat the cold custard until it is thick and creamy.

- In a large bowl, whip cream until thick and then fold into custard.

INGREDIENTS:

CAKE:

5 egg yolks
1-1/2 cups granulated sugar
2 tablespoons cold water
1 cup flour, sifted
10 egg whites
1/2 teaspoon salt
1/2 teaspoon cream of tartar
1-1/2 teaspoons vanilla

FROSTING:

1 envelope unflavored gelatin
1/2 cup cold water
5 egg yolks (reserved from cake)
3/4 cup sugar
1-1/2 cups cold milk
1 tablespoon flour, sifted
1-1/2 teaspoons vanilla extract
1-1/2 cups chilled whipping cream
2 cups grated coconut

- Spread some of the custard frosting on the top of the bottom portion of sliced cake and sprinkle with coconut, then add top half and spread frosting on top and around sides sprinkling with remaining coconut.

- Note: Abby likes to add a large red or yellow rose from her garden in the center of the cake "for a touch of drama."

- Makes 10 slices.

IN PERSON! MARCH 24
'Dear Abby'
Abigail Van Buren
WORLD-FAMOUS ADVICE COLUMNIST OF
THE DALLAS TIMES HERALD
DALLAS MEMORIAL AUDITORIUM
8 PM   ADMIT ONE

Join famed psychic Irene Hughes at my birthday tea

July 25, 2007

It's been a few years since I've done a tea room event, but they are always popular.

So when Don and Nancy Johnson, owners of the quaint Annie's Tea Room and Ice Cream Parlor in neighboring Crete, Ill. asked to host a birthday tea for me on Aug. 13, 2007 for my 37th birthday, I was honored to oblige.

A full menu with favorite recipes from my second cookbook published in May 2007 will be served, such as Mary Beth Schultz's Pillsbury Bake-Off-winning Chicken Fajita Quiche and my mom's Mock Hostess Ho-Ho Cake, which will serve as my birthday cake. Also, we'll have the tea room's signature salad, served with its secret celery-seed salad dressing. Trays of finger desserts, including friend Phyllis Diller's Yummy Refrigerator Lemon Cookies, featured in my first cookbook from 2004, also will accompany the hot and cold tea served.

And, as a special surprise, my friend Irene Hughes, the famed psychic, will attend both seatings to help with the celebration (and a few predictions).

Today's recipe is one my mom has been making quite a bit lately. Even though blueberries aren't doing well because of the early frost and now dry weather, the

The rooms in my friend psychic Irene Hughes' lofty and impressive Chicagoland home are decorated with an interesting and eccentric flair. Here we are in January 2004, in deep conversation in her "Egyptian Room."

(Photo by Tasos Katopodis)

blackberries along our lane and around the mailbox at the farm are plentiful.

In fact, for my older brother Tom's 50th birthday on Monday, rather than birthday cake, my mom made him one of her blackberry pies.

Peggy's Blackberry Pie

- Heat oven to 400 degrees. To make crust, combine flour, oil, milk and salt, and form dough into a ball. Chill for a few minutes, before rolling out top and bottom 9-inch pie crusts between two pieces of waxed paper.

- Line a 9-inch pie pan with one crust.

- In a medium bowl, mix sugar, flour, cornstarch, nutmeg, salt, cinnamon and lemon juice.

- Add the mixture to berries and gently combine to make filling. Pour filling into pie crust.

- Dot berry filling with butter. Moisten edge of pastry with water and cover with remaining crust. Trim excess and press edges together with a fork.

- Cut plastic drinking straw into four sections and insert into top crust for ventilation. (Straws may curl slightly from heat, but won't harm pie.) Cover edge of pie crust with strips of aluminum foil to prevent over-baking.

- Bake 50 to 60 minutes or until brown.

- Makes 8 servings.

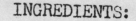

INGREDIENTS:

CRUST:

2 cups all-purpose flour
1/2 cup cooking oil
1/4 cup milk
1 teaspoon salt
Waxed paper
Drinking straws
Aluminum foil

FILLING:

2/3 cup sugar
2 tablespoons flour
1 tablespoon cornstarch
1/4 teaspoon nutmeg
1/8 teaspoon salt
1/4 teaspoon cinnamon
1 teaspoon lemon juice
1 quart or 4 heaping cups fresh blackberries
1 tablespoon butter

Howard Hughes' theme for birthday tea

August 1, 2007

After helping my parents pick an entire bushel basket of green beans last Friday, we decided to deliver some to friendly and famous psychic Irene Hughes. She is helping me host my birthday tea celebration this month at Annie's Tea Room and Ice Cream Parlor in neighboring Crete, Ill.

I was meeting with Irene to complete the menu details for the tea, and she reminded me of some of the famous clients she's worked for, from Merv Griffin and Eva Gabor to the eccentric and reclusive billionaire Howard Hughes (no relation to Irene).

We decided at the tea we will talk a little about the strange and fascinating life of Hughes, who was dubbed "the bashful billionaire."

And in his honor, Don and Nancy Johnson, the owners of Annie's Tea Room, are going to serve guests samples of their "Cherry Vanilla Ice Cream," which was Hughes' favorite. (At the event, we'll share an interesting story about why this ice cream was his stand-out favorite during the early 1970s while he was living in the penthouse of the Desert Inn Hotel and Casino, which he owned, in Las Vegas.)

For any readers still interested in attending one of the Aug. 13 tea seatings, but haven't called yet, there are only a few seats that remain for the two tea times (and, yes,

Irene and my parents will attend both) -- 2 and 7 p.m.

Reservations are required and the price is all inclusive (yep, even the tip) for $25 a person. The seating is limited to 50 people.

This week's recipe is from one of the first-place winners at last week's Porter County Fair pie contest. Linda Curley of Valparaiso created this delicious peach pie which took home top honors.

Tagged by the media as "the Bashful Billionaire," Howard Hughes, shown here golfing in Southern California in 1938, dated some of Hollywood's most beautiful women, including actresses Ava Gardner, Terry Moore, Jane Russell, Olivia de Havilland and Katherine Hepburn. He died April 5, 1976 at age 70, leaving behind a worth of more than $2 billion.

Summertime Peach Pie

- Heat oven to 400 degrees.

- For the crust: Place all crust ingredients, except water and vinegar into a large bowl.

- Use a knife or pastry blender and cut ingredients together to combine.

- Mix water and vinegar and add water slowly and continue to blend (do not overwork). Adjust flour and liquid as necessary for proper consistency.

- Form into a ball, chill for a few minutes and roll on floured board or between two pieces of wax paper to create bottom crusts for a 9-inch pie. Chill any unused dough.

- Line a 9-inch pie pan with the bottom crust and place in freezer for 15 minutes.

- For the filling: Mix all filling ingredients together and place in chilled pie shell.

- Place pie on center rack of a oven and bake for 25 minutes.

- Combine all topping ingredients and cut together in a bowl to create a crumb topping or place in a food processor and pulse several times.

- Remove pie from oven and reduce temperature to 375 degrees.

- Gently spread topping over and to the edges of warm pie.

- Return pie to oven for 30 minutes.

- Cool 1 hour before serving warm with vanilla ice cream.

- Makes 8 slices.

INGREDIENTS:

CRUST:

1-1/4 cups flour

1/2 cup shortening

1/2 teaspoon salt

1 egg, beaten

2 to 3 tablespoons cold water

2 teaspoons vinegar

FILLING:

4 cups peeled, pitted, ripe, sliced peaches

1/3 cup frozen lemonade concentrate

1/4 cup sugar

2 tablespoons quick-cooking tapioca

TOPPING:

3/4 cup flour

1/3 cup sugar

1/4 teaspoon ground cinnamon

1/8 teaspoon salt

5 tablespoons unsalted butter, cut into 1/4-inch pieces

Small town of Toto now nearly a memory

August 8, 2007

Today's recipe is from one of my favorite reporter colleagues from the "old days."

If you're a reader who is from the Porter County area, then you're familiar with Ken Kosky's byline.

I met him back when we both still worked for The Vidette-Messenger newspaper in Valparaiso, Ind. before we were bought out by The Times in 1995. He started in 1988 and I began writing after I graduated from Valparaiso University in 1992.

For nearly two decades, Ken has covered the crime and police beat, including writing his popular police blotter column.

I tested out Ken's recipe (pictured in color section page II) and just slightly changed a thing or two and the results are out of this world.

However, as I mentioned in an earlier column, it's not been a great blueberry season and even our own blueberry patch is now bare.

I suggested to my mom that we could always take a ride to Waldrop's Produce in the tiny town of Toto, Ind. for extra blueberries. I was surprised to find out that the family recently closed the more than five-decades-old business.

Shuttering stores has been an ongoing trend for Toto, which used to be a very popular discount retail destination on Sundays, with many customers coming from as far as Chicago and Michigan looking for bargains.

In fact, one of the popular advertising slogans used years ago was "All roads lead to Toto."

First, it was Harold Weinberg's "Big Store" that closed in 1998. Then, the curtain store, dress shop and shoe stores all closed in 2005.

Now, with Waldrop's closed, all that remains is Joey Weinberg's Wallpaper Store, run by his widow Doretha, and Richard's of Toto, which was originally owned by the late Richard Hazelton, who was a great pal of our family friend Irene Jakubowski.

It's been said for decades that author Frank L. Baum of "Wizard of Oz" fame, who had a cottage on nearby Bass Lake where he wrote, named Dorothy's little dog after this tiny shopping stop in the road.

So despite the color of today's delicious recipe, there's no reason to feel blue. Memories of Toto will always live on.

Ken's Police Blotter Blueberry Buckle

● For crust: Cream together butter, sugar, egg and vanilla with a fork or wire whisk. Add flour and coconut and combine.

● Press half of the mixture into the bottom of an 11-inch-by-7-inch baking dish coated with cooking spray. Reserve the other half of crust mixture.

● For filling: Mix 2 tablespoons of water with cornstarch to make a thin paste. In a medium saucepan, heat the cornstarch mixture with sugar until dissolved and bubbling. Add rinsed blueberries, spices and lemon juice, and stir to coat berries until shiny and sauce is thick, yet berries have still retained their shape.

● Pour filling over bottom crust and spread evenly.

● Pinch off pieces of reserved crust and begin to form a very thin top crust, building it by working from the edges of the pan toward the center. (Some of the filling might still be visible, which is fine.)

● Bake uncovered at 350 degrees for 45 minutes or until coconut in top crust appears golden brown.

● Makes 12 servings.

INGREDIENTS:

CRUST:

3/4 cup butter, softened

1/2 cup sugar

1 egg

1 teaspoon vanilla

1-1/2 cups flour

1-3/4 cup coconut flakes

FILLING:

2 tablespoons water

2 tablespoons cornstarch

1/3 cup sugar

2 pints blueberries

1/2 teaspoon cinnamon

1/4 teaspoon nutmeg

3 teaspoons lemon juice

Our newspaper's longtime crime and police writer Ken Kosky, shown here in 1996 with our courts reporter Susan Emery, has made many people feel "blue" after having to publish names in his "cop check" police report blotter of arrests. His easy blueberry buckle recipe is even better than bail.

Reader has great idea for diet cheesecake

August 29, 2007

Reader Lynn Anthony of Crown Point, Ind. contacted me earlier this month with two requests.

First of all, she's a reader eager for some recipe options that are low in calories and low in sugar, ideal for diabetic menus or anyone counting calories.

Secondly, she was adamant that I provide some recipes that do not require the use of an oven during the steamy days of August.

Today's recipe will make Lynn very happy, especially since she can take credit for helping to develop this gem.

It's very light, delicious, and easy to whip up and, best of all, in addition to not having to use an oven, there's no "artificial" aftertaste, something very familiar to anyone who uses sugar substitutes.

Dieter's Delite No-Crust Cheesecake

- In a small bowl, dissolve both boxes of gelatin with 1 cup boiling water. Add 1 cup cold water and place in freezer for 15 minutes to chill until cool.

- In another bowl, combine the 3 packages of cream cheese with Splenda Sugar Blend. Add vanilla to mixture and cream together until smooth.

- Using an electric mixer, add a little of the evaporated milk to cream cheese mixture and beat until smooth. Continue process at intervals until all of the milk is combined with cream cheese mixture.

INGREDIENTS:

2 (.3-ounce) boxes sugar-free lemon gelatin
3 (8-ounce) packages "light" cream cheese
1/2 cup Splenda Sugar Blend (see note)
1 tablespoon vanilla
1 (12-ounce) can 2 percent evaporated milk

- Pour chilled liquid gelatin into filling mixture and beat quickly just a few times until blended.

- Pour into an ungreased 13-inch-by-9-inch baking pan and chill for 2 hours until set.

- Note: This new variety of Splenda, found in the baking aisle, blends this natural sugar-free sweetener with a reduced amount of real sugar.

- Makes 24 (2-inch-by-2-inch) slices. Each slice contains only 106 calories and just 7 grams of fat.

Pumpkin pie contest at this weekend's fall fest

September 26, 2007

The good folks at South Lake Community Services have asked me to be a judge at this Saturday's Covered Bridge Harvest Fest Pumpkin Pie Bake-Off, sponsored by Strack and Van Til's grocery stores.

The contest is part of the larger three-day festival at the fairgrounds in Crown Point, Ind. to raise money to benefit Special Olympics of Lake County and historical rehab projects at the fairgrounds.

The contest is simple.

Bake your best pumpkin pie, which must use pumpkin as the main ingredient.

Bring two examples of your created pie recipe to the pie area at the festival between 9 and 9:30 a.m. this Saturday for the 10 a.m. judging.

Pies should be in disposable pie pans and have one recipe card with name, address and phone, and a separate card with the complete recipe.

The judging panel will cast votes for two categories, amateur and professional, using a criteria that includes appearance, taste and texture.

The prizes are grocery-store gift certificates and, after the judging, the pies will be sliced and sold for charity.

As for today's pumpkin recipe, it's from one of my students at Purdue University North Central, who is enrolled in my public speaking class.

Christopher Iliff, 20, of Valparaiso, made his mother Sylvia's family recipe for pumpkin roll last week for his demonstration speech assignment, impressing both teacher and fellow students.

This is a favorite fall photo with friends visiting the farm on this September 1999 Sunday afternoon. Ranking among my newspaper buddies are sports writer, Jim Rusnak, holding a pitchfork and news editor Tom Davies.

Christopher's Pumpkin Roll

- Preheat oven to 375 degrees.

- Grease a 10-by-15-inch jelly roll pan, then line with wax paper

- Lightly grease and flour the wax paper.

- To make batter, sift the first six dry ingredients together, set aside.

- Beat eggs and sugar together in a large bowl until fluffy; slowly beat in pumpkin.

- Stir the dry ingredients all at once with wet ingredients and pour into the pan, spreading evenly.

- Sprinkle batter with nuts (if desired).

- Bake for 15 minutes or until center springs to touch. Remove from oven and run a knife around the edges while still warm.

- Meanwhile, make filling by combining all ingredients together and beat until smooth. Set aside.

- Remove cake from oven and invert onto a clean damp towel dusted with confectioner's sugar. Peel off wax paper and trim any small amounts from sides.

- Carefully roll up the cake while still warm (otherwise, it will crack) with damp towel still inside.

- Unroll cake, spread with cream cheese filling. Then, re-roll cake and refrigerate until ready to serve.

- Makes 10 servings.

INGREDIENTS:

CAKE ROLL:

3/4 cup all purpose flour

1/2 teaspoon nutmeg

2 teaspoons cinnamon

1 teaspoon pumpkin pie spice

1 teaspoon baking powder

1/2 teaspoon salt

3 eggs, slightly beaten

1 cup sugar

2/3 cup canned pumpkin

1 cup chopped walnuts (optional)

FILLING:

1 cup sifted confectioner's sugar

1 (8 ounce) package softened cream cheese

6 tablespoons butter

1 teaspoon vanilla

Long before Martha Stewart's craft magazines and television series boasting decorating ideas were ever launched, my Auntie Lill and Auntie Lottie already were creative forces, such as using small gourds in 1964 to make a face and horns on everyday farm pumpkins.

Avon lady a
regular farm visitor

October 17, 2007

Over the weekend, I saw a TV report about Fortune magazine's releasing the names of the business world's top 50 most successful and powerful women.

The new CEO for Avon, Andrea Jung, age 49, ranked right at the top in ninth place.

"The stock is finally showing life, up 15 percent in the past year, as Jung has proved to investors that she is serious about reinvigorating growth at the $8.7 billion cosmetics company," announced the folks at Fortune.

"Among other initiatives, she has increased ad spending and is launching Avon's first worldwide ad campaign, 'Hello tomorrow,' with Reese Witherspoon as the new spokeswoman. The company is also cutting jobs and doing away with less-profitable products."

This reminded me of Esther Lake, who is now retired and in her mid-90s (she NEVER would reveal her age) and living in a retirement home in Rochester, Ind.

Mrs. Lake was my mom's Avon lady for more than two decades.

My mom, who still collects Avon perfume bottles, always had a standing order with Mrs. Lake, who would drive out to our house every two weeks either to bring my mom a new catalogue or to drop off an order.

Besides the "Wild Country" Avon aftershave my dad would wear, my mom's standing order always included Avon bubble bath and bath oil for herself and little tubes of lip balm for all us kids.

My mom would also always comment on how Mrs. Lake made "the perfect Avon lady."

An older and elegant little lady, Mrs. Lake always wore all the products she was featuring, from pins to new perfumes, and carried what seemed like a HUGE display suitcase filled with products.

And when she left, her definite perfumed scent stayed for hours, until my dad would come home for supper and start to sneeze.

Since my mom would always serve something while Mrs. Lake was visiting, I decided to use this favorite brownie recipe from friend and farmer's daughter from down the road Amy Scamerhorn. (For years, Amy's father Steve also farmed Mr. and Mrs. Lake's ground for them, usually planting peppermint.)

"I really like the frosting -- it's almost as good as your mom's!" Amy wrote me, while sharing the recipe.

"I also like the fact that you don't have to mess around with cocoa powder, since whenever I use it, the powder always gets all over the kitchen!"

Amy's Smooth Frosted Chocolate Chip Brownies

- Preheat oven to 350 degrees.

- To make brownie batter, in a large mixing bowl, cream butter and sugar. Add eggs, one at a time, beating well after each addition.

- Beat in chocolate syrup and vanilla. Stir in flour, salt and chocolate chips (and nuts, if desired).

- Pour into a greased 13-by-9-by-2-inch baking pan. Bake for 35 to 40 minutes or until a toothpick inserted near the center comes out clean. Cool.

- To make frosting, in a microwave-safe bowl, melt chocolate chips and butter; stir until smooth. Cool for 5 minutes. Whisk in sour cream and vanilla. Gradually stir in confectioner's sugar until smooth. Frost brownies. Cut into bars. Store in the refrigerator.

- Makes 1 dozen large brownies.

INGREDIENTS:

BROWNIES:

1/2 cup butter, softened

1 cup sugar

4 eggs

1 (16 ounce) can chocolate syrup

2 teaspoons vanilla extract

1 cup all-purpose flour

1/2 teaspoon salt

1 cup semisweet chocolate chips

1 cup chopped nuts (optional)

FROSTING:

1 cup semisweet chocolate chips

1/4 cup butter, cubed

1/2 cup sour cream

1/2 teaspoon vanilla extract

2-1/4 cups confectioner's sugar

Walking the red carpet in Chicago at the June 18, 2009 film premiere for "Public Enemies," I was joined by Amy Scamerhorn and many camera flashes, while wearing the hat once owned by Walter Winchell (inset photo), which I also wore for my filmed scenes.

Prisoner's 'Shoo-Fly Pie' recipe better than bail

October 24, 2007

As many readers know, on Fridays, I teach two college courses in public speaking for Purdue University North Central at the Westville Correctional Center.

I've been doing this for five years, and I've found the offenders, whose families are paying for them to be enrolled in college classes, are serious about both rehabilitation and turning their lives around.

Most have decided when "life gives you all lemons, make lemonade."

Sometimes, a little humor also can go a long way.

For instance, Ron Edwards #135928, who is serving time until 2016 for armed robbery, was pleasantly surprised that for the past year, he was receiving a subscription to Gourmet magazine, the monthly publication filled with photographs of delicious food and sumptuous menu possibilities.

He figured one of his family members provided the gift mailing.

Then one day, he met Ronald Edwards, head of the prison facility's dining-services program, who had wondered why he hadn't been receiving his magazines for the past 12 months.

Today's recipe was given to me more than a year ago by one of my student success stories, Robert Parker #966733, who has paid his dues and is free.

He always bragged (and with good reason) about his Aunt Mary's old fashioned "Shoo-Fly Pie," printed here.

It serves as proof that something good can come from a prison sentence.

INGREDIENTS:

1 unbaked 9-inch pie shell
1/4 cup shortening
1 cup brown sugar
1-1/2 cups flour
3/4 teaspoon baking soda
1/4 teaspoon salt
3/4 cup molasses
3/4 cup hot water
1/8 teaspoon nutmeg
Pinch of cinnamon
Pinch of ginger
Pinch of ground cloves

Shoo-Fly Pie # 966733

● In a small bowl, use a fork to gently combine shortening with flour and brown sugar until crumbly. Set aside.

● In another bowl, combine all remaining ingredients and pour into an unbaked pie shell.

● Pour crumb mixture on top of pie filling and bake for 15 minutes in a hot 450-degree oven (or 20 minutes at 350 degrees, if preferred.)

● Makes 10 slices.

Brownie recipe worthy of praise

November 21, 2007

Matt Dudzik, director of Purdue University Calumet's intramurals program, came up with a great idea last week.

The campus launched a search for the best brownie recipe whipped up by a member of the student body or staff.

When I was asked to be a judge, of course, I couldn't pass on an opportunity to be part of a brownie bake-off.

Raquel Perez won top honors after presenting her glass pan of fresh-baked brownies last Thursday to our judging panel in the PUC cafeteria.

You're getting the exclusive recipe first, right here.

Thank you for reading my columns and to all readers, a happy and blessed Thanksgiving!

Raquel's Perfect Purdue Brownies

● In a small saucepan, combine butter and chocolate chips over a low flame until combined and smooth.

● Remove from heat and add sugar; stir to combine.

● Add eggs and vanilla to chocolate mixture. Set aside.

● In a separate bowl, combine flour and baking soda and mix with warm chocolate mixture. Lastly, fold in butterscotch chips with batter.

● Spray a 9-by-11-by-2-inch baking pan with cooking spray and pour brownie batter, spreading evenly.

● Bake at 350 degrees for 20 minutes, testing with a toothpick, and then baking an extra 10 minutes if necessary.

● Makes 18 brownies.

INGREDIENTS:

1 stick butter
3 ounces semi-sweet chocolate chips
1 cup granulated sugar
2 eggs
1 teaspoon vanilla
2/3 cup flour
1/4 teaspoon baking soda
1/2 cup butterscotch chips

Pumpkin cake squares a favorite request

November 28, 2007

One of the recipes I often get requests for comes from my mother's recipe file.

I'm amazed at how many readers remember my mom's recipe for moist pumpkin cake bars.

We first shared this recipe in 2005 when I hosted a "Thanksgiving From the Farm" cooking class at the little cooking school that used to be in Highland, Ind.

And ever since I mentioned it in those columns from a couple years ago, I've received requests for it since it never appeared in any of my columns or cookbooks.

So this week, I've decided to share it.

Whenever my mother makes her pumpkin pies, she always has mashed pumpkin left over. She learned long ago not to make too much filling and "over fill" her pies, so they don't run over in the oven.

So, this recipe is the ideal way to use up any leftover pumpkin.

My mom was given this recipe more than 25 years ago when she was still working as a school teacher's aide at our farm town's local elementary school.

One of the second grade teachers, Mrs. Mary Brown (who also happened to be the wife of my older sister Pam's girl's basketball coach, Kevin Brown), made this recipe as one of her specialties.

Ever since my mom sampled it in the teachers' lounge, it's been a favorite in her recipe file.

I think you'll like it just as much as she does.

There also was a great quote written on the bottom of my mom's recipe card that I'll share.

"No man's opinion is entirely worthless; even a watch that won't run is right twice a day."

I have fond memories of this May 1992 college graduation from Valparaiso University. With my Auntie Lilly and my parents along to share the day, it was the first day of a bright career future I knew awaited.

INGREDIENTS:

CAKE

2 cups flour

1/2 teaspoon baking powder

1 teaspoon baking soda

2 teaspoons cinnamon

2 cups sugar

4 beaten eggs

1 cup salad oil

1 cup canned pumpkin

1 teaspoon vanilla

1 cup chopped walnuts or pecans (optional)

FROSTING

1 (8 ounce) package cream cheese

1 stick margarine

1 pound box powdered sugar

1 teaspoon milk

1 teaspoon vanilla

1/4 cup chopped walnuts or pecans (optional)

Frost on the Pumpkin Bars

• To make cake batter, combine sugar, eggs, oil, pumpkin and vanilla.

• Sift flour, salt, baking powder, baking soda and cinnamon together and beat into pumpkin mixture.

• Fold in the chopped nuts and mix well.

• Pour batter onto a large greased and floured 15-by-11-inch jelly roll pan.

• Bake at 350 degrees for 20 minutes.

• While cake is cooling, make frosting by creaming together cream cheese and margarine.

• Add powdered sugar, milk and vanilla.

• Blend at a low speed until smooth.

• Frost cake and sprinkle with chopped nuts for decoration.

• Makes 20 squares.

Grandpa Potempa is making hay in this July 1948 photo memory.

'Dairy-free' brownies get extra recognition

December 5, 2007

When I told my family friend Irene Jakubowski about the recent brownie competition I judged last month, she was especially fascinated by the "vegetarian" brownie recipe that finished close to first place.

Irene, 85, has spent the last month in a hospital bed as she awaits further tests about possible heart surgery.

Over the weekend, she finally was moved to the specialty heart hospital in Indianapolis.

I drove down to see her Sunday and brought her a sample of one of these special brownies, as well as some of my sister Pam's recipe for delicious chicken chili, which was featured in my second cookbook "More From the Farm."

Not only did my care package put a smile on Irene's face, but also the added surprise of a small fresh poinsettia to brighten her room and Christmas tree star ornament autographed by one of her favorites: Martha Stewart.

Irene remains in good spirits.

She's watching lots of CNN news, and she told me how amazed she is by the new plastic "shampoo caps" used in hospitals today. I have to admit, I was pretty impressed by this invention as well. I remember when Grandma Potempa was in the hospital during the 1980s and couldn't have a complete shampoo over a sink. They used to use a "dry, water-free" powder shampoo kit. The new shampoo shower cap Irene showed actually uses a water solution and seems to work like a charm.

I ask that readers continue to keep Irene in their thoughts and prayers.

And as promised to reader Debbie Schmidt's request last month, here's that finalist "vegetarian friendly brownie" recipe from Purdue University Calumet student Audrey Weaver.

"This recipe is GREAT for anyone abstaining from animal products (vegans) or for those with food allergies," Audrey said.

"And the bonus is these brownies are also cholesterol-free and you can lick the bowl when you're done since there are no raw eggs in the recipe."

Of course, I sampled these brownies when I was a judge last month for Purdue's First Brownie Bake-off.

And as mentioned, I also whipped up my own batch over the weekend.

Audrey's correct that these brownies do have a lighter "cake quality" to them. And without the eggs in the recipe, these brownies are still so moist,though a little bit crumbly. But the end result is still quite nice, considering the ingredient limitations based on diet.

INGREDIENTS:

1 1/4 cups white sugar

3/4 cup soybean stick margarine (try Willow Run brand, found at Meijer or Healthy Horizons on Indianapolis Boulevard in Hammond)

1/2 cup cocoa powder

1/2 cup applesauce

2 teaspoons baking powder (divided use)

1 teaspoon vanilla

1-1/2 cups all-purpose flour

1 teaspoon baking powder

1-1/4 cup soymilk (original or vanilla flavor)

1-1/4 cups chopped walnuts

Powdered sugar for garnish (optional)

Audrey's Vegetarian Cake Brownies

- Grease a 9-inch-by-13-inch baking pan with vegetable oil; set aside.

- In a sauce pan, heat sugar, margarine and cocoa powder over medium heat until melted, stirring constantly to avoid scorching. Remove from heat.

- Add applesauce and 1 teaspoon baking power to cocoa mixture. (This serves as the substitute for eggs. If you are ever out of eggs, 1/4 cup applesauce and 1/2 teaspoon baking powder will equal 1 medium egg.)

- Add vanilla and stir just until combined.

- In a mixing bowl, combine flour, 1 teaspoon baking powder and baking soda.

- Add flour mixture and soymilk alternatively to the chocolate mixture, stirring well after each addition. Fold in walnuts.

- Pour batter into the prepared baking pan. Bake in a 350-degree oven for about 20 minutes, checking to see if a toothpick inserted near the center comes out clean.

- Let cool at least a half hour and sprinkle with powdered sugar.

- Note: You also can replace an egg with 1/4 cup mashed banana and 1/2 teaspoon baking powder, but unlike the applesauce this does add a hint of additional flavor (banana) and may not be suitable for some recipes.

- Makes 25 bars.

Vegetarian Brownies (Photo by Michael Berkos)

Red Velvet Cake
an age-old favorite

December 12, 2007

After reading last week's food cover story about the tradition of red velvet cake written by writer Jane Ammeson, Mary S. Wallace of Munster, Ind. wrote me to share yet another version of what she believes to be the real recipe from the famed historic New York hotel.

As for the interesting reader letter and recipe I received from Mary, I decided to share it with readers in this week's column:

"After reading the food section, I believe I actually have the TRUE Waldorf-Astoria Hotel Red Velvet Cake recipe which my mother has, and her mother had," Mary wrote me.

"I've been using this recipe for many years. The real frosting is not a cream cheese base. It has the texture of very thick whipped cream."

Thank you, Mary. As a big fan of traditions and heirloom recipes, I've always been a fan of red velvet cake. I'm eager to give this recipe, with all of its lore and connection to the famous hotel of the Big Apple, a try for the holidays.

Of course, when I think of red velvet cake, the first image I think of is the custom "groom's cake" design featured in the favorite 1989 film "Steel Magnolias," which starred Dolly Parton, Julia Roberts, Sally Field, Shirley MacLaine, Daryl Hannah and Olympia Dukakis.

When Roberts' young bride character Shelby planned her big southern wedding, she had a special groom's cake (an old-fashioned tradition started back during the Victoria Era) made in the shape of an armadillo.

"It's made out of red velvet cake, so they'll get a surprise when they start hacking into it," said Roberts, as Shelby, sporting a devilish grin.

Oscar-winning actress Olympia Dukakis, pictured with me in Chicago in August 2003, has earned critical praise for many roles, but among my favorites are her turn in "Moonstruck" with Cher in 1987 and "Steel Magnolias" in 1989.

INGREDIENTS:

CAKE:

1/2 cup shortening

1-1/2 cups sugar

2 eggs

1 teaspoon vanilla

2 tablespoons unsweetened cocoa powder

1/4 cup red food coloring

1 teaspoon salt

1 cup buttermilk

2-1/4 cups sifted flour

1 tablespoon vinegar

1 teaspoon baking soda

FROSTING:

1 cup milk

5 tablespoons flour

1 cup softened butter

1 cup powdered sugar

1 teaspoon vanilla

NOTE: Must add ingredients the way they are listed.

True Waldorf Astoria Hotel's Red Velvet Cake

- Cream shortening and sugar until fluffy.

- Add eggs and beat one minute.

- Place cocoa and red food color in a cup and make a paste. Add that to shortening mixture. Add salt.

- Place the vanilla in the buttermilk and add slowly to the creamed mixture alternately with the flour.

- Place vinegar and soda in a cup. Add that to the cake batter.

- Pour batter in 2 greased and floured 9-inch round layer cake pans.

- Bake at 350 degrees for 25 to 30 minutes. Cool completely before frosting.

- To make frosting, cook milk and flour over a low flame until thick and pasty. Cool completely in refrigerator.

- Beat butter, powdered sugar and vanilla with electric mixer.

- Add the cooled flour mixture to the butter and sugar a little at a time while beating.

- Frost the cooled cake. Store cake in refrigerator.

- Makes 12 serving slices.

'Powdered Sugar' Pound Cake a holiday gift

December 26, 2007

I hope everyone enjoyed Christmas and the holiday feasting is still continuing with delicious leftovers to enjoy in the days to come.

Whenever I think of leftovers, I always think of my Uncle Joey, who died in August 1996.

He was married to my dad's older sister, my Auntie Judy, who died two years ago this month in 2005.

When Auntie Judy was always the busiest was during this time of year.

She would bake dozens and dozens of assorted Christmas cookies as well as her wonderful signature "Powdered Sugar Pound Cake," all of which she would mail to Grandma Potempa and Auntie Lilly at the farm, as well as sharing with us and the rest of the family.

I particularly like that in Auntie Judy's recipe steps, she uses the empty powdered sugar box as her means of measuring the necessary amount of cake flour used.

Whether you're Polish like my family, or even if you're not, even Auntie Judy's "transformed box" measurement tradition is enough to bring a smile.

Auntie Judy's
Powdered Sugar Pound Cake

- Preheat oven to 350 degrees.

- Cream together powdered sugar and butter, using an electric mixer and beat for 5 minutes.

- Add eggs, one at time, beating well after each addition.

- Add vanilla and then gradually add flour, beating batter on medium speed for 5 minutes.

- Pour batter into a lightly sprayed or lightly greased and floured loaf pan or bundt pan.

- Bake in 350 degree oven for 1 hour and 15 minutes or until toothpick inserted comes out clean.

- Makes 12 servings.

INGREDIENTS:

1 (16 ounce) box powdered sugar

1 pound butter

2 heaping cups cake flour (or Auntie Judy would fill the empty powdered sugar box with cake flour exactly to the top)

6 eggs

1 teaspoon vanilla

Christmas church services filled with memories

January 2, 2008

Happy New Year!

While attending Christmas Eve Mass with my parents, we were excited to welcome Dec. 25 at a very special church service for our town.

Rev. Robert Gehring, a member of the large farming family that's a part of Starke County history, returned to our town for the first time in 40 years to celebrate Christmas Eve Mass.

During the Christmas Eve service, Father Gehring said one of his most vivid memories in our town while he was growing up is from 1940 when Two Joe's Grocery Store, which also was owned by his family, burned down that Christmas Eve.

"The next day, I'll never forget when we went to Grandma Dolezal's house and she had all of the money saved from the store hanging over the radiators in the house to dry out from all of the firemen's water hoses," he said with a smile.

On the day after Christmas, I also attended daily Mass with my mom in the beautiful 1940s marble chapel of Our Lady of Holy Cross Nursing Home (formerly Little Company of Mary) in our town, which sadly, will close in February.

In the story I wrote about that closing earlier this month, my parents reminded me I neglected to include that the 377 acres of land the convent and nursing home sit on was donated, along with his farm, by John J. Tierney, described in our town's history records as "a recluse philosopher and wealthy philanthropist."

After being cared for by the Sisters of Little Company of Mary, an order of nuns based in Evergreen Park, Ill., up until his death at age 91 on Dec. 2, 1941, he left his estate to the nuns.

Sister Solace, in her memoirs, described Tierney as "a darling man whom I called St. Joseph."

Both my mother and the farmer's wife neighbor down the road, Joann Scamerhorn, have made many cookie and sweets trays to donate and serve as refreshments while volunteering for functions at the nursing home during the past three decades since I can remember.

I decided to share one of my favorite candy recipes often included on Mrs. Scamerhorn's sweet trays: a simple candy hash.

White Chocolate Candy Hash

- Melt white chocolate in a double boiler over boiling water or in a microwave.

- In a separate bowl, combine all remaining ingredients and toss to mix.

- Pour melted white chocolate over combined ingredients and stir until well blended and evenly coated.

- Line a cookie sheet with wax paper and drop candy by the teaspoonful onto the lined cookie sheet.

- Chill candy in refrigerator until candy is firm to the touch. Place in air-tight container, and keep refrigerated until serving.

- Note: This candy freezes well.

- Makes 3 dozen.

INGREDIENTS:

1 pound melting chocolate, white variety

1-1/2 cups sweetened corn and oat breakfast cereal, such as Captain Crunch cereal

1-1/2 cups crisp rice breakfast cereal, such as Rice Krispies cereal

1-1/2 cups dry roasted peanuts

1-1/2 cup miniature marshmallows

I snapped this photo of one of the nuns from the order of the Sisters of Little Company of Mary, praying in the beautiful marble chapel of the nursing home facility in 1992. It was taken on the eve before her order had to vacate to return to its mother house convent in Evergreen Park, Ill.

Apples, carrots, onions last the winter

January 23, 2008

When I asked my mom what vegetable she was making with her mashed potatoes and beef roast for the family Sunday dinner, I was surprised when she answered me with "your dad's fresh carrots from the garden."

After all, over the weekend it was below-zero, and it's not often you can talk about enjoying "fresh vegetables" from a garden when the calendar shows it's near the end of a snowy and cold January.

On Christmas Eve, for example, I was still picking parsley from the garden and fresh sage (though it was nestled under the snow), with the parsley used for homemade clam chowder to have before midnight Mass and the sage seasoning our roast turkey and stuffing for the next day's Christmas dinner.

I also had fresh chives from near the fence to use in a soft cheese ball recipe.

My Dad and Auntie Lottie still remind me how Grandma and Grandpa Potempa used the underground root cellar at our farm to store Grandma's canning, including pears, beans, tomatoes, jam and sauerkraut, and also bushels of winter apples, black walnuts, pears, carrots, potatoes, onions, dried herbs and even heads of cabbage, to use to feed a big Catholic Polish family of nine children all winter.

Today, my dad still keeps apples (if there's a bounty in the fall), walnuts, carrots, onions and potatoes for Mom to use during the winter.

And leaving the dirt on all the root vegetables helps with preservation.

Today's easy apple cake recipe was given to me by Karen Kallok of Griffith, Ind. Your fired-up oven, and the cake that will come out once the door is opened, will help warm up hearts and homes.

INGREDIENTS:

3 eggs
1-3/4 cup sugar
1 cup cooking oil
2 cups sifted flour
1 teaspoon cinnamon
1 teaspoon baking soda
1 dash salt
5 apples, peeled and diced
1 cup chopped walnuts

Simple Kitchen Apple Cake

- Preheat oven to 350 degrees.

- Grease and flour a 9-by-13-inch baking pan. Set aside.

- Blend eggs, sugar and oil together in a mixing bowl.

- Sift together flour, cinnamon, baking soda and salt, and stir into egg mixture.

- Fold in apples and nuts.

- Pour batter into prepared pan and bake at 350 degrees for 1 hour or until it tests done.

- Makes 16 slices.

Third grade teacher knew 'a smart cookie'

January 30, 2008

I received plenty of mail and nice comments about a column I wrote earlier this month mentioning my third-grade teacher Erna Eckert.

Mrs. Eckert was always a very stern and traditional teacher.

Since I had struggled through Mrs. Paulsen's second-grade class, my mom was particularly concerned I would have even a harder time with Mrs. Eckert, who also had taught my two older sisters and two older brothers. I was especially a very poor reader and lousy speller, and aware of this fact since in second grade, I was in the "plum-colored" reading group for "the worst readers." (I always longed to be in the Canary-yellow group.) And since I have an August birthday, I also was very young for my class, since my mom decided to have me start school early.

Well, despite my nervousness about moving on to third grade, even though it had been recommended that I repeat second grade, I found a very valued and surprising supporter in Mrs. Eckert, who rather than having me remain in the lowest reading group, decided I should be challenged and motivated more by pushing me into the "middle" reading group, "the tangerine-orange readers." This small nod gave me new self-confidence.

And even more, what always stood out in my mind was one particular day early on in the school year when I got a perfect score on my spelling test (thanks to lots of at home studying with my mom, and Mrs. Eckert said in front of the whole class: "That Phil Potempa is one smart cookie."

From this early point in my school career on, I never seriously struggled with studies and just realized the importance of hard work.

So today, I'm not only happy to share this teacher story, but I'm also sharing her old-fashioned chocolate-chip cookie recipe.

In my mind, Mrs. Eckert, who now is in her 80s and was always a member of the adult home economist club, is also a great cook as well as a great teacher.

Erna's "Perfectly Chocolate" Chocolate Chip Cookies

- Heat oven to 375 degrees.

- Mix flour, cocoa, baking soda and salt and set aside.

- In a slightly larger bowl, beat together margarine, sugars and vanilla until creamy, using an electric mixer set on medium.

- Beat in eggs and then gradually add in the flour mixture until combined.

- Fold in chocolate chips and nuts, if desired.

- Drop dough by rounded teaspoonfuls onto an ungreased cookie sheet.

- Bake 8-10 minutes or until set as desired. Cool slightly and remove to wire rack.

- Makes 5 dozen.

INGREDIENTS:

2-1/4 cup flour

1/3 cup cocoa

1 teaspoon baking soda

1/2 teaspoon salt

1 cup (2 sticks) margarine, softened

3/4 cup white granulated sugar

3/4 cup packed light brown sugar

1 teaspoon vanilla

2 eggs

1 (12 ounce) package semi-sweet chocolate chips

1 cup chopped walnuts or pecans (optional)

Here's Erna Eckert at one of my mom's many children's birthday parties we were so lucky that she planned for us over the years. This one was on July 23, 1961, and my mom can be seen in the background with Auntie Lilly and neighbor Sue Paulsen, along with my sister Carol and Mackie Paulsen.

Mom's home perms meant helping hands

February 20, 2008

When you're a little kid, seeing ladies clucking and fussing over a home permanent seems pretty strange.

One winter memory I have from my youth is when my mom would annually get a home permanent at the start of the new year.

And since, despite how many mirrors might be propped all around, my mom couldn't see the back of her hair to evenly roll up the little pink, blue and yellow color-coded plastic curlers, that meant she'd always have a friend over and they'd help roll up each other's hair.

I'd know it was home-permanent day if, besides being greeted by the smell of chemical solutions, I spotted small, plastic needle-nose bottles and stacks of curlers on the basement table next to the concrete laundry tub. Meanwhile, my mom and her friends had plastic aprons around their necks and plastic bonnets on their heads, with cotton tucked around their ears and over their foreheads.

(By late afternoon, once their new curly hairdos were finished and dry, they would be playing Yatzee, and I'd hear them grouse they had "railroad tracks" along the crown of their head from rolling the curlers too tight.)

Over the years, Pat Royce, Joann Scamerhorn and Mary Roy would all spend an afternoon helping with "beauty duty."

And of course, there was also good ol' Marie Skuderna, the farm wife who just lived one field away down our road.

Marie, who died at age 71 on Nov. 30, 1997, also had a cake specialty she loved.

In fact, her recipe for moist and delicious "Harvey Wallbanger Cake" is included in a small homemade booklet my mom still keeps with all her cookbooks. The faded construction paper cover of the booklet reads, "Picnic with Marie in '73," and the pages are filled with the recipe specialties of our town's local ladies home economics club.

INGREDIENTS:

Cake:

1 (18.25-ounce) package orange cake mix

1 (3.75-ounce) package instant vanilla pudding

4 eggs

1/2 oil

1/2 cup orange juice

1/2 cup Galliano liqueur

2 tablespoons vodka

Glaze topping:

1 cup powdered sugar

1 tablespoon orange juice

1 tablespoon Galliano liqueur

1 teaspoon vodka

Marie Skuderna's Harvey Wallbanger Cake

● Preheat oven to 350 degrees.

● To make cake, in large mixing bowl, combine cake mix and instant pudding, also adding eggs, oil, 1/2 cup orange juice, the Galliano liqueur and the vodka, beat on low speed for 30 seconds and then on medium speed for 5 minutes.

● Pour in a greased-and-floured 10-inch fluted tube pan and bake for 45 minutes. Cool slightly in pan.

● While cake is baking, to make glaze, combine all ingredients and pour over cake while still warm from the oven.

● Serves 12.

It's one of my many childhood memories while growing up, seeing (and hearing) Marie Skuderna sitting with my mom at our kitchen table drinking coffee chatting about everyone and anyone. So often, I'd hear them advise one another about a bit of secret "news," which they would remind each other to "keep it on the QT," which later, I found out was code for "quiet."

My goodbye to
dear friend Irene

March 12, 2008

As I'm writing this column, it's Monday at 8 p.m. and I've just returned with my parents from our good friend Irene Jakubowski's visitation and Rosary service in Monticello, Ind.

Irene, 85, died one week ago from today, at 1:30 p.m. March 5 at Monticello Rehabilitation and Care Center.

One of the many things that makes writing this column emotional for me is realizing that it was 15 years ago in this same building, here in our Valparaiso office, that I met Irene, who was working her usual early evening shift selling newspaper subscriptions as her past-time, and a reason to get out of the house to make a little extra money. When she'd decide to take a little break and stroll over to the water fountain (which was near the desk I sat at during the evenings writing my stories), she'd always chat with me, and soon, we became fast friends. We both liked to say we had newspaper ink that flowed through our veins.

And whenever I had to drive some place far for a story or to do an interview, I could always depend on Irene to be at my side as "My Girl Friday," yep, just like the 1940 movie with Cary Grant playing a reporter and Rosalind Russell as his assistant. In my Friday offBeat column, I mentioned a few of the famous folks Irene met during my assignments, but I neglected to also mention her other encounters with people like Lucie Arnaz, Ann Jillian, David Letterman's mom Dorothy Letterman, "Garfield the Cat" creator Jim Davis, and Ruth Handler, "Barbie's Mom," inventor of Mattel's Barbie Doll.

When I went to see Irene last Wednesday with my parents, I had the last three weeks of my "From the Farm" columns in one hand for her and in my other hand, a vase with a dozen pink roses, set off by a big bowl and a tiny robin nestled in a small bird's nest.

And though she was peacefully sleeping and not conscious enough to talk, I know she heard me talking with her and holding her hand for that half an hour. While standing near her bed and talking with Irene, as my mom stood on the other side of the bed saying prayers, I told Irene that when my next cookbook was published [the book you are now holding in your hands as you read this], on the first page it would read with a dedication to her.

After we left and I was driving my parents back to the farm, we received a call while driving that Irene died less than an hour after we said good-bye.

As I had shared with readers around the holidays, Irene hadn't been feeling well.

So many readers also know Irene from this

Wednesday "From the Farm" columns and my two previous cookbooks, "From the Farm" (2004) and "More From the Farm" (2007).

Irene was born and raised in LaPorte, but spent most of her life living in Valparaiso, attending St. Paul's Catholic Church and living in a beautiful cottage on Long Lake, before she retired to Monticello about a decade ago.

In addition to all the wonderful recipes and memories she shared with me and my readers, over the years, Irene also would be at my side at my Times events as well. She was with me at some of the stories I would cover, often meeting and chatting with folks from all over, including many famous faces like President Jimmy Carter, singer Helen Reddy, Lassie, comedian Pat Paulsen, former hostage Father Lawrence Martin Jenco, Bobby Vinton, household hints columnist Heloise and so many others.

We met in 1991 while she worked in the circulation department for The Vidette-Messenger and then for The Times, and Irene traveled with me at a moment's notice to any assignment, from a trek to Evansville, Ind., to visit the on-location filming for "A League of their Own" starring Geena Davis and Madonna, to the Chicago Broadway November 2000 press opening of "Tallulah," the stage play based on the life of Tallulah Bankhead starring Kathleen Turner and then dinner at the elegant Walnut Room at Marshall Field's.

If I had to bake 10 dozen muffins for a weekend event, I knew I could always ask Irene for help.

And when I'd double-check with her to see if she really was able to help me out in a pinch, she'd always reply with: "I'll do something kiddo, even if it's wrong."

And in the end, she'd always come through for a friend.

It's rare, if ever, that I reprint a recipe that's already been published in one of my previous columns or has already appeared in one of my earlier cookbook. But today is a special exception, since this recipe I am once again sharing was one of Irene's favorites, which she provided for me and readers, in this column in May 2003, and then appeared in my second cookbook. It seems like the perfect one to reprint today in honor of Irene, whose memories and smile will continue to live on the pages of my books and the paragraphs of my past and future columns.

Irene's Go-to-Sleep Mints

INGREDIENTS:

2 egg whites (room temperature)

1/2 teaspoon cream of tartar

3/4 cup sugar

Pinch salt

3 drops green food coloring

1 (6-ounce) package semisweet mint-flavored chocolate chips

- Preheat oven to 375 degrees. In a medium bowl, beat the egg whites and cream of tartar while gradually adding sugar, salt and coloring.

- When stiff peaks are formed, stir in the chocolate chips. Drop by teaspoonfuls onto ungreased cookie sheets. Turn the oven off and place mints into the oven to set overnight. Mints will be ready the next morning.

- Note: If regular chocolate chips are used, use 3/4 teaspoon of peppermint extract mixed into batter.

- Makes 50 mint drops

Saturday's library party
a green scene

March 26, 2008

If you haven't made your reservations yet for my free program and party at noon this Saturday welcoming spring and celebrating the grand opening of the new Wanatah Public Library, 114 S. Main St., Wanatah, Ind., I hope you'll join the fun.

A recipe sampling (including today's featured moist, green cake recipe), music, contests, a book signing and plenty of prizes will welcome guests.

Remember, you have to RSVP for your seat. The quaint, tiny library is just about 15 minutes east of Valparaiso, Ind. right down U.S. 30.

Not only will my parents attend, but adding to our green, "think spring" theme, will be a selection of my dad's homemade wren, bluebird and yellow finch bird houses, which he makes from dried gourds and hollowed tree limbs from our woods.

And as a grand prize door drawing giveaway, I have two of the much-sought-after front and center seats for the Broadway hit musical "Wicked," for the date of your choice for this popular stage sensation, which is playing in Chicago through June 2008.

Tickets for "Wicked," which is the story of how all of the popular characters from "The Wizard of Oz" were first brought to life and their origins before Dorothy "dropped in," seemed like a perfect prize since Wanatah is famous for an annual Scarecrow Festival every fall.

On the subject of origins, today's cake recipe comes from 92-year-old Ann Civiletti of Prescott, Ariz., who passed it along decades ago to her neighbors Pat and Jean Tuleja, of Schererville, who are dedicated readers of this column. The Tulejas have remained great neighbors of Ann and still visit her every winter. Not only does Ann still drive, they tell me, but she also is "a firecracker of energy."

Could the secret of her magic spell be in this green cake recipe?

INGREDIENTS:

1 (14.5-ounce) box yellow cake mix

1/2 cup vegetable oil

1 (3.4-ounce) box pistachio instant pudding

4 eggs

1/2 pint sour cream

3 tablespoons sugar

1/2 cup ground pecans

1 teaspoon cinnamon

Spring's Green Bundt Cake

● Combine cake mix, oil, dry instant pudding, eggs and sour cream in a mixing bowl and beat 4 minutes with electric mixer. Set aside.

● In a small bowl, mix together sugar, pecans and cinnamon.

● Using a coated bundt pan, pour in 1/2 of the nut mixture, then adding 1/2 of the cake batter on top of nuts. Repeat process, adding remaining nut mixture and ending with last of batter.

● Bake 1 hour at 350 degrees.

● Makes 14 serving slices.

Further From the Farm

County fair gal wins $1 million for cookies

April 16, 2008

DATELINE -- **Dallas** -- Philip Potempa is reporting from Texas this week while on assignment.

Carolyn Gurtz, of Gaithersburg, Md., sent in a selection of four recipes last year in hopes of being a finalist at the 43rd Annual Pillsbury Bake-Off.

Instead, it was her recipe for a quick and tasty peanut butter cookie that captured the tastebuds of the preliminary judges and won her a spot among the 100 finalists from around the country.

On Tuesday, Gurtz, 59, and her peanut butter cookie recipe took home the $1 million grand prize, in addition to a complete set of GE Profile kitchen appliances valued at $10,000. She also won "The JIF Peanut Butter Award" worth $5,000, an earlier prize awarded during the ceremony hosted by Food Network TV personality Sandra Lee.

Pillsbury's (more than) $1 Million Double Delight
Peanut Butter Cookie Recipe

- Heat oven to 375 degrees. In small bowl, mix chopped peanuts, granulated sugar and cinnamon, set aside.

- In another small bowl, stir peanut butter and powdered sugar until completely blended. Shape mixture into 24 (1-inch) balls.

- Cut roll of cookie dough into 12 slices. Cut each slice in half crosswise to make 24 pieces; flatten slightly. Shape 1 cookie dough piece around 1 peanut butter ball, covering completely. Repeat with remaining dough and balls.

- Roll each covered ball in peanut mixture; gently pat mixture completely onto balls. On ungreased large cookie sheets, place balls 2-inches apart. Spray bottom of a drinking glass with Crisco Original No-Stick Cooking Spray; press into remaining peanut mixture. Flatten each cookie dough ball to 1/4-inch thickness with bottom of glass. Sprinkle any remaining peanut mixture evenly on tops of cookies; gently press into dough.

- Bake 7 to 12 minutes or until edges are golden brown. Cool 1 minute; remove from cookie sheets to cooling rack. Store tightly covered.

- Makes 24 cookies.

- Recipe courtesy of Carolyn Gurtz, Gaithersburg, Md. and Pillsbury/General Mills.

INGREDIENTS:

1/4 cup Fisher Dry Roasted Peanuts, finely chopped

1/4 cup Domino or C&H granulated sugar

1/2 teaspoon ground cinnamon

1/2 cup JIF creamy peanut butter

1/2 cup Domino or C&H confectioners powdered sugar

1 (16.5 ounce) roll Pillsbury Create 'n Bake refrigerated peanut butter cookies, well chilled

Green salad dessert great for counting calories

April 22, 2008

On Sunday, I joined my sister Pam and my parents to share a nice and relaxing noon meal down the road with my oldest brother Tom and his wife Linda.

Along with my niece Bethany, and her two sons (my great nephews), we enjoyed a terrific roast turkey dinner with all the fixings, including the light and delicious dessert salad recipe of Linda's I'm sharing with readers this week.

Many of you might be familiar with it, since it's an old and favorite combination of simple ingredients that have been whipped together for years.

But the longer I write this column, I find more and more younger readers aren't always familiar with some of the simple basic recipe greats.

I also receive countless requests each week to print more light and healthy recipes.

Another favorite part of Sunday was the chance to enjoy the beautiful weather, while strolling through the back woods to the pond, which is filled to the very top because of all the rain. While frogs and turtles are already out, thankfully, the mosquitos haven't emerged yet.

On the subject of sightings, it was easy to smile after spotting the asparagus, rhubarb and chives all up and soon to be ready for recipes, a promise of more good things to come.

Linda's Light Fluffy Green Cloud Dessert Salad

- In a medium bowl, combine dry pudding mix with undrained pineapple.

- Fold in whipped topping, and if desired, marshmallows.

- Chill for 2 hours before serving.

INGREDIENTS:

1 small (1-ounce) box sugar-free and fat-free pistachio pudding

1 (20-ounce) can crushed pineapple, in juice, undrained

1 (8-ounce) carton fat-free thawed frozen nondairy whipped topping

1 cup miniature marshmallows (optional)

- Note: 65 calories per 1/2 cup serving, with no fat and low sugar and sodium. With marshmallows, 85 calories per 1/2 cup servings.

- Makes 6 servings.

Mom finally gets chance to work an election day

May 14, 2008

I hope all our readers had an enjoyable and relaxing Mother's Day.

For my own mom, her Mother's Day gift came extra early.

For as long as I can remember, my mom has always talked about working the election-day table as the faithful voters file in to cast their ballots.

Her good farm-wife friend Marie Skuderna never missed working an election day.

Finally, after all these years, my mom had her chance last week for the May Primary.

When her farm-wife friend down the road Debbie Wappel asked her if she wanted to train and work Indiana's voting day earlier this month, my mom quickly accepted. (I think she forgot about the part of having to get up at 4 a.m. to be to the town firehouse by 5 a.m. to get everything ready for voters to pull their party's lever.)

"I get to see all my neighbors in one day and catch up with them," says Debbie, explaining one of the reasons she enjoys working at election time.

Seated right next to my mom at the table with "the official sign-in books" was another great family friend, Ruth Dolezal Smolek, whose late mother Jeanne Dolezal was close to both my mom and Marie Skuderna and who died far too young at age 62 in 1989. (Recipes from both Jeanne and Marie have been featured in some of my earlier columns and included in both my cookbooks.)

It's always a tradition to have lots of baked goods for the election workers to enjoy, especially a very old recipe called "Election Day Cake," a delicious, dense, spiced, raisin coffee bread, which dates back to the 1700s.

(In Hartford, Conn., known as the Nutmeg State, it's been baked and served on election day for centuries, a fact confirmed by ledgers hundreds of years old that show records of ladies being reimbursed for the ingredients for this cake.)

My mom's version that I'm sharing today is a variation that, according her written out recipe card, dates back to 1957.

I joined Debbie Wappel and Lorraine "Blondie" Wappel for this photo snapped with my mom in February 2005 after they "shadowed" me by sitting in on one of college lectures at Valparaiso University.

INGREDIENTS:

SPONGE DOUGH:

3/4 cup milk

1 envelope/package (1/4 ounce) active dry yeast

1/4 cup warm water

1 teaspoon sugar

1 cup sifted flour

- Stir in raisins and nuts.

- Sift together dry ingredients and stir into creamed mixture, beating well.

- Mix the sponge dough and cake batter together (will be heavy), until well blended.

- Turn into two greased 5-1/2-inch-by-9-1/2-inch loaf pans or one 10-inch greased tube pan. Pans should be no more than half- filled. Let rise in warm place until doubled.

- Bake in moderate oven, 375 degrees, for 45 minutes. Frost while warm with confectioner's sugar icing.

- Makes 16 servings.

Election Day Cake

- To create sponge dough, scald milk and cool until lukewarm. Set aside.

- Sprinkle granular yeast over warm water (at least 110 degrees). Stir in 1 teaspoon sugar and let stand until bubbly, about 5 minutes.

- Add yeast to milk and stir in 1 cup sifted flour and beat until smooth. Let stand in warm place (at least 85 degrees) until doubled in size.

- Meanwhile, to create cake batter, cream butter and brown sugar and add egg and beat well.

INGREDIENTS:

CAKE BATTER:

1/2 cup butter or margarine

1 cup brown sugar

1 egg, beaten

1 cup raisins (can be rum-soaked if desired)

1/3 cup chopped nuts

1-1/2 cups sifted flour

1 teaspoon cinnamon

1/4 teaspoon cloves

1/4 teaspoon nutmeg

1 teaspoon salt

ICING GLAZE:

2 to 3 tablespoons milk

1 cup confectioner's sugar

1 tablespoon butter, softened

1/2 teaspoon vanilla extract

Further From the Farm

Time for spring's favorite strawberry-rhubarb pie

May 21, 2008

In the past six years I've been writing this farm column, I've never shared my mom's strawberry-rhubarb recipe.

My Dad, Auntie Lottie and Auntie Wanda all agree that while growing up on the farm, their mom, my Grandma Potempa, never grew rhubarb. Although, their good next door farm neighbor, Anna Skuderna, who I knew as Granny Skuderna while growing up, would sometimes bring Grandma and Grandpa Potempa some of her rhubarb.

However, much like the case with Grandma Potempa's gooseberry bushes that I wrote about a couple years ago, Grandma Potempa rarely would can, cook or bake with rhubarb because she said it required too much sugar, which was a waste of money.

INGREDIENTS:

CRUST:

2 cups flour

1/2 cup cooking oil

1/4 cup milk

1 teaspoon salt

Wax paper

Drinking straws

Aluminum foil

FILLING:

1-1/2 cups granulated sugar

4 tablespoons cornstarch

1/4 teaspoon salt

3 cups fresh strawberries, rinsed and sliced

3 cups fresh rhubarb, rinsed and sliced small

Peggy's Strawberry-Rhubarb Pie

● To make crust, combine flour, cooking oil, milk and salt and form dough into a ball. Chill for a few minutes, before rolling out a top and a bottom 9-inch pie crust between two pieces of wax paper.

● Line a 9-inch pie pan with the bottom crust.

● To make filling, combine sugar, cornstarch and salt in a medium bowl. Add sliced strawberries and rhubarb, mixing well to coat.

● Spoon filling into a prepared 9-inch pie pan lined with crust.

● Lightly moisten edge of bottom crust with water and cover pie with top crust and seal edges with fork and then finger flute the pie edges.

● Cut two plastic drinking straws into four sections and insert into top crust for ventilation. (Straws may curl slightly from heat, but won't harm pie.) Cover edge of pie crust with strips of aluminum foil to prevent over-baking.

● Bake in hot oven at 450 degrees for 15 minutes. Reduce heat to 350 degrees and bake an additional 30 to 40 minutes until juice begins to bubble through slits or until evenly brown.

● Makes 8 servings.

Auntie Lottie celebrates 85th birthday with rice pudding recipe

June 4, 2008

It's hard to believe, but my dad's sister, my Auntie Lottie, celebrated her 85th birthday on Monday.

She's been retired and living near Sarasota, Fla., for more than 15 years.

When my friend Dennis Deany of Kankakee, Ill., wrote to me last month requesting a good recipe for yummy old fashioned rice pudding, it was Auntie Lottie who came to the rescue.

I remembered it was a favorite of Grandma Potempa's.

Growing up, I always preferred bread pudding or tapioca (both of which my mom despises, along with rice pudding, for that matter), but never cared much for rice pudding.

After calling Auntie Lottie to search her own recipe tins, she wrote me a long letter and enclosed her own recipe.

She mentioned this recipe was also a favorite that she would make for Uncle Swede, before he died in 1997.

I'm sure it also will become a favorite for readers to save and pass along as well.

Note, the consistency for this homemade pudding recipe is more thin rather than thick. For a thicker consistency, a little cornstarch can be added.

Tomorrow, I will speak as a special guest at a church luncheon hosted by St. Stanislaus Catholic Church in East Chicago, Ind.

I'm not sure what's on the dessert menu, but I know fried chicken, fellowship and good will are sure to be served up as our main course.

INGREDIENTS:

6 cups whole milk

1 large (12 ounce) can evaporated milk

2-1/2 cups water

1 cup regular white rice

4 large eggs

1 cup sugar

1 teaspoon vanilla

2 teaspoons cornstarch (if desired for thicker consistency)

Cinnamon

Nutmeg

Auntie Lottie's Rice Pudding

- Bring both types of milk, water and rice to a boil and boil for 40 minutes or until rice is soft and mixture is thick and creamy, stirring often.

- In a large bowl, mix eggs, sugar and vanilla until very frothy. Add the rice mixture to the egg mixture and fold together. Chill for 2 hours.

- Serve sprinkled with a dash of cinnamon and nutmeg and/or a dollop of whipped cream.

- Serve chilled.

- Makes 6 servings.

Join me at my local library for a mint-inspired event

June 18, 2008

I've hosted many free library events during the past six years I've been writing this "From the Farm" column.

Yet, for some reason, I've never been featured at my own home county's library for an event.

So, this Saturday is finally the day to enjoy presenting a free program closer to my own backyard and roots.

If you're interested in a quiet and peaceful Saturday drive through farm country, I'd like to invite readers to our "new" Starke County Public Library, 152 W. Culver Rd. in Knox, Ind. for a free "From the Farm" program and recipe sampling from 12 noon until 2 p.m. (CST) this Saturday, June 21.

I'll be sharing farm stories, introducing family members and giving away more than $800 in prizes in a free drawing.

And even better, I'll be serving up some of the past winning recipes from our annual mint festival, which are featured in my second cookbook, "More From the Farm."

At the urging of the Knox town librarian Diantha Upham, I'll also share some details from my three days of filming the new Universal Pictures movie "Public Enemies" with actor Johnny Depp, which opens in July 2009.

One very important note, even though the event is free, reservations are required so we can have the appropriate amount of chairs and refreshments.

Please call the library with your name, telephone number and the number in your party attending. The deadline date for the RSVP is Friday morning.

From Valparaiso, this library in our "county seat" of Knox is about 35 minutes away.

As for this week's featured recipe, it's one that was in the spotlight last weekend

when I judged our 31st Annual Mint Festival's "Cooking with Mint" contest.

It's the creation of Mary Gumz of Medaryville, Ind.

It's not only both easy and delicious, but it's also a light and refreshing minty sweet surprise to serve guests.

I've learned one of the keys for making "the perfect mojito" is to use a premium rum. Mount Gay Rum ranks at the top, and is billed as "the world's oldest rum."

So I've included this historic label's traditional mojito recipe, a true buried treasure from Barbados.

Mint Mojito Cake

- Heat oven to 350 degrees.

- Spray bottom of a 9-inch by 13-inch baking pan.

- Mix together all cake ingredients for 2-1/2 minutes using a medium setting on electric mixer. Bake for 30 minutes and allow to cool for 15 minutes.

- While cake is baking, mix together all of the glaze ingredients in a small saucepan and bring to a boil. Reduce heat to medium and heat 2 more minutes stirring frequently.

- Use a fork and poke holes into top of cake for every inch of cake surface. Pour glaze over cake.

- Once cake is completely cool and set, fold peppermint oil into whipped topping. Lastly, add drop of green food coloring and swirl to make a green design while lightly frosting cake with topping. Garnish with leaves.

- Makes 20 serving slices.

- 2008 First Place Winner, North Judson Mint Festival "Cooking with Mint" Contest, by Mary Gumz of Medaryville, Ind.

MINT MOJITO CAKE INGREDIENTS:

CAKE:

1 (18.25 ounce) white cake mix
1 cup club soda
1/3 cup vegetable oil
1/4 cup rum
3 tablespoons rinsed, chopped, fresh spearmint or peppermint leaves
2 teaspoons grated lime zest
3 eggs whites

GLAZE:

1/2 cup butter
1/4 cup water
1 cup sugar
1/2 cup rum

TOPPING:

1 (8 ounce) carton of thawed, frozen nondairy whipped topping
1/2 teaspoon peppermint oil extract
1 drop green food coloring
Fresh spearmint or peppermint leaves for garnish

MOUNT GAY RUM MINT MOJITO INGREDIENTS:

1-1/2 ounces Mount Gay Eclipse Silver Rum
12 fresh spearmint leaves
1/2 of a lime
2 tablespoons simple syrup (or 4 teaspoons sugar)
Splash of club soda

Mount Gay Rum Mint Mojito

- Muddle mint leaves and lime in a tall chilled glass.

- Cover with simple syrup and fill glass with ice

- Add Mount Gay Rum and top with club soda; stir well.

- Garnish glass with lime wedge and sprigs of mint.

- Makes 1 cocktail.

- Recipe courtesy of Mount Gay Rum.

Old-fashioned drugstore soda fountains missed

July 9, 2008

The summer before my sixth-grade year, I became one of the few kids in my school to have braces.

It was 1980 and in a small farming town, you didn't see many kids wearing braces because of the expense.

David Paulsen, Rodney Yost and Ann Scamerhorn, all in my class, also smiled with wires and brackets, as did Amy Ledvina and Jason Danford, who were one year younger than us.

Most of us went to the same dentist and orthodontist in the neighboring town of Winamac, Ind. wearing silly T-shirts that said "The Tin Grin is In."

At the time, I hated it, never realizing that my metal smile was actually a kind of status symbol and that my parents had to make an extra sacrifice by working harder for us to have a better smile. (My older brothers and my oldest sister Carol also had braces.)

Today, I'm grateful.

But the one thing I do remember enjoying most about my every-three-week visit to the orthodontist for three years, is that all the mothers would take turns car-pooling to save money. And at the end of those visits, we'd get to stop for ice cream (which felt good on throbbing teeth and gums) at the next door corner drugstore in Winamac, which had an old-fashioned soda fountain.

This was at the same time that our own family-owned neighborhood drugstore and soda fountain had just closed, after a Hooks Drugstore chain came to our town.

Petry's Drugstore was a favorite haunt for many kids in our town after school and before basketball practice.

Pharmacist Jack Petry died years ago, and last Thursday, his wife Lucille L. Petry, who was 85, also died.

The Petry's daughter Sue is still in our town, and I wrote about her just last month, talking about how she owns our town's roadhouse restaurant, Brantwood, with her husband Jerry Jonas.

There was a time when every town had a drugstore or five-and-dime store with a soda-fountain counter and coffeeshop.

In LaPorte, there used to be Woolworth's and in Valparaiso, Ind. in the court-house square, it was Harvey's Mart Dime Store. In Hebron, Ind. there was Buchanan's Drug Store and Soda Fountain, with it's cozy booths and main counter, which remained until the early 1970s.

Even Porter Memorial Hospital used to have its own coffeeshop with a soda fountain and sandwich counter.

Even if they're all gone now (like my braces), at least the memories remain.

Today's recipe is for a dessert that is perfectly served in an old soda-fountain sundae parfait glass.

Pastries & Dessert Favorites

Like two of last month's recipes, this one is also a winner from when I judged our town's "Cooking with Mint" contest.

This was the first-place winner from the youth category from the kitchen talents of six-grader Ellie Eccles of North Judson, Ind. the daughter of Gregory and Beth Eccles.

Minty Chocolate
Mousse Parfait

● Melt chocolate in a double boiler over simmering water.

● Remove from heat and pour into a mixing bowl.

● Lightly beat egg yolks and blend into the still-warm chocolate.

● In a separate bowl that has been slightly chilled, beat egg whites into soft peaks. Add sugar and beat again for stiff peaks.

INGREDIENTS:

6 ounces semisweet chocolate chips
3 eggs, separated
2 tablespoons sugar
3/4 cup heavy cream
1/2 teaspoon mint extract
Whipped cream
Fresh mint leaves

● Fold 1/3 of beaten whites into the chocolate mixture, continuing with remaining white a little at a time.

● Using another chilled bowl, whip heavy cream with mint extract until stiff, and fold into chocolate mixture. Chill thoroughly.

● Spoon into tall dessert classes, layering with whipped cream (or Dream Whip, if desired) and topped with a final dollop of whipped cream.

● Garnish with fresh mint leaves.

● Makes 4 to 6 servings.

Chocolate-cherry bars perfect for picnics

July 23, 2008

While describing in last week's column the farm barbecue and corn boil I attended with my parents at the neighboring "retired" dairy farm earlier this month, I ran out of space before I made it to the subject of desserts.

Harry and Sandy Maranowicz were the party hosts and the terrific couple whose family has worked so hard to keep alive their Polish family traditions started by Harry's father Bruno, who died in 1989.

It was Bruno's parents who came from Poland and purchased the tiny 80-acre dairy farm near our farm. Today, Harry and Sandy come down from "the city" aka Downers Grove, Ill. and spend their weekends at the farm, including their 10-year tradition of hosting this large July gathering, which features favorite Polish meats and recipes from both the city and farm.

Harry and four of his siblings attended Saturday's party, along with our neighboring farm friends the Wappels and the Scamerhorns. Harry always gives all of the ladies pairs of corn cob earrings to display the true spirit of the season, with "ears (of corn) adorning ears."

As for today's recipe, I'm showcasing some very easy and delicious chocolate cherry bars whipped up by my friend Ann Scamerhorn for Harry's picnic. Because of their color blend, she likes to call them "Blackhawk Bars."

Annie's Blackhawk Chocolate Cherry Bars

- In a mixing bowl, combine flour, oats, sugar and butter until crumbly. Set aside 1-1/2 cups for the topping and then press the reserved crumb mixture into an ungreased 13-inch by 9-inch baking pan. Bake at 350 degrees for 15 to 20 minutes or until edges begin to brown.

- In a small bowl, combine the cherry pie filling and extract and carefully spread over the crust. Sprinkle with reserved crumb topping mixture. Return to oven and bake another 20 to 25 minutes longer or until edges and topping are lightly browned.

- In a microwave or heavy saucepan, melt chocolate chips and shortening and stir until smooth. Drizzle over the warm bars. Cool completely before cutting into bars.

- Makes 36 bars.

INGREDIENTS:

- 2 cups all-purpose flour
- 2 cups quick cooking oats
- 1-1/2 cups sugar
- 1 1/4 cups butter or margarine, softened
- 1 (21-ounce) can cherry pie filling
- 1 teaspoon almond extract
- 1/2 cup semi-sweet chocolate chips
- 1-1/2 teaspoons shortening

Apricot pie better than birthday cake

August 13, 2008

Today is my 38th birthday.

It's hard to believe I'm inching closer and closer to my fourth decade.

I already received a nice card and note last week with birthday blessings from good friend and funny lady Phyllis Diller, who just turned 91 last month.

Phyllis, who lives in the Brentwood, Calif., neighborhood of Los Angeles next to Judy Garland's former house, originally hailed from Lima, Ohio, where my older brother David lives.

David and his wife Patty came with their son, my nephew Quentin, from Lima over the weekend to visit us at the farm and pick blueberries at our oldest sister Carol's farm near Culver, Ind.

I gave them a helping hand and by the end of the day Saturday, we had 50 pounds of berries, which will be used for blueberry pancakes, jelly, pies and healthful fruit smoothies.

It was wet picking in the patch, because we had 5 inches of rain last week. Since we were standing in water most of the time, it felt more like being in a cranberry bog.

But rather than blueberry pie on the dessert menu, I received something even better in place of an early birthday cake.

Patty baked one of her fresh homemade apricot pies to share, using apricots given to her by her neighbor in Ohio. She also brought some of her delicious apricot preserves.

Today, I'm sharing Patty's delicious apricot pie recipe, along with her easy-as-1-2-3 pie crust recipe.

And thank you to all The Times readers for making my 37th year so much fun at all the parties, book-signing events and programs I've hosted and so many of you have attended during the past year.

Rather than counting candles on a cake, I count my blessings each and every day.

PIE CRUST INGREDIENTS:

4 cups flour

2 teaspoons salt

1-3/4 cup shortening

1 tablespoon sugar

2 tablespoons vinegar

1 egg

1/2 cup water

Patty's No-Fault Pie Crust

- In a large bowl, combine flour and salt. Use a knife or pastry blender to cut shortening into flour mixture until it becomes coarse with pea-size bits.

- In small bowl, mix together sugar, vinegar, egg and water and pour over flour mixture.

- Turn dough onto a floured surface and roll into four pie crusts. Do not worry about over-working dough or if it appears too sticky or dry.

- Extra crusts can be frozen or kept in refrigerator up to one week.

- Makes 4 pie crusts.

Patty's Old-Fashioned Apricot Pie

- Heat oven to 425.

- Prepare pie crusts (see above recipe) and line the bottom of a 9-inch pie pan. Reserve top crust and set aside.

- Mix sugar, flour and cinnamon together in a large bowl and stir in apricots, lemon juice, tossing to coat. Pour into bottom pie crust and dot butter.

- Cover with top crust, make slits for ventilation and flute. Sprinkle with sugar if desired. Cover edges with foil, removing last 15 minutes for even baking.

- Bake until crust is brown and juice bubbles through slits in crust, about 35 to 40 minutes. Makes sure pie bubbles before removing from oven.

- Makes 1 (9-inch) pie with 8 slices.

APRICOT PIE INGREDIENTS:

2 prepared pie crusts

Filling:

1 cup sugar

1/4 cup all-purpose flour

1 teaspoon cinnamon

5 cups fresh apricots, do not peel, just pit and slice

1 teaspoon lemon juice

2 tablespoons margarine or butter

My older brother David and his wife Patty, shown here in 1998, love working around their home in Lima, Ohio and decorating for the holidays.

Church gathering a blessing of abundance

August 27, 2008

I know there are many Times readers in our region who are Catholic and who receive the region's weekly Catholic newspaper The Northwest Indiana Catholic.

In last week's issue, readers who also receive this mailed publication from the Catholic Diocese of Gary might have noticed a story about the 150th anniversary of our little red brick All Saints Catholic church in San Pierre, Ind.

I was interviewed for the story and I explained that the reason I became a newspaper reporter was because of my Sunday school teacher Stanley Pieza, who taught my high school catechism classes.

He was a retired religion reporter for William Randolph Hearst's Chicago Daily American Newspaper. He always told many wonderful stories about the famous and interesting personalities he met and interviewed during the course of his journalism career. The walls of the library in his home were filled with photos of himself interviewing everyone from popes to actors and actresses like Eddie Cantor and Irene Dunne.

While at Sunday's anniversary Mass and dinner at Strongbow Inn in Valparaiso, both led by our bishop Rev. Dale J. Melczek's and our priests Rev. William Spranger and Rev. Theodore Mens, I reflected on my many blessings and how fortunate I've been with the many gifts in my life.

Today's recipe is from my high school algebra teacher Mrs. Mary Kay Powell, who was at Sunday's event and who also lectors with me on weekends at my church. I don't know of too many people who can say they still see their high school algebra teacher from 25 years ago each week and still smile. I remember Mrs. Powell had a delicious homemade caramel corn recipe that she would bring us as a treat. And this week, she shared the recipe with me to share with you, just in time for next weekend's Popcorn Festival in Valparaiso.

INGREDIENTS:

1-1/2 cups unpopped popcorn (7-1/2 quarts popped corn)

2 cups brown sugar

1 cup butter, melted

1/2 cup corn syrup

1 teaspoon salt

1 teaspoon baking soda

1 tablespoon vanilla

Mrs. Powell's Caramel Corn

● Pop corn and set aside.

● Combine sugar, butter, corn syrup and salt and heat until boiling for 5 minutes and stirring. Remove from heat.

● Add baking soda and vanilla.

● Pour popped corn into a large roasting pan. Pour warm caramel syrup over popped corn, mixing thoroughly to coat.

● Bake uncovered in roasting pan for 1 hour at 200 degrees, stirring every 15 minutes.

● Stores well in cool dry area in sealed container.

● Makes 7 quarts of delicious caramel corn.

Join me for Times' 'Taste of Home'

September 17, 2008

With worries of poor weather and a struggling economy, it's nice to know features like my farm column give our readers the chance to take their minds off the concerns of the moment, even if it's only a temporary reprieve.

I'm excited to be part of an event sponsored by The Times next week in Merrillville, Ind. which will bring to life the stories and recipes I share with you in this column. It also will give you a fun, relaxing, carefree evening that is sure to put a smile on your face.

I will join professional culinary specialist Dana Elliott on stage at Star Plaza Theatre at 5 p.m. Sept. 25, when the doors open to a world of excitement, prizes and first-class cooking demonstrations on stage at "The Taste of Home Cooking School."

Guests will receive a complimentary cookbook to follow along with as the recipes are whipped up on stage.

And before the 6 p.m. show begins, area businesses and sponsors will greet arriving guests in the outer lobby with free samples and great ideas starting at noon.

Tickets are $9 to $16 and available at the Star Plaza Theatre Box Office. There aren't many left.

Today's featured recipe comes from the warm and inviting family kitchen of my desk neighbor here in the features department of our newsroom. Katie Higley, who designs our Food section each week, brought in this easy and delicious family recipe for peach cobbler last week. She grew up enjoying this recipe, which has been made by her mom, aunt and grandmother for years.

Katie's Old-Fashioned Peach Cobbler

- Melt the butter and add to the bottom of 9-by-13-inch baking dish or any large casserole dish, swirling to cover the bottom of the pan.

- Peel and core peaches before cutting in to halves, then quarters.

- In a medium bowl, mix sugar, flour, baking powder and milk until combined. Add batter to the buttered pan.

- Add peaches to the batter, arranging in a single layer. (Peaches will sink into batter during baking.)

- If desired, sprinkle up to 1/2 teaspoon of cinnamon and a scattering of sugar over layered peaches.

- Bake at 375 degrees for 30 to 40 minutes or until golden brown.

- Makes 10 servings.

INGREDIENTS:

2 tablespoons butter

4 cups peaches, slices plus juice

1 cup sugar

1 cup all-purpose flour

1 teaspoon baking powder

1 cup milk

Cinnamon and sugar to taste (optional)

Pineapple pie a true pastry favorite

September 24, 2008

While judging the third annual Pie Baking Contest at last weekend's Bizarre Bazaar festival in downtown Hammond, Ind. it was easy to see the only thing that goes better with a piece of warm fresh pie than a cup of coffee, is a good story about the pie recipe's origin.

Our big winners from Saturday were Rada Velligan of East Chicago, Ind. for her old fashioned Mince Meat Melody Pie; Rhonda Lynn Halper of Hammond for a savory Zucchini Pie garnished with dollops of sour cream and Emma Hayes of Hammond for her picture perfect Pumpkin Pie.

But there was also one other pie that captured my attention and tastebuds submitted by Hayes that ranked second place after all of the judges' votes were counted.

However, in my mind this delicious pineapple pie was also more than ribbon worthy. She named it after her Serbian hairdresser Michael Rateich (or "Mr. Michael" as she calls him) because he loves this recipe and often requests she make it for him.

Michael's Favorite Pineapple Pie

- Line a 9-inch pie pan with bottom pie crust and bake for 10 to 12 minutes at 375 degrees or until golden brown.

- Drain pineapple, reserving liquid.

- Heat orange juice and pineapple liquid in a saucepan over low heat.

- In a bowl, combine sugar, cornstarch, salt and water and egg yolks and stir until smooth. Slowly pour this mixture into the hot juice liquid in saucepan, cooking over medium heat, stirring constantly, until thick.

- Remove filling from heat and add drained pineapple and butter to the filling in saucepan, stirring and allowing to cool slightly.

- Pour filling into baked bottom pie crust and cover with top pie crust, pinching edges and flute.

- Bake at 350 degrees for 12 to 15 minutes, until golden brown.

- Makes 10 slices.

INGREDIENTS:

2 (9-inch) pie shell crusts
1 (20 ounce) can crushed pineapple
1 cup orange juice
1/2 cup sugar
1/4 cup cornstarch
1/8 teaspoon salt
1/4 cup water
3 egg yolks
1 tablespoon butter

This mince meat pie appeals to reindeer

October 1, 2008

As promised in last week's column, this week, I'm showcasing the other winning recipes from the third annual Pie Baking Contest at last month's Bizarre Bazaar festival in downtown Hammond.

Rada Velligan, of East Chicago, Ind. was a big winner for her old fashioned Mince Meat Melody Pie, which is also referred to as a "Father Christmas Mince Meat Pie."

And since this particular old recipe contains carrots as part of the filling, the old wives' tale says this was a particularly popular pie to make on Christmas Eve. People would leave it out for Father Christmas, aka Santa Claus, as well as for his hard-working reindeer, who especially enjoy carrots.

I remember from my youth that my mom would often tell me how her mom, my Grandma Green always made Mince Meat Pie for Thanksgiving and Christmas. Grandma Green was continuing the tradition of her own mother.

On a sad note today, it was just over a year ago this week that I printed a recipe from our good farm family friend Mrs. Ann Boilini for her Zucchini Parmesan Cheese Pie while writing about this same Hammond pie event.

She died Sunday, at age 80, after a long fight with leukemia. She was in the hospital as a result of a blood clot. Ann had been married to beloved husband Richard for more than 50 years and their daughter Mary Anne went to school with my oldest brother David. My prayers and sympathy to the Boilini Family. My mother will especially miss her.

Father Christmas' Mince Meat Pie

- Preheat oven to 425 degrees.

- Cook carrots in salted water until barely tender. Drain and discard water.

- In a large bowl, combine carrots with all remaining filling ingredients, including 3 tablespoons of flour and lightly toss.

- Line a 9-inch pie pan with bottom pie crust and pour filling in, then sprinkle with the 1 remaining tablespoon of flour, dotting with 1 teaspoon of butter.

- Cover pie with top pastry crust, press edges to flute and cut slits in center to ventilate.

- Bake in very hot 425 degree oven for 30 minutes, covering top or at least edges with foil, baking until apples are tender.

- Makes 8 slices.

INGREDIENTS:

1 cup young carrots, cleaned and diced

1-1/2 cups sliced raw apples

1 teaspoon grated orange rind

1 cup sugar

3 tablespoons plus 1 tablespoon flour, divided use

1/8 teaspoon cinnamon

1/8 teaspoon nutmeg

1/2 cup seedless raisins

1 teaspoon butter

Pastry for 2, 9-inch pie crusts, a top and bottom

Apples and potato share notoriety

October 22, 2008

Thank you to all the readers who made reservations for this Friday's "Halloween From the Farm" party in Crown Point.

It's going to be a great time. Remember, the free evening runs from 6 to 9 p.m. at the Crown Point location of South Shore Arts, 138 S. Main St. which is the old, historic People's State Bank in Crown Point, right on the corner across from the courthouse. This event is sponsored by our own Shore Magazine and the Crown Point Mayor's Office as part of 4th Friday Arts. Many readers have asked about attire. Costumes are NOT required.

You've probably noticed something unusual about this week's column.

I've included a photograph, something I've only ever done once before in the six years I've written this column.

I thought readers could use a smile. While digging potatoes at the farm over the weekend, my father found a spud that he thinks looks exactly like Mickey Mouse's profile. I'll let you judge it for yourself.

As for this week's recipe, it comes from one of my Purdue students Anne Kabaj. Her apple pie won first place in 2004 while I was judging a pie contest as part of the Harvest Moon Festival in LaCrosse, Ind. Now, four years later, I'm finally sharing it with readers.

Here's a photo of the potato my dad dug up at the farm that we believe resembles the profile of Walt Disney's Mickey Mouse.

Anne Kabaj's Apple Pie

- Preheat over to 375 degrees and prepare an 11-inch large pie pan.

- To make pie dough, place flour, sugar and salt in a large mixing bowl or food processor.

- Cut up chilled butter into small pieces and add to processor or cut into mixture in bowl. If using a food processor, "pulse" mixture until it is crumbly and you can feel the butter in little pieces incorporated throughout the dough.

- Working quickly, continue to pulse while adding the cold water and blending it until the mixture almost forms a ball. (If it's a little on the crumbly side, it's still okay. Just work it with hands.) If working dough by hand, use a knife or pastry cutter to work in the butter and shortening. Add the water a bit at a time until mixture begins to come together, but is not sticky.

- Turn out dough on a floured work surface and separate. Keep 2/3 to roll out to make bottom pie crust and refrigerate the smaller portion left to roll out later as top crust.

- To make filling, peel, core and slice apples and place in a large mixing bowl with flour and sugar, adding more or less sugar as needed depending on sweetness of apples. Add the cinnamon and salt and toss dry ingredients with apples.

INGREDIENTS:

PIE CRUST:

3 cups flour
1-1/2 tablespoons sugar (optional)
Pinch of sea salt
9 ounces unsalted butter, chilled
3 ounces shortening, chilled
3 ounces ice water

FILLING:

4 1/2 pounds assorted Granny Smith and/or Gala apples
1/2 cup flour
1-1/2 cups sugar
2 teaspoons cinnamon
1/2 teaspoon sea salt
4 tablespoons unsalted butter
Baking glaze:
1/4 cup heavy cream or whole milk
1/4 cup sugar

- Roll out bottom pie crust to 1/8- inch thickness and place in bottom of pie pan. Pour in filling and dot with pieces of butter. Roll out top crust and place on pie, trimming an excess and crimping edges to seal. Make slits for ventilation on top of pie.

- Brush top of pie with milk and sprinkle with sugar.

- Cover edges with foil to avoid burning and bake for 1 1/2 hours until golden brown and filling begins to show in slits of top crust. Remove foil for even baking.

- Remove from oven and cool slightly before serving.

- Makes 10 slices.

Cool weather a great time for baking

October 29, 2008

When the weather turns cool, there's nothing better than warming up the house by turning on the oven and baking something delicious.

And if it's an easy recipe, all the better.

Since we have apple trees at our family farm, apples have been both on my mind and on our menu.

A favorite memory I have from growing up on the farm during autumn is not only raking leaves, but also raking up and gathering apples.

This is also a favorite time of year for deer, hungry visitors who love to munch on apples, especially at night, when the farm dogs are sleeping.

One of the best apple trees at our farm for decades is pictured in my first "From the Farm" cookbook from 2004 in a photo of my father standing next to it while holding Grandpa Potempa's horse-hitch plow.

Sporting a gnarled and bumpy trunk, this apple tree was celebrated and prized by my grandparents because it bore "winter apples," small, very hard, tart apples that easily stored all winter in the underground root cellar without rotting.

And since my dad loved Grandma Potempa's homemade fresh-baked apple pies, it's easy to see why he's smiling in that photograph from the first book that features him standing next to this particular apple tree.

Today's showcased recipe, for a scrumptious apple cake, comes from librarian Donna Hohl of Valparaiso, a familiar and smiling face at Valparaiso Public Library for 18 years before she retired earlier this year.

"This recipe is from my mother-in-law, passed along through the family for many years," Hohl said.

"Wisconsin this time of year is beautiful, with all the changing leaves. And what makes this recipe especially good is that it is delicious any time of day, though some describe it as a coffeecake. It is a family favorite."

INGREDIENTS:

CAKE:

4 Granny Smith apples, peeled and sliced

1/2 cup of butter

1-1/2 cups all-purpose flour

2 tablespoons sugar

1 teaspoon baking powder

1 egg, beaten

2 tablespoons milk

1 teaspoon vanilla

CRUMB TOPPING:

3/4 cup sugar

3 tablespoons flour

1/2 teaspoon cinnamon

Dash of nutmeg

3 tablespoons butter

Wisconsin Apple Crumb Cake

● Precook sliced apples in a nonstick skillet with a little water over low heat until tender; cool completely.

● For the cake batter, in a large bowl, mix butter, flour, sugar and baking powder until finely crumbled and combined.

● In a smaller bowl, combine egg, milk and vanilla and add to the dry butter mixture.

● Press cake batter mixture into a greased and floured 8-by-10-inch baking pan.

● Spread prepared apples evenly over the cake pastry layer.

● Combine all the crumb-topping ingredients and sprinkle on top of the apples.

● Bake cake at 375 degrees for 35 to 40 minutes, until toothpick inserted comes out clean.

● Makes 9 serving slices.

Grandpa Potempa has plenty of apples to peel and keep himself busy while sitting at the table in the original farmhouse in this 1946 photo.

As American and incarcerated as Apple Pie

November 5, 2008

After our 2008 Presidential Election, it's time to start a new chapter in America's history.

As many readers know, for the last seven years, I've spent my early Friday mornings as a part-time adjunct professor for Purdue North Central teaching public speaking at the Michigan City State Prison and Westville Correctional Facility, both in Northwest Indiana.

And even though the offenders can't cast votes, they definitely can cook and bake.

I've always been fascinated by a special culinary arts program at Westville, run for the past 12 years by Ron Edwards of Valparaiso.

Inmates are taught both basics and advanced methods of food preparation and serving techniques in a neat little kitchen and mock restaurant dining room in the education building, preparing inmates for future careers in food service.

Of course, the students have limited access to sharp objects and all fresh fruit, sugar, yeast and juices must be kept under lock and key.

I'm always impressed how the inmates are able to keep their minds off their day-to-day woes and worries by diverting their attention to learning new skills or often times, just watching the world outside.

Last Friday, one of the students noticed something outside our classroom window, a fat and furry identity -- one of the inmates favorite pastimes to spy on.

Chuck is the name the inmates have given to a very large groundhog (or often called a "woodchuck") that lives just outside of their reach on the other side of the high fences in the prison yard. With bristled whiskers, he stares at these inmates eye to eye through the safety of the barbed wire-topped fence eating bugs and scurrying back and forth to his hole.

And just beyond this high fence is the double gate called a "Sally port," which is where the title of today's prison recipe comes from. A Sally port is the small secured entry way that forces a person or car to enter an enclosed gate or doorway in prison and have the behind door or fence gate close first before the next doorway is opened.

Today's featured pie recipe is from 23-year-old Brian Feely, inmate No. 180005 of Granger, Ill., who made this recipe during a food projects test and passed with very high marks. Brian is due to be released in May after a three-year sentence for "operating a vehicle while intoxicated resulting in death."

Sally Port Apple Pie No. 180005

- To make crust, mix flour and shortening together on lowest speed of an electric mixer for 1 minute, using a flat beater, scrape down the sides of bowl and continuing to mix until shortening is evenly distributed, about 1 to 2 minutes.

- Dissolve salt in a small amount of the water, reserving the remaining water and adding to the flour and shortening mixture as needed and mixing on a low speed until the dough is formed, usually after about 40 seconds.

- Portion the dough into 2 balls, about 5 ounces each for the bottom crusts for two pies and into two balls, about 4 ounces each, to make two top crusts for two pies.

- To make filling, combine sugar, flour and cinnamon in a small bowl and add to apples, tossing to coat.

- Line the bottoms of two 8-inch pie pans with the bottom crusts and divide the filling evenly between the two pies.

INGREDIENTS:

CRUST:

1 cup all-purpose flour

3/4 cup shortening

1/4 cup cold water

1-1/2 teaspoon salt

FILLING:

3 pounds tart apples, peeled, cored and sliced

12 ounces granulated sugar

2 teaspoons all-purpose flour

1 teaspoon cinnamon

1 tablespoon butter or margarine

- Divide the butter or margarine between the two pies and dot the tops of each of the spread filling.

- Cover each of the pies with the top crusts, moisten and seal the edges, flute and add slits to the top crust to vent.

- Bake at 400 degrees for 45 minutes or until apples test soft and done.

- Makes 2 pies, each serving into 8 slices.

I love this rare photo taken of me taken May 21, 2008, standing near the "Deadline Sign," with a guard tower looming behind me, while at the Westville Correctional Facility in Westville, Ind..

(Photo by Jon L. Hendricks)

Fudge contest nets rich reward of recipes

November 26, 2008

Last weekend's 25th anniversary celebration festival for the 1983 film "A Christmas Story" held in Downtown Hammond was a great success.

My favorite part, of course, was the "Oh, Fudge! Recipe Contest" which attracted a wide variety of different fudges.

Today, I'm sharing two of the first place winning recipes.

Altamae Blick, of Highland, won in the "old fashioned" cooked fudge category (see color recipe photo on book cover) and Marilyn McDonald, of Hammond, won in the "quick set-up" fudge category.

Scott Keith of Keith's Restaurant in Whiting and Terry Zych, a chef/instructor for Ivy Tech of Michigan City also served on the judging panel. (See color photo on page XI)

Next month, as we get closer to the Christmas holidays, I'll share the other two first place fudge recipes.

Congratulations to all the participants and thank you to everyone who attended the festival.

From my family to yours, have a blessed, wonderful and relaxing Thanksgiving.

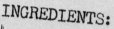

INGREDIENTS:

4 cups white granulated sugar
1 cup milk
1 teaspoon vanilla
25 large marshmallows
1 cup butter
11 ounces milk chocolate chips
13 ounces semi-sweet chocolate chips
2 ounces unsweetened baking chocolate
1 cup chopped walnuts

Mock Fannie May
Fudge with Walnuts

- Mix sugar, milk, butter and vanilla in a large pan and bring to a boil for 2 minutes, stirring constantly so it doesn't burn. Remove from heat.

- Add marshmallows to mixture and stir until dissolved and evenly combined.

- Add each of the various chocolates, one at a time, stirring to evenly blend into fudge.

- Pour fudge into an ungreased cookie sheet or jelly roll pan (for small thin squares) or into a 9-inch by 13-inch pan (for larger, thicker squares).

- Yields 4 pounds of fudge.

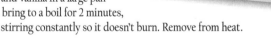

Mrs. Blink's Old-Fashioned Creamy Cooked Fudge

- Mix sugar, milk, cocoa and butter together in a saucepan and cook gently over a low flame. Do NOT stir while cooking.

- Cook mixture (about 10 to 15 minutes more or less) until a very soft ball stage (testing the liquid by dropping just a drop into a clear glass of cold water and watching to see if it forms a ball. If the mixture disperses and the water becomes cloudy, the liquid must be cooked longer.)

INGREDIENTS:

2 cups white granulated sugar

2/3 cup milk

3 tablespoons baking cocoa powder

1 tablespoon butter

1 teaspoon vanilla

Chopped nuts of choice (optional)

- When mixture tests ready, remove pan from heat and set the pan into 2 inches of cool water and allow the pan of fudge to "rest" for 25 minutes. Do NOT touch or disturb the pan during this 25 minutes.

- Remove pan from water and beat fudge until it looks "dull" and creamy in appearance. Fold in vanilla and nuts (if desired).

- Line a cookie sheet or tray with waxed paper and spoon the fudge out, dropping it as small dollops on the wax paper. Allow to set in a cool, dry place.

- Makes 2 pounds of fudge.

Here's a perfect photo memory of Auntie Loretta and Uncle Ed, with my cousins Ronny and Ricky.

This cookie recipe is 'all heart'

December 3, 2008

As many readers might have read last month, I served as a judge at Purdue Calumet's competition for the campus' second annual baking championship.

Ellie Chen, of Hammond, called it "a sweet victory."

The 21-year-old Chen won an intramural bake-off Monday at Purdue University Calumet and now holds the title of "best Boilermaker baker."

Chen was one of two finalists among students and staff at the competition.

Her recipe for heart-shaped strawberry jam-filled shortbread cookies (see color photo on page III) not only took home top honors but also will be served as a standing menu item in the PUC cafeteria.

Ellie's Strawberry Valentine Cookies

- Note: These are heart-shaped "sandwich-style" cookies with jam filling in between.

- In a large mixing bowl, combine butter, sugar, egg whites and extracts and cream together until smooth.

- Slowly mix in flour, baking soda and cream of tartar, blending well to create a stiff dough. Divide the dough into 4 parts to make it easier to work with and roll out.

- On a lightly floured surface, roll out the first piece of dough to a 1/4-inch thickness. Cut out as many heart shape cookies as possible and place on a cookie sheet. Remember, for each cookie cut out, it will need another cookie so there is a top and bottom. If desired, for the top half of each cookie cut out, use a knife or a smaller heart-shape cookie cutter to make a cut-out "window" for each top cookie, so jam will show through. Gather dough scraps and continue to roll out all of the dough until all of the cookies have been cut out to bake.

INGREDIENTS:

1 cup unsalted butter, softened

1 cup confectioner's sugar

2 egg whites

1 teaspoon vanilla

1 teaspoon almond extract

2 1/2 cups all purpose flour

1 teaspoon baking soda

1 teaspoon cream of tartar

1 cup strawberry jam (preferably seedless variety)

1 heart-shaped cookie cutter

- Bake at 350 degrees for 12 to 15 minutes, or just until cookies are turning golden. Remove from oven to cookie rack.

- If jam is firm, gently heat in microwave a few seconds to soften and place a little in the center of each of the "bottom" cookie shapes and then cover with one of the "heart window" cut -out cookie shapes, gently pressing together to seal.

- Makes 20 cookies.

Town barber changing with the times

December 10, 2008

In May 2006, I wrote about our small farm town's barber retiring after 45 years of crew-cuts and making sure the sideburns of the men in our family were even (most of the time.)

I mentioned a young man from our town bought Curly's Barbershop, including the old-fashioned spinning, lighted barber pole outside the front door.

I had an interesting chat recently with the new owner (even after nearly three years of haircuts, for our town, he's still considered new), Edison McDaniel.

The son of Moses and Velva McDaniel, Ed, as he's known to most, is helping to keep a great small-town tradition alive by continuing this cut-and-snip business with $9 haircuts.

Ed graduated from my same high school in North Judson, Ind. in 1997, about nine years after me and enrolled in the Indiana Barber/Stylist College in Indianapolis to earn his certificate in 2001.

But like every other business, times are changing, along with styles.

Ed said since longer hair is the style for the young men of today, there are fewer new and younger customers, and visits are less frequent.

And women also have an influence on his business, with many wives and girlfriends pushing the men in their lives to go to their beauty salons.

"I often say that even though the men still 'wear the pants,' it's the women who decide which pants they wear," Ed said.

As promised, today's recipe is the "healthy" finalist cookie creation (see photo in color section page III) from Purdue Calumet's competition for the campus' second annual baking championship.

It's a terrific blend of ingredients whipped together by Diana Virijevich, of Schererville, Ind.

Healthy Banana Oatmeal Cookies

- Sift together first six dry ingredients.

- Combine oil, water and mashed bananas and add to dry ingredients.

- Add rolled oats and walnuts and stir until blended.

- Drop by rounded teaspoons on greased baking sheet.

- Bake at 350 degrees for about 10 to 15 minutes.

- Note: These cookies do not brown on top so check the bottoms during baking and remove when they are lightly browned on the bottom.

- Makes 2 dozen cookies

INGREDIENTS:
1/2 cup sugar
1-1/2 cups flour
2 teaspoons baking powder
1/4 teaspoon cinnamon
1/4 teaspoon nutmeg
1/4 teaspoon mace
1/4 cup vegetable oil
1/3 cup water
1 cup mashed bananas
1-3/4 cups rolled oats
1/2 cup chopped walnuts

Goldblatt's cheesecake recipe a buried treasure

December 17, 2008

I've heard from readers many times over the past seven years I've been writing this column, with many requesting the same recipe.

All desire the fabled recipe for a cheesecake sold at the bakery of the old Goldblatt's Department Store in Hammond, Ind.

After I wrote about this request in my column last month, I was fortunate to have readers aid me in my search.

Reader Alice Graban of Hammond knew someone who worked at the department store and was familiar with this recipe for the cakes sold there.

And though it took some searching, she was kind enough to send the recipe along to share. She said some versions were "plain without a crust" and others were sold with a "traditional graham cracker crust."

So, for this provided recipe, the filling can be baked in a springform pan with or without the prepared graham cracker crust, as desired.

Goldblatt's High Cream Cheesecake

- To make crust, combine graham cracker crumbs, sugar and flour. Use a fork to blend thoroughly. Add melted butter.

- Firmly press crumb mixture into a 9-inch pie pan, or, even better, a 9-inch springform pan.

- For this cheesecake, set unbaked prepared crust aside to prepare cheese filling. (Normally, when using this crust for recipes that call for an already cooked filling, you would bake the crust at 375 degrees for about 10 minutes.)

- To make filling, in a large bowl, cream the cream cheese and sugar together and then add sour cream.

- Add the egg YOLKS only, one at a time, to filling mixture.

- In a separate bowl, beat the egg whites until stiff, and fold them into the filling.

- Pour filling into crust (or into plain, greased springform pan if making the crust-less version) and bake at 350 degrees for 1 hour.

- After one hour, turn oven off and allow cake to remain undisturbed in oven and slowly cool for 1 more hour before removing.

- Makes 14 slices.

INGREDIENTS:

GRAHAM CRACKER CRUST:

10 ounces crushed graham cracker crumbs

2 ounces plus 3 ounces sugar

1 teaspoon flour

4 ounces melted butter

FILLING:

1-1/2 pound cream cheese (3 of the 8-ounce packages)

3/4 cup granulated sugar

1/2 pint sour cream

2 tablespoons flour

1 teaspoon vanilla

6 eggs separated

Old-fashioned graham cracker cake a holiday hit

December 24, 2008

Thank you to the many readers and friends who called or e-mail offering thoughts and prayers after my older brother Tom's only son, my nephew and godson Thomy passed away Dec. 13 from an undiagnosed heart ailment at just 28 years old.

His passing came on the same day as our late and beloved Auntie Lilly's birthday and she happened to be Thomy's godmother.

As is a farm and good neighbor tradition for so many people, the other farm families around us were kind enough to bring food and baked goods to our home.

Joanne Scamerhorn brought some delicious thinly sliced roast beef and crusty rolls, along with her famous Mocha Drop cookies. Debbie Wappel brought a large, brimming platter of cold cuts, cheese and a basket of fancy mustard and spreads.

Joanne brought a terrific recipe that I've been after for months.

She first told me about this old recipe over the summer, after her daughter Ann casually mentioned it after they enjoyed it at the family's 63rd annual Teske Family Reunion.

The batter of this Graham Cracker cake is moist and delicious. The recipe comes from the files of the Scamerhorn family's cousin Nancy Lacina of Berwyn, Ill.

"When I was growing up, Saturday morning was always baking day at our house," Nancy writes with her recipe.

"My mother loved to bake, and she was always trying new recipes. Most of them were very good, but there were some that didn't quite make it. I remember a Chocolate Sauerkraut Cake that was on the 'please-don't-ever-make-that-again' list.

"After my mom passed away, I got most of her recipes. Among them was a recipe for this Graham Cracker Cake. This one is a real keepers. What makes it unusual is that you don't use any flour, only crushed graham crackers. I don't know how she originally dreamed this up, but it sure is good."

Thank you for sharing this heirloom recipe.

And a blessed and Merry Christmas and Happy Holidays to all readers.

This family photo of my oldest brother Tom, wife Linda and Thomy and Bethany is the way I always remember them, smiling and ready for long walk through the woods to see their pond nestled out back.

Graham Cracker Cake with Buttercream Icing

- Preheat oven to 375 degrees.

- Cream butter and sugar; add egg yolks and beat well.

- Combine graham cracker crumbs and baking powder; add to butter and sugar mixture, alternately, with milk and vanilla, starting and finishing with graham cracker crumbs.

- Fold in 3 stiffly beaten egg whites.

- Pour mixture in two greased and floured 9-inch round cake pans. Bake 30 to 35 minutes at 375 degrees or until a toothpick put in the middle comes out clean.

- Cool completely before frosting and assembling layer cakes.

- Note: You can also use a greased and floured 9-by-13-inch pan for this recipe.

- Serves into either 12 slices or 20 squares, depending on pan(s) used.

INGREDIENTS:
1/2 cup butter
1 cup sugar
3 egg yolks
3 cups graham cracker crumbs
3 teaspoons baking powder
1 cup milk
1 teaspoon vanilla
3 egg whites, stiffly beaten

INGREDIENTS:
1/2 cup vegetable shortening
1/2 cup butter, softened
1 teaspoon vanilla extract
4 cups sifted confectioner's sugar (about 1 pound)
2 tablespoons milk
3 tablespoons light corn syrup (for thinner icing)

Everyday Buttercream Icing

- Cream butter and shortening with electric mixer.

- Add vanilla and gradually add sugar one cup at a time, while beating well on medium speed.

- Scrape sides and bottom of the bowl often. When all sugar has been combined, the icing will appear dry.

- Add milk and beat at medium speed until light and fluffy. For thinner icing, add corn syrup.

- Keep icing covered with a cloth until ready to use.

- Icing can be stored in an airtight container in the refrigerator for 2 weeks. Re-whip before using.

- Makes 3 cups.

Homemade fudge a sweet gift idea

January 7, 2009

Happy New Year!

I want to start off the new year right, wrapping up any unfinished recipe business from last year.

Reader Anna Daniels of Wheatfield wrote me asking about the remaining winning fudge recipe from the November fudge contest I judged in downtown Hammond, Ind. in November for the first "A Christmas Story Festival," which celebrated the 1983 film's 25th anniversary.

Anna had good reason to remind me I had promised readers before the holidays I would run the other two first-place recipes for the holidays.

It was her delectable recipe, featuring dried cranberries, which netted one of the these first-place honors.

So today, you'll find Anna's.

With St. Valentine's Day around the corner and the economy still unsteady, these homemade candies would make a nice gift, wrapped in retro red cellophane.

Once again, congrats to all the contest winners.

Anna's Favorite Fudge

• Use a double boiler (or a smaller pot submerged in a large pan of boiling water to prevent burning) to melt chocolate chips and butterscotch chips and combine with sweetened milk.

• Once chocolate and butterscotch mixture is smooth, add vanilla and cranberries. Blend well.

• Pour mixture into a buttered 6-by-10-inch rectangular glass pan. Refrigerate for 2 hours to set.

• Cut into squares and keep refrigerated.

• Makes 1 pound.

INGREDIENTS:

1 (14-ounce) can condensed sweetened milk

1 (12-ounce) bag semisweet chocolate chips

6 ounces of butterscotch chips

6 ounces of dried cranberries

1 teaspoon vanilla

Join me for 'Babs' Valentine's Day weekend luncheon

January 14, 2009

As many faithful readers have reminded me in recent months, it's been more than a year since I've had any tea or luncheon party events.

It's time to mark your calendars for St. Valentine's Day weekend.

I'll be presenting a Valentine's Day full luncheon from noon to 3 p.m. on Sunday, Feb. 15, in the large connected joining salon dining rooms at Teibel's Restaurant.

The seating is limited to 200 guests, with reserved seating at each of the 25 tables, which seat eight.

Doors open at noon with lunch served at 1 p.m.

On the day of the luncheon, guests will be asked to pick from a choice of three main course entrees: Teibel's Fried Chicken or Beef Sirloin Tips or Teibel's Famous Boned and Buttered Lake Perch. Each will come with a dinner roll and cole slaw first course, and the entrees served with baby red potatoes, and a vegetable blend of young yellow summer squash, red peppers, onions and green zucchini. Each lunch also comes with choice of beverage, including coffee, hot tea, iced tea or milk.

And for dessert, fresh peppermint ice cream served with the showcased recipe featured in today's column: Coca-Cola Cake.

The luncheon presentation tickets are $25 per person, which includes the tax and tip. A portion of each ticket sold benefits one of my favorite nonprofit groups, The Caring Place, the shelter in Valparaiso for victims of domestic violence.

Since seating is limited, reservations are required by leaving name, contact telephone number and the number in your party attending.

As for the theme and topic I'll be talking about at the luncheon, it's a look at the fascinating and eccentric life of five-and-dime heiress Barbara Woolworth Hutton, who squandered a $750 million family fortune trying to buy love with seven unhappy marriages, including nuptials to a prince, a count, a baron and movie star Cary Grant.

During her later years, after she gave up drinking, she became addicted to Coca-Cola (which she insisted only be served to her over round ice cubes), which is why my mother thought if would be fun to bake this special dessert to serve for the Valentine's Day weekend luncheon.

INGREDIENTS:

CAKE:

2 cups flour

2 cups sugar

1 cup Coca-Cola (not diet)

2 eggs beaten

1 teaspoon vanilla

1 cup butter or margarine

2 tablespoons unsweetened cocoa powder

1/2 cup buttermilk

1 teaspoon baking soda

1-1/2 cups miniature marshmallows

FROSTING:

2 tablespoons butter or margarine

6 to 8 tablespoons Coca-Cola

1 cup chopped pecans

2 tablespoons unsweetened cocoa powder

1 pound powdered sugar

The recipe comes from her teacher and farm wife friend from down the road from our farm, Marilyn Lukac, who has been teaching first grade at our town's little elementary school for more than 25 years.

Marilyn Lukac's Coca-Cola Cake

● Heat oven to 350 degrees.

● Grease and flour 13-by-9-by--inch pan.

● Combine flour and sugar in large bowl.

● In saucepan, melt butter; add cocoa and Coca-Cola, heat to the boiling point. Cool slightly, pour over flour and sugar and stir by hand until well blended.

● Add buttermilk, eggs, baking soda and vanilla. Mix well. Stir in marshmallows. (Batter will be thin and marshmallows will rise to top.)

● Pour batter in pan. Bake 40 minutes or until tests done.

● Once cake is removed from oven, make frosting by mixing all frosting ingredients well and spread over cake while still warm, since frosting will set fast.

● Makes 24 slices.

Enjoying some tropical relaxation in this June 10, 2009 photo, the Lukac Family, Wesley, Marilyn, Erika, Ken and Kyle, have a great view from Paradise Point at St. Thomas in the Virgin Islands.

Chocolate pie recipe a reward

January 21, 2009

I'm pleased that after 16 years of writing our annual holiday help series for the Porter County editions of The Times, this year, a record of more than $46,000 was raised in four weeks for the Porter County Visiting Nurse Association, thanks to readers' generosity.

It was in 1970 that nurses from Porter Memorial Hospital in Valparaiso voiced their concerns about patients who were discharged but still needed medical care. In answer to their plea, the VNA opened in September 1970 to become the first home health care agency in Porter County.

Laura Harting, an RN for the Lake County VNA, became the pioneer to start the Porter County VNA, and still continues as executive director.

As promised, for reaching a new record, this week, Laura is sharing her delicious recipe for her homemade chocolate cream pie.

As a bonus, I've paired her recipe with another family favorite: the perfect pie crust for this type of cream pie created by our farm-wife friend Joann Scamerhorn.

Joann's Perfect Pre-Baked Pie Crust

PRE-BAKED PIE CRUST INGREDIENTS:

1 cup all-purpose flour

1/2 teaspoon salt

1/3 cup shortening

1 tablespoon butter

Splash of milk

● In large bowl, combine flour and salt with shortening and butter and work ingredients together with a fork until consistency of crumbles about the size of peas.

● Add just enough of a splash of milk until a smooth dough consistency is created.

● Roll all the dough out on a floured surface to create a circle large enough and just thick enough for the bottom and sides of a 9-inch pie pan.

● Form to pan and flute edges as desired. Using a fork, gently poke holes throughout the bottom and sides of the unbaked pie crust so dough bakes evenly.

● Bake in a 375 degree oven for 10 to 12 minutes or until a delicate, light golden brown.

● Remove from oven and allow to cool slightly before filling.

● Makes 1 bottom 9-inch pie crust.

Laura Harting's
Chocolate Cream Pie

- Heat chocolate and milk in double boiler.

- When chocolate is melted, beat with an electric egg beater until blended.

- Combine sugar, flour and salt and add gradually to chocolate mixture, stirring after each addition. Cook until thickened, stirring constantly; then cook 10 minutes longer, stirring occasionally.

- Pour small amount of mixture over egg yolks in separate bowl, stirring vigorously to temper yokes before adding to cooked filling.

- Return the tempered yokes to chocolate filling in saucepan and cook about 5 minutes longer.

- Add butter and vanilla; blend.

- Cool only about 5 minutes, stirring once or twice.

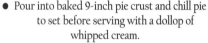

CHOCOLATE CREAM PIE INGREDIENTS:

2 squares unsweetened chocolate

2-1/2 cups milk

1 cup white granulated sugar

6 tablespoons all-purpose flour

1/2 teaspoon salt

2 egg yolks, slightly beaten

2 tablespoons butter

1 teaspoon vanilla

1 baked 9-inch pie shell
(see above recipe)

Whipped cream for garnish

- Pour into baked 9-inch pie crust and chill pie to set before serving with a dollop of whipped cream.

- Note for success: Cook filling on medium heat. Do NOT double recipe, instead, cook filling for each pie in a separate pan. To avoid egg yolks from cooking when added to hot filling, be sure to mix them with just a small amount of hot liquid before adding in entirety to saucepan. To avoid having tough layer of "skin" from forming on top of pie filling as pie chills, cover with plastic wrap, slowly starting on one side, to assure no air bubbles are trapped.

- Makes 8 serving slices.

Robert Wagner joining Valentine Teibel's lunch

February 4, 2009

I have a special surprise for readers planning to attend this month's Valentine's Day weekend luncheon event at Teibel's.

Actor Robert Wagner and his beautiful wife, actress Jill St. John, will be joining us following lunch by telephone to answer questions from guests.

I've had the pleasure of knowing the famous Hollywood couple through a mutual famous friend, funny lady Phyllis Diller.

Wagner met Phyllis through his late first wife, actress Natalie Wood, while she was filming the 1961 film "Splendor in the Grass" with actor Warren Beatty, which earned Wood an Oscar nomination. While visiting his wife on the set, Wagner met Diller, who also starred in the film playing saloon owner Texas Guinan.

The last time I visited with Wagner and St. John it was May 2005 backstage at the Rialto Theatre in Joliet where the couple performed together in "Love Letters."

At that time, the play marked the first time St. John had been back on her feet performing since a terrible ski accident at her Aspen home in January 2005 -- the same time my own mother Peggy had her terrible automobile accident.

The couple was kind enough to give me notes of encouragement and autographed photos for my mother's homecoming which was that Mother's Day weekend.

As I've mentioned in previous columns describing this event, the luncheon's theme will be the fascinating life of five-and-dime heiress Barbara Woolworth Hutton.

St. John's first husband was Lance Reventlow, Hutton's only son by her second marriage.

Jill St. John's Creamy Chocolate Filled Tea Cakes

- Melt chocolate chips, combined with butter and vanilla in a double boiler pot over hot water, stirring until blended. Remove from heat.

- In a separate bowl, use an electric mixer and beat eggs until frothy and gradually add sugar, beating until dissolved and then gradually adding flour.

- Fold chocolate mixture into flour mixture.

- Spoon batter into paper-lined muffin tins, filling cups half way full.

- Bake at 350 degrees for 25 to 30 minutes.

- Cool small cakes on wire rack before serving.

- Makes 2 dozen.

INGREDIENTS:
2/3 cup semisweet chocolate chips
3/4 cup butter
1-1/4 teaspoon vanilla
4 eggs
1-1/2 cups granulated sugar
1 cup all-purpose flour

Family wedding announcements bring joy

February 18, 2009

There's nothing that compares to the romance of an engagement announcement on Valentine's Day.

Last weekend's charity luncheon event at Teibel's included a surprise that even I wasn't expecting.

My sister Pam, who lives in South Bend and who is just four years older than me, announced she received an engagement ring on Saturday for Valentine's Day from her boyfriend, Darrell. And I had the privilege of sharing the just-announced news with the readers who were gathered as guests at the Sunday event.

Many thanks to the 200 readers who gathered over the weekend at the sold-out luncheon to share the day with our family and friends.

On the subject of red and Valentine's Day, today's showcased family recipe is from Leona Jackomis of Portage for a simple, rich and decadent ruby red fruit cobbler.

Ann Scamerhorn, who was the gracious face who welcomed guests at the registration table at Sunday's luncheon, sampled this hit and managed to get the recipe, which I've also enjoyed in recent months.

Since it features cherries, it's ideal for Sunday's celebration of George Washington's birthday.

Leona's No-Mix Easy Cherry-Pineapple Cobbler

- Preheat oven to 350 degrees.

- In a greased 9-by-13 glass baking dish, evenly spread the pineapple with its syrup.

- Spoon pie filling evenly over pineapple.

- Sprinkle dry cake mix evenly over the other ingredients.

- Cut the chilled butter or margarine into thin slices and place them evenly on top of the already layered ingredients.

- Bake at 350 degrees for 50 minutes or until golden brown.

- Serve warm with ice cream or whipped cream.

- Makes 16 servings.

INGREDIENTS:

1 (20 ounce) can crushed pineapple in heavy syrup

1 (21 ounce) can cherry pie filling

1 (14 ounce) package yellow cake mix

1/2 cup (1 stick) butter or margarine, chilled

Poppyseed cake recipe answers reader request

March 4, ,2009

Saturday was my Auntie Wanda's 84th birthday.

To celebrate, my parents sent me to Auntie Wanda and Uncle Bob's house in Chicago with some bottles from the farm cellar of our homemade Dandelion Wine. The recipe, from Uncle Swede and Auntie Lottie, is featured in my original "From the Farm" cookbook from 2004.

While visiting with Auntie Wanda, instead of my mind being on birthday cake, my attention was focused on her old-fashioned recipe for poppyseed cake.

INGREDIENTS:

CAKE:

1/4 pound butter

1-1/2 cups granulated sugar

4 eggs, separated

1 cup sour cream

1 (12 ounce) can poppyseed filling

2 teaspoons vanilla

2 cups cake flour

3/4 teaspoon salt

1 teaspoon baking soda

1/2 teaspoon cream of tartar

SIMPLE WHITE ICING:

2 to 3 tablespoons milk

1 cup confectioner's sugar

1 tablespoon butter, softened

1/2 teaspoon vanilla extract

Auntie Wanda's Poppyseed Cake

● In a large bowl, cream together butter and sugar.

● Separate eggs and add beaten egg yolks to the butter and sugar mixture.

● Add sour cream, poppyseed filling and vanilla to batter.

● In a separate bowl, sift together flour, salt and baking soda.

● Gradually add the blended dry ingredients to the batter.

● In a small separate bowl, combine egg whites with cream of tartar and beat until stiff and then fold into batter.

● Grease a 10-inch tube pan or two small loaf pans.

● Bake for 1 hour at 350 degrees.

● Remove from oven and allow to cool slightly before using a butter knife to gently separate edges of cake from pan before removing.

● Combine all icing ingredients and drizzle over cake or simple dust cooled cake with powdered sugar.

● Makes 10 slices.

Days of telephone party lines long past

April 15, 2009

Despite the stretch of rainy cool weather, there's plenty of plant promise already offering a glimpse of the good things to come.

I've spotted leafy rhubarb and tender asparagus tips poking through the cold garden ground.

In fact, I was so excited over the weekend, I wasted no time calling my dad's sisters, Auntie Lottie in Florida and Auntie Wanda in Chicago, to tell them about one of the first finds of the farming season.

This made me think about how my family still follows the frugal tradition of making long-distance calls on Sundays for the advantage of a cheaper rate. And even though we are now a family with cell phones, I also can still recall my mom waiting until "after 6 p.m." to make telephone calls during the weekdays for the same cheaper rate.

In fact, my grandma Potempa never really talked on the telephone that I can recall from when I was growing up. And as for my dad's sister Auntie Lilly, she also would never have dreamed of picking up the phone to chat or gossip or to report something as minor as spotting asparagus sprouts, even if it was just a local "free" call.

At the farm, my dad's family treated the telephone as a "necessary expense" used only for practical and quick communication.

Today, I've retired and stored the original black rotary phone.

But ironically, its more modern replacement still sits on a doilie on the same little telephone table in the hallway with only a wooden straightback chair adjacent. After all, you were never intended be TOO comfortable while talking on the telephone because you weren't supposed to be talking or gossiping for any length of time.

On the subject of gossip, I still laugh when I think of a source of constant irritation for my grandma, auntie Lilly and even my mother, that I recall from my youth: the party line.

For anyone unfamiliar, in rural farm areas, neighbors all shared the same phone line. And at any given time, picking up the telephone might mean hearing a gabby, gossipy neighbor chatting for extended lengths, which would tie up the phone line for everyone all the way down the road (unless you were rich and important enough to pay for a private line).

For Auntie Lilly and Grandma, it was always their new younger just-married neighbor with a new house just a couple fields away, Linda Skuderna, whose mother-in-law was the farm wife down the road, Marie Skuderna, who was my mom's best friend.

When it came to eavesdropping, which also happened frequently with these party lines (I'm not referring to neighbor Linda Skuderna, she simply just liked talking a lot on the phone, including at times, with my own Mom), Auntie Lilly, Auntie Lottie and others found the perfect solution by switching to their native Polish language once they heard the always-audible nosey "click."

Today's recipe is so good, you might be compelled to call your own neighbor to pass it along.

These moist brownies not only contain coffee, but they also go great with a cup of fresh hot brewed coffee.

The recipe comes from Agnes Sech, who is from Poland, a former student from my Purdue public speaking class in 2006 and whose pierogi recipe is featured in my second cookbook.

INGREDIENTS:

1 (19.5 ounce) package brownie mix

1/2 cup oil

1/4 cup water

2 eggs

1 cup of milk

2 tablespoons of granulated coffee (can be decaf)

3 cups fresh whipped-up cream (or a 12-ounce container prepared whipped topping)

2 (3.4 ounce) packages instant vanilla pudding

20 vanilla-filled chocolate sandwich cookies, coarsely chopped

2 tablespoons chocolate shavings, or a handful grated chocolate morsels

Cinnamon for garnish

Agnes' Easy Coffee Brownies

● Bake and cool the brownies, adding oil, water and eggs and following directions on package.

● Combine coffee granules with milk, stir well.

● Add half of the whipped cream and dry pudding mix to the milk mixture, blending until smooth.

● Fold in crushed cookies and spread the cookie and cream mixture over brownies.

● Fill a cake decorator (or a sealable plastic bag with a corner tip cut off) with the remaining plain whipped cream to decorate the creamy top layer with rows of whipped cream over the top, or createany other design you like.

● Add chocolate shavings and cinnamon.

● Chill before serving.

● Makes 12 brownie bars.

Agnes Sech and her daughter are shown at a book signing event March 20, 2009 in Merrillville, Ind. Sech also is featured in the 2007 cookbook "More From the Farm: Family Recipes and Memories of a Lifetime."

Further From the Farm

Sugar Cream Pie a topic at 'old school' annual town dinner

April 22, 2009

There's been plenty of talk in recent months that the state of Indiana should have its own state pie.

After all, the red Cardinal is our state's bird and the Tulip Tree is the state's tree.

So, after much discussion, apparently the Sugar Cream Pie has won out for this delicacy designation.

This isn't a pie I grew up with, since mother was never a fan of baked custard pies.

However, by the time I was in high school and working as a bag boy stocking shelves and carrying out groceries at our only store in our town, I was introduced to this type of pie since we sold them.

My store manager, Patty Avery, who went to high school with my oldest brother Tom and had also worked with my other older brother David and my oldest sister Carol at our town's grocery store, loved this type of pie. Her mother loved to bake them.

Over the weekend, I attended our town's annual "old school" banquet dinner with my parents and Tom and his wife, Linda.

I have been after Linda to share her grandmother's recipe for this old-fashioned pie and finally, I have it to also share with readers today. More than 60 years old, the recipe was preserved by Linda's aunt, Phyllis Swinehart of Crown Point, Ind.

Mrs. Calvert's Sugar Cream Pie

- Preheat oven to 375 degrees.

- The first three ingredients: 1 cup sugar, 1/4 cup cornstarch, 2 cups milk are combined in a saucepan and cooked until blended but NOT brought to boiling.

- The softened 1 stick of butter and 1 teaspoon of vanilla are blended into the filling, which is poured into an unbaked pie crust and sprinkled with cinnamon before baked at 375 degrees 15 to 20 minutes or until center of pie is firm.

- Edges of pie crust can be covered with foil to prevent over-browning.

- Makes 8 slices.

INGREDIENTS:
1 unbaked 9-inch pie shell

1 cup sugar

1/4 cup cornstarch

2 cups milk

1 stick butter, softened

1 teaspoon vanilla

Sprinkle of cinnamon

Join me at St. Anthony's for free recipe event

April 29, 2009

I made the wonderful recipe for Old-Fashioned Sugar Cream Pie earlier this week, since it was the recipe featured in last week's column.

I made this simple and delicious pie on our rainy Monday this week to share with my parents over a cup of coffee, and it turned out perfect.

Remember, this is an old recipe, so whole milk must be used, not skim or lesser percents. It only takes a few minutes to heat those first few ingredients over a low heat before it begins to thicken and the butter and vanilla are added. You don't want to scorch the milk.

On the subject of old-fashioned recipes, a number of readers called and e-mailed about how much they enjoyed my interview with Dolly Parton featured Sunday. While visiting with her in Tennessee last month, we exchanged cookbooks.

Some of my co-workers got a kick out of a photo of my Mom and Dolly paging through my "More From the Farm" cookbook, whose forward was written by friend Jim Nabors, who starred with Dolly and Burt Reynolds in the 1982 comedy musical, "The Best Little Whorehouse in Texas."

Today's recipe is from Parton.

I'll serve samples of this recipe and share stories about other heirloom recipes at a special free event next week at 6:30 p.m., May 7, at Franciscan Communities at St. AnthonyCampus, 203 Franciscan Drive, Crown Point, Ind.

Hello Dolly Dessert Bars

- Preheat oven to 350 degrees.

- Pour melted butter into small baking pan, such as a square 8-by-8-inch pan.

- Evenly spread the Graham cracker crumbs in the bottom of the pan over the butter.

- Scatter chocolate chips, then coconut and, lastly, the pecans, evenly over the Graham cracker layer.

- Finally, pour the condensed milk over the pecan layer.

- Bake until golden on top, about 20 minutes, and then remove from oven while bars still appear soft and warm.

- Allow pan of bars to cool on a rack until they cool and firm up; cut into bars.

- Makes 12 bars.

INGREDIENTS:

1 stick butter, melted
1 cup Graham cracker crumbs
1 cup chocolate chips
1 cup shredded coconut
1 cup chopped pecans
1 (14 ounce) can sweetened condensed milk

Rhubarb patch is ready and welcomed

May 13, 2009

Last spring, we planted a brand new patch of rhubarb at our farm and just one year later, the bounty is plentiful.

My mom made a delicious lattice top rhubarb pie last week and some home-made rhubarb preserves are also on the way.

As mentioned in some previous columns, Grandma Potempa never did much with rhubarb over the years, believing that the vast amounts of sweetening required to "do anything with rhubarb" was "a waste of sugar."

However, I, along with my parents, love rhubarb. And our new patch is just a few feet away from the strawberry patch.

And my mom already has her mind set on making her delicious strawberry rhubarb pie as soon as we finally get enough warm weather to make our strawberries grow and ripen.

Readers who attended my event last Thursday at St. Anthony's received a special treat because of a surprise special guest who was sitting in the front row.

Judy Gudeman of Kouts, Ind. is a farm gal friend (and nurse) I met through the one and only Ann Scamerhorn. Both, of course, are familiar names from both my columns and cookbooks. Judy was kind enough to attend my presentation and graciously helped sign cookbooks, along with my parents.

And even better, she dug in her files to find a great rhubarb pie recipe I have been looking for.

Nicole's Rhubarb Pie with Crumb Topping

- Sprinkle 1 tablespoon flour in the bottom of the pie crust.

- Evenly spread cut up rhubarb in pie crust.

- Mix the sugar, 1/3 cup flour, salt and 1 cup egg/milk mixture together.

- Bake (without topping) at 375 degrees for 15 minutes.

- Combine topping ingredients until crumbly. Pour over warm rhubarb filling and then bake at 350 degrees for another 40 to 45 minutes more or until pie tests done.

- Makes 8 slices.

INGREDIENTS:
1 (9-inch) unbaked pie crust

FILLING:

3 to 4 cups of rhubarb, cut up
1 cup of sugar
1/3 cup flour plus 1 tablespoon
1/8 teaspoon salt
2 eggs beaten in a measuring cup
3/4 cup milk (OR enough milk to add to beaten eggs to make 1 cup of liquid)

Crumb topping:
1 cup Flour
2/3 cup sugar
1/2 cup butter, softened

Friends share recipes and good and bad times together

May 27, 2009

When readers are looking through my cookbooks, they often comment on how nice it is to see photos of the faces of the family and friends I write about in this weekly recipe column.

This year's Memorial Day weekend included the passing of the uncle of my good friends Ann and Amy Scamerhorn.

Their Uncle Byron, who died Thursday, and Aunt Alice have appeared in previous columns, often with grilling recipes, in addition to their photos featured in both the 2004 and 2007 cookbooks.

Alice, who is their mother Joann Scamerhorn's sister, loves to cook and bake, just like all of the ladies in this family.

While visiting Alice and Byron at their beautiful home in North Carolina last summer, Joann and the girls gathered fresh figs and made a delicious fig jam with Alice to bring home to share with my parents. Since Amy is a high school teacher in Indianapolis, she has plenty of time during the summer to cook, bake and fine tune recipes.

This week, I'm dedicating this column to Byron and the family while sharing one of Amy's favorite easy and delicious treats which are perfect for sharing.

Teacher's Pet Rocky Road Bars

● In a microwave-safe bowl, melt the butter, chocolate and syrup on high for 30 seconds. Stir.

● Keep heating in 30-second intervals until melted, stirring each time.

● Fold the graham cracker pieces and peanuts into the melted chocolate mixture, and then add the marshmallows.

● Pour into a 9-inch square pan lined with aluminum foil and flatten mixture with a spatula. Refrigerate for about 2 hours or overnight.

● Makes approximately 24 bars.

INGREDIENTS:

1 stick plus 1 tablespoon soft unsalted butter

1 12-ounce package semi-sweet chocolate chips

1/4 cup corn syrup

8 ounces graham crackers, broken into bite-sized pieces

2 cups miniature marshmallows

1 cup cocktail peanuts

You're invited to Dad's 80th birthday party

June 10, 2009

It's not every day there's an 80th birthday to celebrate.

And when it's your dad celebrating the beginning of his ninth decade, it's even more special.

On Sunday, July 12, my dad will turn 80 years old and Times readers are invited to join the fun and surprises at a special birthday dinner in the beautiful Somerset Garden Room of Avalon Manor on U.S. 30 in Merrillville, Ind.

My mother and all my older siblings, Carol, Tom, David and Pam, in addition to all the family and friends you so often read about in this column and my cookbooks, will be there to share in this special day.

One of the first things my dad mentioned about having a birthday celebration was that he did NOT want gifts. Instead, just sharing the day with guests is a gift better than any of the rest.

As for today's featured recipe, for as long as I can remember, my dad has always ended every dinner meal asking "What's for dessert?" with vanilla ice cream always the first request on his list.

In recent years, he's cut back on his ice cream, but you can see it's included on his birthday dinner menu.

About 10 years ago, one of my Purdue students shared a great and easy recipe for homemade ice cream, which she made for her demonstration speech assignment.

INGREDIENTS:

1 pint half and half

1/2 cup sugar

1 teaspoon vanilla (or 2 tablespoons chocolate syrup or 1/4 cup mashed strawberries)

Ice

Rock salt

1-pound coffee can with lid

3-pound coffee can with lid

Duct tape

"Roll-With-It" Easy Homemade Ice Cream

- Rinse and dry both empty coffee cans.

- In a small bowl, mix together half and half, sugar and vanilla or desired flavor.

- Pour mixture into the small coffee can, snap on lid and seal with duct tape.

- Place small, sealed coffee can in larger coffee can and surround with ice and a generous scattering of rock salt, until tightly packed and seal with lid and more tape.

- Roll the sealed coffee can back and forth along the floor 10 times and check to see if ice cream is combined, creamy and solid. If ice cream has not completely formed, re-seal and repeat rolling process.

- Makes 6 servings.

Reader gets help with butterscotch recipe

June 17, 2009

Everyone seems to have their minds on birthdays these days.

Last week, I wrote about my dad's birthday party event for readers next month.

And as the reservation calls come in, I also received a nice note from reader Elaine Phillips, of Griffith, Ind. with a reader birthday request:

"Dear Phil: I love reading your column. I cook and bake a lot, often bringing it to my work. I am a nurse. I had someone request a special cake for an August birthday. It is called "Butterscotch Candy Cake." Can you help me find a recipe for it please? I can't even find anything even close. Thanks! Elaine"

Thank you for the letter Elaine. My mom has a very easy and similar recipe that might help out. On weekends, she simply adds one box of instant butterscotch pudding to a yellow cake mix, uses four eggs, and then follows the rest of the box instructions, and bakes it in her bundt pan. She frosts it with a yellow buttercream frosting and it makes a yummy, rich and very moist "Butterscotch Candy Cake."

Speaking of birthdays, my mom's older sister, my Aunt Ruby, also turns 80 this summer, on July 10.

She'll also be at next month's party.

This week, I'm sharing her terrific and very old recipe for her butterscotch snack bars.

Aunt Ruby's Easy Butterscotch Bars

- In mixing bowl, beat together sugar and butter/margarine.

- Add eggs and vanilla and beat well. (Batter might appear slightly separated or curled.)

- In a separate bowl, mix together flour, pudding mix and salt.

- Add dry ingredients to the creamed mixture and mix well.

- Stir in oats.

- Spread batter into a greased 9-inch by 9-inch by 2-inch baking pan.

- Bake in 350-degree oven for 30 to 35 minutes or until tests done. Cool in pan.

- Sprinkle with powdered sugar using a tea strainer or sifter and cut into bars.

- Makes 2 dozen bars.

INGREDIENTS:

2/3 cup packed brown sugar

1/2 cup butter or margarine

2 eggs

1 teaspoon vanilla

1/2 cup all-purpose flour

1 (3.5 ounce) box of instant butterscotch pudding

1/4 teaspoon salt

3/4 cup quick cooking rolled oats

Powdered sugar

Reader recommends 'from scratch' butterscotch cake

June 24, 2009

Last weekend included some additional reasons to celebrate at the farm, in addition to our annual Father's Day family barbecue.

My mom and her twin sister, my Aunt Patty, attended their 60th high school reunion in the tiny town of Wheatfield.

And following the Saturday evening Mass at our farm church, we gathered at our church hall for a potluck to honor our parish priest, the Rev. William Spranger, on his 80th birthday.

My mom made one of the butterscotch bundt cakes I described in last week's column. She added a cup of butterscotch chips to the cake-mix batter as well as a package of instant butterscotch pudding. It was even more moist, rich and delicious.

On the subject of butterscotch recipes, I received the following letter this week:

"Hello, Philip,

I was visiting in the Northwest Indiana area this past week, I happened to read your column. Your mom's recipe might be good, but you may have missed the boat in not checking out a most tempting recipe for this Butterscotch Fudge Cake. I think this may be the one your reader was hoping to find. It is a scratch recipe, rather than a box easy out. Not that there's anything wrong with a box cake. I still prefer fresher ingredients, even for a decadent dessert unless I'm in a time crunch. I am going to try your recipe next week. I hope you enjoy this recipe. Sincerely, Mary Boudjalis."

My mom and her twin sister, Aunt Patty, celebrated their shared birthday with a towering cake in this Aug. 17, 1957 photo.

Butterscotch Fudge Cake

- Preheat oven to 325 degrees.

- Grease a 10-inch tube or bundt pan.

- To prepare cake, in a large bowl, cream the butter with the brown sugar, continuing to beat until the sugar is fully incorporated.

- Beat in the eggs very well.

- Beat in the milk and vanilla.

- In another bowl, stir together the flour, butterscotch candy, baking powder and salt.

- Add to the creamed mixture, beating or stirring until the dry ingredients are incorporated.

- Spread the batter evenly in the prepared pan. Bake 1 hour, 20 minutes, or until a toothpick inserted in the highest part of the cake comes out clean.

- Transfer the pan to a rack to cool. Allow the cake to cool completely before frosting it.

- To prepare frosting: Place the brown sugar, butter, evaporated milk and salt in a medium saucepan. Bring to a boil. Boil, stirring continuously, for 3 minutes.

- Remove the pan from the stove and add the baking powder and vanilla.

- Beat with an electric mixer 5 minutes, or until thickened.

- Immediately drizzle over the cake.

- Makes 16 to 20 servings.

INGREDIENTS:

CAKE:

2 sticks (1 cup) butter, softened

2 cups dark brown sugar

5 eggs

1 cup milk

1 teaspoon vanilla

3 cups flour

1/2 cup crushed butterscotch candy

2 teaspoons baking powder

1/4 teaspoon salt

BUTTERSCOTCH FUDGE ICING:

1 cup dark brown sugar

4 tablespoons butter

5 tablespoons evaporated milk

Pinch salt

1/4 teaspoon baking powder

1/4 teaspoon vanilla

The quaint bridge to our mailbox at the farm.

Prison banana cake
better not behind bars

July 1, 2009

The opening scene of Universal Pictures' "Public Enemies" has Johnny Depp as John Dillinger in black and white prison stripes breaking out of the Michigan City Prison in 1933.

Yep, Dillinger was once housed in the same prison where I teach courses for Purdue North Central, in addition to also teaching at Westville Correctional Center, not far from Michigan City, Ind.

I sampled today's recipe for "Behind Bars Banana Cake" at an honors luncheon last year for students who had earned good grades.

This delicious cake was served for dessert.

This delicious "from scratch" banana cake is much better than visions of "bread and water rations," as depicted in media stereotypes of incarceration. Note the beautiful origami prison butterfly crafted by an inmate as a paper garnish.

I'll never forget it.

While seated with some of the inmate students, one of the men serving time for arson passed the creamer packets and sugar to me for my coffee.

He casually mentioned those tiny powder packets of creamer are highly flammable, "just look at the warning on the packet."

And sure enough, he's right.

On the subject of cake, the photo I snapped of this cake includes a paper garnish of an origami (Japanese folded paper art) prison butterfly. Many of the inmates learn this paper craft as a way to pass the time. At this month's reader dinner event on July 12 for my father's 80th birthday celebration, this prison origami art is among some of the more than $1,000 of free drawing prizes to be given away.

Behind Bars Banana Cake
No. 147612

- Cream shortening, butter, sugar and vanilla using an electric mixer on a medium speed, for about 10 minutes.

- Add bananas (and extract, if desired) and eggs and continue mixing for another 5 minutes.

- In a separate bowl, combine flour, salt, baking powder and baking soda.

- Add dry ingredients, alternately, with buttermilk, using a low mixing speed.

- Pour batter into a greased 9-inch by 13-inch pan, baking 20 to 30 minutes at 350 degrees.

- While cake is cooling, make frosting by creaming butter until light and fluffy using an electric mixer on low speed.

INGREDIENTS:

CAKE:

1/4 cup shortening

1/4 cup butter

1 cup granulated sugar

3/4 teaspoon vanilla

1 cup mashed bananas

1/2 teaspoon banana extract (optional)

3 eggs, beaten

4 cups flour, sifted (or slightly more if needed for batter consistency)

1/4 teaspoon salt

1 tablespoon baking powder

1/2 teaspoon baking soda

1/4 cup buttermilk

INGREDIENTS:

FROSTING:

2 sticks of butter, softened

1 egg

2 cups sifted powdered sugar (1 pound box)

1 teaspoon vanilla

- Beat in egg and gradually add in sifted sugar, frequently scraping down side of the bowl.

- Lastly, add vanilla, beating frosting until smooth and light.

- Frost cake generously and serve.

- Makes 20 slices.

Dillinger's favorite pie recipe revealed

July 8, 2009

Food and family go hand in hand.

Public Enemy No. 1 John Dillinger and his clan are no exception.

But remember, Dillinger was a farmboy raised just outside Indianapolis in Mooresville, Ind.

A new book written by crime writer Carol Sissom shares intimate details of this elusive man famous for robbing banks and escaping jail cells. "Banking with Dillinger" by Carol Sissom (March 2009 Carol's Adventures Publishing $17.95) is a 200-page paperback with rare photos and facts never before made public.

One of my favorite surprises in this clever book is the inclusion of 20 Dillinger family recipes, including recipes for John Dillinger's favorite fried chicken, mashed potatoes and coconut cream pie. The author and the Dillinger Family graciously allowed me to publish the following recipe for readers.

According to Mike Dillinger, John's nephew and closest living male relative, many recipes featured in the book were dishes included at the Dillinger Family Reunion held April 8, 1934. That's the last time the family saw John alive.

John Dillinger's Favorite Coconut Cream Pie

- Combine sugar, cornstarch and salt.

- Heat milk in a saucepan and gradually add sugar, cornstarch and salt mixture, stirring until smooth.

- Bring to a boil, stirring over medium heat and allowing to boil for 2 minutes. Remove from heat.

- *Place beaten egg yolks in a bowl and stir half the hot mixture in with yolks to temper, before returning all of the tempered egg mixture back to saucepan. Cook, stirring over a low heat, until boiling and thick enough to mound to spoon, about 5 minutes.

- *Remove from heat and pour filling into a bowl and stir in extracts and half the coconut.

- Cover filling with wax paper and refrigerate for one hour.

- Pour filling in prepared pie shell and chill for 3 hours.

- Top with whipped cream and remaining coconut.

- Makes 8 slices.

- Recipe courtesy of Dillinger Family and "Banking with Dillinger" by Carol Sissom (March 2009 Carol's Adventures Publishing $17.95)

INGREDIENTS:

1 (9-inch) pie shell, baked and cooked

1 cup sugar

1/2 cup cornstarch

1/2 teaspoon salt

3 cups hot milk

3 egg yolks, beaten

1 teaspoon vanilla extract

1/2 teaspoon almond extract

2 cups grated coconut

1 cup heavy cream, whipped for topping

Join me Saturday in Crown Point for free farmers market demo

August 12, 2009

I hope lots of readers will join me, along with my parents, 10 a.m. Saturday in the middle of the Crown Point, Indiana's Farmers Market (right off the courthouse square) while I host a free cooking demonstration using much of the wonderful harvest around me.

I'm pleased and honored to be a guest of Crown Point Mayor David Uran for this event and I've made sure to confirm with his office that there will be chairs set up for guests to relax while they enjoy both the show and samples, along with some surprises and free prizes.

However, I'm told only 50 chairs will be set up and made available for "first come, first serve."

As for the recipes I'll be demonstrating, I've selected two summer favorites from my second cookbook "More From the Farm: Recipes and Memories of a Lifetime" (2007 Pediment Press $29.95). Millie's Favorite Linguine Salad, featuring diced cucumbers and tomatoes, and Roasted Eggplant-Tomato Dip which highlights sun-dried tomatoes, fresh parsley and fresh basil as key featured ingredients.

For more information about the event, contact Jennifer Young at the Crown Point Mayor's Office of Special Events.

Today's recipe is in answer to a reader's request from a favorite

Newspaper columnist and radio personality Mary Margaret McBride was a trusted source for consumers, often lending her name and support to various product endorsements.

media name in the Chicagoland area. Jackie Swike, of Merrillville, Ind. is best know to millions of listeners as one of the popular radio news personalities on Chicago's WBBM 780 radio station. I, like many readers, also remember Jackie from her days with our own local television outlet Channel 56, which I how I first met her 15 years ago.

"Dear Phil: Do you have a good orange cake recipe? My family says my grandmother made a delicious orange cake for special occasions, but this was years ago, before my time, and the recipe was probably in her head. Also, did Betty Crocker have an orange cake mix in a box? I wish they had such retro flavors now. Thanks, Jackie Swike"

I'm sure many readers can recall enjoying orange cake as a refreshing sweet summer favorite from years ago. My second cookbook even included a great recipe for grapefruit cake, another retro favorite. Jackie is correct - Betty Crocker, Pillsbury and Duncan Hines all manufactured orange-flavored cake mixes for years, until the 1980s when orange seemed to fall out of "favor flavor." (Some stores still carry a Duncan Hines cake mix version called "Orange Supreme.")

The recipe I'm including today is 50 years old, but is simple and delicious. It comes from the 1958 kitchen of culinary legend Mary Margaret McBride (who died in 1976), the popular radio and television personality long before Martha Stewart.

INGREDIENTS:

CAKE:

2-1/2 cups cake flour

2 teaspoons baking powder

1/4 teaspoon salt

3/4 cup butter or margarine

1-1/2 cups sugar

3 eggs

1/2 cup orange juice

1/3 cup water

Grated rind of 1 orange

FROSTING:

1/4 cup butter

2 cups confectioners' sugar

3 tablespoons milk

1 teaspoon vanilla

Dash of salt

2 drops yellow food coloring

Mary Margaret McBride's Frosted Orange Cake

● To make cake, sift flour, baking powder and salt together. Set aside.

● In a second bowl, cream together butter or margarine with sugar, beating until light and fluffy.

● Add eggs one at a time and beat thoroughly after each addition.

● Add dry ingredients alternately to creamed egg mixture, while alternating with orange juice and water, beating batter until smooth. Fold in orange rind.

● Pour batter into a well-greased 9-inch-by-13-inch cake pan and bake in a moderate oven at 375 degrees for 25 to 30 minutes.

● Allow to cool 10 minutes before frosting.

● To make frosting, cream together butter and sugar, gradually adding the milk and remaining ingredients until desired consistency, color shade and taste.

● Makes 20 serving slices.

Readers eager for more orange cake opportunities

August 26, 2009

A column I wrote earlier this month featuring a reader's request for an old stand-by recipe for Orange Cake by famed 1940s radio and TV home economist Mary Margaret McBride was a big hit for readers.

A number of readers wrote to me saying it ranks only second to the recipe for the lush, moist layered frosted Grapefruit Cake that was a favorite of the late, great Hollywood gossip columnist Louella O. Parsons, who worked for the legendary William Randolph Hearst.

I received a nice typewritten letter from reader Janet Krygoski of East Chicago, Ind.

"Dear Phil: Read about the request for orange cake. I know my baby sister Diane has written you a few times. My mother made this recipe many years ago, beginning during World War II, for us when we were little. I remember one time, she made one and took it downstairs to her in-laws to enjoy. And when my uncle came home from work at midnight and saw the loaf on the kitchen table, he thought for sure that Ma made fresh bread, since that's what it looks like. I love it and I hope your readers will too. Sincerely, Janet Krygoski, East Chicago"

INGREDIENTS:

2 cups cake flour

1-1/4 cups sugar

1-1/2 teaspoon baking powder

1/2 teaspoon salt

1/2 cup vegetable shortening

1/2 cup fresh orange rind/liquid (created from the grated fresh orange rind from 1 orange and then just enough of the juice, so together, it makes 1/2 cup and add a bit of pulp for an even better taste)

3 large eggs, unbeaten (equals about 1/2 to 2/3 cup eggs)

Janet's Mom's World War II Fresh Orange Loaf Cake

- In a bowl, sift together flour, sugar, baking powder and salt.

- Add shortening and orange rind/liquid and beat batter vigorously with a spoon for exactly 2 minutes (which equals 150 strokes per minute).

- If using an electric mixer, mix on slow speed for 2 minutes.

- Add eggs and beat for 2 more minutes.

- Pour batter into a greased 8-by-4-inch loaf pan or, if desired, into an 8-by-8-inch or 9-by-9-inch square pan and bake at 350 degrees for 1 hour or until tests done when knife is inserted.

- Once cooled, cake will have an "almost sugary glaze appearance," so a dusting of powdered sugar or light icing can be added if desired.

- Makes 16 slices.

Blueberry Pie garners praise and top honors at Hammond Fest

September 23, 2009

It was great weather and a great weekend for winners and contestants at this year's Downtown Hammond, Ind. Pie Baking Contest.

While sampling pies during the judging and hearing the band down the street playing "76 Trombones," it really did feel like a scene from "The Music Man."

As for top honors, the most ribbons went to Marilyn Kmak, of Munster, Ind. for her very flaky pie crust and delicious blueberry pie, which also took home the grand prize. The ribbon for "best savory pie" went to Melissa Garcia, of Highland, Ind. for her pumpkin-apple pie and "creative use of ingredients" went to perfect blend of thinly sliced apples and delicate spices used by 8-year-old Dominc Velligan, of Whiting, for a scrumptious fall apple pie.

A Strawberry Angel Pie, entered under by 5-year-old twins Julie and Jasmine Lopez, of East Chicago, Ind. won a special ribbon for "wackiest pie presentation."

As for our overall winner, whose recipe is showcased today, she first began cooking and baking on the family farm for wheat thrashing as a young girl. Marilyn's daughter Lisa Kmak Beatty told me: "Growing up, we always had homecooked meals and fresh baked goods. And to this day, it is hard to find a restaurant that can do it better than my mom."

A selection of picture-perfect pies await ribbon honors at the 2008 Hammond, Ind. festival weekend pie contest.

Marilyn Kmak's True Blueberry Pie

INGREDIENTS:

CRUST:

2 1/2 cups flour

1 teaspoon salt

1/2 cup shortening

1/2 cup cold butter

6-7 tablespoons cold water

1 tablespoon scattering of plain, unseasoned breadcrumbs

1 egg yolk plus 1 tablespoon water for egg wash

FILLING:

4 cups fresh blueberries

1 cup granulated sugar

1/2 teaspoon salt

1/4 cup cornstarch

1/4 cup cold water

3/4 cup hot water

1 tablespoon lemon juice

1 tablespoon butter

- To make crust, combine cold butter and shortening by using a pie blender or knife to cut it into the dry ingredients.

- Add enough water to form a workable dough.

- Divide dough into two rounds and refrigerate for 1 hour before rolling into the two pie crusts.

- To make filling, add the 1/4 cup cold water to cornstarch and dissolve, combining with sugar, salt and 1/2 cup blueberries and the 3/4 cup hot water, all placed in a saucepan and simmered for about 5 minutes and crushing berries with back of a spoon to burst. Remove from heat and add lemon juice to make a glaze.

- Place remaining berries in a large bowl and pour glaze over berries and mix to coat.

- Allow filling to stand until cooled. If filling appears too thick, a little water may be added.

- Remove chilled dough and roll out to create a top and bottom crust, to line a 10-inch pie pan.

- Sprinkle dry bread crumbs on the bottom of pie shell and then pour filling into the crust. (Crumbs will help absorb extra liquid during baking for ideal slicing consistency.)

- Dot filling with 1 tablespoon of butter. Apply top crust and seal and flute edges, allow with cutting slots for pie to vent.

- Mix one beaten egg yolk with 1 tablespoon water to make an egg wash to brush over top of pie.

- Place foil along edges of pie and on bottom rack under pie and pack for 30 minutes at 350 degrees on bottom rack.

- Move pie to middle rack and bake another 15 minutes. Remove foil from pie and increase oven to 400 degrees and bake another 15 minutes or until top crust is golden.

- Makes 8 serving slices.

Time for Times 'Taste of Home' cooking school

September 30, 2009

If your cookbooks are anything like those passed along in my family, including those of my mom, in addition to my grandmothers' and aunts' collections, there are probably quite a few scattered favorite recipe cards and notes tucked away inside the pages, almost like random bookmarks.

Whenever I see one of my own "From the Farm" hardcover cookbooks in this condition, cradled by a reader, I know my book is valued.

Recipes are the equivalent of fond memories preserved as our food favorites.

I'm always excited to see how many young people, both men and women, have an interest in cooking and baking these days.

In fact, while teaching at Valparaiso University, during my public speaking courses, I usually stumble across a few great recipes that students share during their demonstration speech assignments.

This month, I was particularly impressed by a recipe presented by Gabriele Bladdick, who hails from St. Louis.

Her recipe for an age-old favorite called "St. Louis Gooey Butter Cake" earned high marks and a round of applause from her fellow students, especially when she provided samples. The legend of the story is the recipe came from a St. Louis bakery in the 1930s after a German baker found he had left out a few of the key ingredients for a traditional coffeecake recipe and accidentally developed this sweet and delicious treat.

Gabby's St. Louis Gooey Butter Cake

- In a large bowl, combine dry cake mix with 1 egg and 1 stick of butter.

- Mix using an electric mixer so mixture is crumbly.

- Pat into the bottom of a lightly greased or sprayed 9-inch by 13-inch baking pan.

- In a separate bowl, combine the confectioner's sugar with cream cheese, 2 eggs and vanilla.

- Mix with electric mixer until creamy and free of lumps.

- Pour over the dry cake bottom layer in pan.

- Bake at 350 degrees for 35 minutes.

- Makes 18 serving slices.

INGREDIENTS:
1 (18-ounce) box white cake mix
3 eggs (divided use)
1 stick of butter
1 (16-ounce) box confectioner's sugar
1 (8-ounce) package of cream cheese
1 teaspoon vanilla

Help me celebrate with Franciscan Sisters and 70th anniversary

October 14, 2009

Thank you to all of the readers who attended Monday's Second Annual Taste of Home Cooking School presented by The Times. It was a nice night to gather together for some food, fun and clever cooking ideas as we ready ourselves for the holidays.

Readers are invited to also join me, along with my parents, when we return to Star Plaza in the Radisson Hotel's ballroom at 6:30 p.m. Oct. 23 as I host a special dinner and dance event for the Franciscan Sisters. This special order of nuns will celebrate the 70th anniversary of Franciscan Communities and the St. Anthony Hospital Campus.

I'll be sharing the remarkable history of these dedicated nuns who began what was then called St. Anthony Home for the Aged in Crown Point in 1939 using the $1,000 purchase of a 40-acre farm, which included a farmhouse, woods, chicken coop, stables, summer house kitchen, orchard, four cows, two calves, two horses and 30 pigs .

On the subject of orchards, fruits and desserts, as promised, this week's recipe is another winner from last month's pie contest in Hammond, Ind. compliments of 8-year-old Dominc Velligan, of Whiting, Ind. Try this scrumptious fall apple pie.

INGREDIENTS:

Prepared top and bottom crust for a 9-inch pie

6 cups of sliced, tart apples

1 teaspoon lemon juice

3/4 cup sugar

2 tablespoons all-purpose flour

3/4 teaspoon ground cinnamon

1/8 teaspoon nutmeg

2 to 3 teaspoons of butter

Dominc's Basic Apple Pie

- Heat oven to 425 degrees.

- In a large bowl, gently toss sliced apples with lemon juice.

- Combine all remaining dry ingredients and mix well with the prepared apples.

- Form bottom crust in pie pan and pour in apple filling mixture.

- Dot top of filling with a little butter and cover with top pie crust. Seal and flute edges, also cutting a few slits in top of pie crust for ventilation.

- Bake 40 to 45 minutes, covering crust edges with foil if desired to prevent over browning.

- Makes 8 serving slices.

All's fair with yummy 'elephant ear' cheesecake recipe

October 21, 2009

It's that time of year when the Sandhill Cranes pay a visit to our farm to frolic and feed in all the now harvested cornfields.

Last week, while my dad was out for a morning walk with Laddie, my parents' dog, he said he counted as many as 100 of these stilt legged, long neck Stork-like birds.

It's a sign that Autumn has really arrived and winter is just down the road.

For my mom, that means she always gets a craving for caramel taffy apples, rolled in chopped peanuts.

Similarly, my mom gets the same craving for the sugar and cinnamon sweet coated deep-fried "flat" batter known to most as "elephant ears."

In the meantime, this week's recipe is sure to provide a fun fair food fix for readers. Kylee Spier, of neighboring Union Mills, Ind. in LaPorte County, one of my Valparaiso University students in my public speaking class this semester, shared her terrific and easy recipe for Elephant Ear Cheesecake for her demonstrative speech and it was a big hit.

Kylee's Easy Elephant Ear Cheesecake

- Preheat oven to 350 degrees.

- Spray a 9-inch by 13-inch baking pan.

- Gently unroll one of the cans of crescent rolls into a single layer of dough and press into bottom of prepared pan, stretching or rolling out dough as necessary to cover bottom of pan.

- In a bowl, mix together cream cheese, 1 cup of sugar, egg and vanilla, beating until smooth and creamy.

- Spread filling over the bottom crescent layer.

- On a very lightly floured surface, gently roll out the second can of crescent rolls to a size that fits over the entire cheese filling layer. Don't press down on cheese layer.

- Pour melted margarine over the entire top crust and spread so it evenly covers before combining cinnamon with 1/4 cup sugar and scattering evenly over the melted margarine.

- Bake 25 to 30 minutes or until golden brown.

- Makes 20 dessert squares.

INGREDIENTS:

2 (8-ounce) canisters of refrigerated crescent rolls

2 (8-ounce) packages cream cheese

1 cup sugar plus 1/4 cup (divided use)

1 egg

1 teaspoon vanilla

1/2 cup margarine, melted

1 teaspoon cinnamon

Non-stick cooking spray

Special chocolate chip cookie recipe is devilishly good

October 28, 2009

I feel fortunate that I don't have to wait until Halloween to look forward to sampling wonderful treats.

Throughout my career, and even before I began writing columns a decade ago, readers have always been generous about sharing wonderful treats and dropping off samples at our newspaper offices or bringing yummy surprises to events I host or attend.

From macaroni salad and fudge to muffins, homemade wine, strombolis, homemade breads, coffeecakes, pickles and dish towels and scouring pads, Times readers are a creative and sharing bunch.

Vickie Brant, of Munster, Ind. brought me a batch of her Cain and Abel Chocolate Chip Cookies last spring for Valentine's Day. She says the recipe was given to her years ago from her friend Theresa Dye, who named them such because "They are so good, you'll do anything for a second one!"

I'll let readers give these biblically branded cookie creations a try so you can decide for yourselves.

Have a happy and safe Halloween!

Cain and Abel Chocolate Chip Cookies

- Preheat oven to 375 degrees.

- Combine flour, baking soda and salt in a large bowl.

- In a separate bowl, beat the melted butter with both sugars and kahlua, until smooth and then add eggs, beating well until mixture is creamed.

- Gradually add flour mixture, while stirring dough and then slowly fold in chocolate chips, pecans and chocolate bar pieces.

- Preferably, cookies should be large, so using an ice cream scoop, scoop dough onto a cookie sheet and bake for 16 minutes, making sure to turn the cookie sheet halfway through the baking time.

- Remove from oven and allow cookies to set (they will look underbaked) for a few minutes. Do NOT overbake.

- Makes 2 dozen cookies.

INGREDIENTS:

2-1/4 cups all-purpose flour
1 teaspoon baking soda
1 teaspoon salt
1 cup butter, melted and cooled
3/4 cup granulated sugar
3/4 cup brown sugar
1 tablespoon kahlua liqueur
2 large eggs
3 cups chocolate chips
1 large (8 or 12 ounces) bar of premium milk chocolate of choice, broken up into pieces
1-1/4 cup whole pecans, lightly toasted

Your chance for resurrected holiday 'Caring Place' baking recipe contest

November 4, 2009

For many of our longtime Times readers, the columnist name "Aunt Maxine" certainly rings a bell.

She was my predecessor who originally began this food cover column concept when hired by The Times in 1993.

After five years, "Aunt Maxine" (who really does have a last name: Ciminillo) retired in 1998 and moved to Florida.

But during her writing tenure at The Times, I did have the good fortune to help her judge at least one of our annual Times holiday recipe contests before her departure.

But just after I joined The Times in 1995, Aunt Maxine began annually helping coordinate and to promote a specific contest for one of her favorite charity causes: The Caring Place, a shelter for victims of domestic violence, based in Valparaiso. Over the years, I've continued her tradition, while adding other organizations as well to my "full plate."

But this year, I'm helping to resurrect one of Aunt Maxine's original efforts.

Joann and Steve Scamerhorn celebrating their 25th wedding anniversary with family in January 1994 at our All Saints Church.

From 1996 to 1998, she helped with The Caring Place's annual Taste of chocolate recipe contest and in a February 1998 column, she wrote: "Every year around this time, I count my blessings, and I think about those individuals who are not as fortunate as I when it comes to personal relationships. My parents loved each other and us kids, and we were never abused. My husband has loved me and our children without abusing us either physically or emotionally. The Caring Place is a shelter for abused women and children. Again this year, its fundraiser is looking for cooks and bakers to enter their chocolate contest."

This month, I'm working with The Caring Place and Wiseway grocery stores to help raise money with a similar recipe contest open to all types of holiday goodies, rather than just limited to chocolate.

The details are explained in today's Wiseway advertisement inside The Times.

And here are more details as well:

The 2009 Holiday Baking and Caring Contest benefiting The Caring Place for Victims of Domestic Violence:

Include your favorite original COOKIE or DESSERT BAR or CONFECTION recipe to be considered for the first place prize in any of the three recipe categories to win baking gift baskets valued at $200, along with runner-up prizes also awarded.

Enter as many recipes as you wish, but only one entry may qualify as a winner.

Mrs. Scamerhorn's Easy Ginger Snap Cookies

- In a large mixing bowl, combine sugar, oil and molasses.

- Add egg and mix well until blended.

- In a separate bowl, combine flour, baking soda, salt and spices.

- Add the dry mixture to the sugar and oil mixture.

- Cover dough and refrigerate at least 4 hours, or preferably, overnight.

- Preheat oven to 375 degrees and pinch off pieces of dough to make 1-inch balls, rolled in hands and then rolled in white sugar before placed 3-inches apart on cookie sheet.

- Bake for 7 to 9 minutes, or until centers "crack" and edges firm.

- Cool cookies for 2 to 3 minutes before transferring to cool further on a wire rack.

- Makes 3 1/2 to 4 dozen cookies.

INGREDIENTS:
1 cup granulated sugar
3/4 cup vegetable oil
1/4 cup molasses
1 egg
2 cups all-purpose flour
2 teaspoons baking soda
1/2 teaspoon ground cinnamon
1/2 teaspoon salt
1/4 teaspoon ground ginger
1/4 teaspoon ground cloves
Additional white sugar as needed

(Food Styling by Philip Potempa / Photo by Michael Berkos)

A minimum of at least three varieties of dried beans make Jennifer's Chili "El Grito" (recipe on page 17) a flavorful favorite, in addition to the unusual garnish of fresh avocado.

I

Blueberries are better than ever when baked into a delicious and easy baked buckle (page 42) topped with a crust featuring coconut as a sweet surprise ingredient.

With garden-fresh zucchini layered with a simple biscuit mix as the ingredient base and then dressed-up with a blend of cheeses, herbs and spices, this basic zucchini and cheese pie (page 174) is a celebration of summer.

A blend of crisp bacon, contrasted with the mildness of crisp cucumber and the juicy goodness of tiny ripe tomatoes, all set off as a creamy dream with toasted tease makes BLT Side Salad (page 227) a certain sensation.

Here's the best of both worlds in a cookie competition: a moist banana oatmeal cookie (page 93) and a beautiful strawberry valentine heart cookie (page 92).

Easy and elegant, followed by rich and delicious, are words that best describe these yummy "quick-pick-me-up" coffee brownies (page 106).

*It's September 1993 and I'm with my parents (who are wearing "real"
Hawaiian shirts from their farm friends Bill and Marie Skuderna) on
the island of Maui in Hawaii, helping them toast their 40th wedding
anniversary.*

*Backstage at the Drury Lane Dinner
Theater in Evergreen Park, Ill. in 2003.
My mom is all smiles, with me at her
side, reunited with the one and only
Jim Nabors, whose macadamia nut
plantation on the island of Maui in
Hawaii we had visited a decade earlier.*

*Phil swapping some business
advice with Donald Trump's
first NBC "Apprentice" reality
show winner Bill Rancic in
Chicago in October 2007.*

(Photo by Christopher Smith)

("Public Enemies" image courtesy of Universal Pictures)

Yep, that's me holding the pencil and wearing legendary gossip columnist Walter Winchell's fabled fedora hat while playing a 1930s newspaper reporter interviewing actor Johnny Depp as gangster John Dillinger in the 2009 Universal Pictures film "Public Enemies."

Here's my idea of what a 1930s newspaper reporter should look like, from head to toe, wearing my dad's wing-tipped shoes and his striped wide tie and topped off with Walter Winchell's actual fedora hat and my Uncle Joe's old camera. I must have been "right on the money," because this February 2008 audition "look" landed me my role with director Michael Mann in his "Public Enemies."

(Photo by Michael Berkos)

For Hollywood royalty, actress Jane Russell, with me in Los Angeles in February 2007 at age 85, ranks right at the top. Her starring breakout role in Howard Hughes' "The Outlaw" in 1943 was scandalous to film censors. But by a decade later in 1953, she was putting her hands in cement with co-star Marilyn Monroe at Grauman's Chinese Theater (inset photo) for the opening of the film "Gentlemen Prefer Blondes")

(Photo by Michael Berkos)

*They don't get any nicer than the legendary Karl Malden, at age 95 here,
and his wife of 70 years, Mona, who invited me to their Brentwood, Calif.
home in November 2007 for afternoon tea and a sit down interview. I
gave them a copy of my second cookbook and they gave me a recipe for this
cookbook, which is found on page 281.*

(Photo by Michael Berkos)

*I'm face to face with a very famous Phil
aka all-around good-guy and Notre
Dame grad Phil Donahue, who spent an
afternoon with me during his Chicago
homecoming visit in May 2008.*

(Author's Collection)

*That's celebrity photographer
Michael Berkos, the man behind
many of the photos in this book,
as well as my second book,
meeting out-of-character Paul
Reubens, known more often as
Pee-wee Herman.*

(Author's Collection)

Nicer than you could ever imagine is how I describe Dolly Parton, who really made my mom's day when she exchanged cookbooks with us while visiting her at her Dollywood theme park in Tennessee in April 2009. You'll find her recipe for "Hello Dolly" bars on page 108.

(Author's Collection)

What a "Golden" opportunity, meeting the wonderful Bea Arthur in May 2001 and "sweet as pie" Betty White in March 2009, after sharing lunch in March 2009 at the historic Empire Room at the Palmer House in Chicago.

(Photo by Michael Berkos)

Does the camera really add 10 pounds? I guess it just depends what I'm whipping up in the studio kitchen that day for my television cooking segments.

(Photo by Michael Berkos)

Blue ribbons are proudly displayed at a book launch party for my second cookbook for Mother's Day Weekend 2007, with my entire family gathered for the unveiling.

(Photo courtesy of Seattle Sutton Healthy Eating)

(Author's Collection)

Weight-loss Guru Seattle Sutton introducing her 10 contestants, including me, on national television for the January 2010 kick-off of her three-month Slim Down Challenge. By April 12, 2010, I was 50 pounds lighter and loving it!

Back row: Denise Akande, Andrea Lasticly, Phil, Michael Koch and Paul Quaglia. Front row: Martha Ibarra, Donna Nelson, Tim Gallivan, Linda Russell, Heidi Wolfrom and Seattle Sutton.

It's May 2000 and I'm back in the gymnasium of my old high school in North Judson, Ind. for the honor of giving the commencement address to that year's graduating class. I'm joined by two of my favorite high school teachers who helped steer my future, Janet Hetterscheidt and Ken Stewart.

Here I am with two fellow classmates, Chad Schumacher (left) and Ann Scamerhorn (far right), and evenly-numbered by our elementary school teachers, Erna Eckert (left), Pam Nielsen (middle) and Lois Haring (right) at an April 2008 banquet honoring our 20 year school reunion. Mrs. Eckert has recipes featured on pages 61 and 231, while Mrs. Haring's recipe is on 146.

It wouldn't be Easter without my mom's lamb cake and our basket of blessed Easter foods. Our pastor for 25 years, Rev. William Spranger did his final blessing for us in 2009, before retiring the following year.

Painting away to create artsy Eastern European Easter eggs, I'm joined by Serbian friend Sanjin Bosnjak as we learn the craft from Theresa Child, whose egg salad recipe is found on page 277.

If it's Christmas, there's always time for family and friends, in addition to a few book signing events, like this December 2006 shopping mall holiday party event hosted with some help by Ann Scamerhorn.

This 1968 photo shows an ideal view ~~from our the~~ *front of the family farm house, including some great details from the "P" initial decorative shutters to the rock garden flower beds on the front lawn and surrounding shrubbery.*

Grandma Potempa displays a bushel basket bounty of fall button mushrooms, against the white paint backdrop of the farm grainery.

This 1968 perspective photo shows the classic farm landscape of memories past, from the curve of a circling lane to the barn (at left) and one of many apple trees.

Here's Grandma Potempa and Aunty Lilly with Skippy, their Chihuahua, in 1968 by the back porch. Note the "P" initial also included on the house awnings.

Every judging event means there must be a winner. In the case of this December 2009 holiday baking contest, that winner is Cathy Kallok, of Griffith, for her peanut butter brownie cups (see page 134).

The race is on, for an exciting birthday adventure when my Auntie Wanda and cousin Patty (left) joined me and my parents at Balmoral Horse Racing Track in Crete, Ill. for my mom's birthday celebration. This photo was taken in "the winner's circle."

Scott Keith (left) joined me and Terry Zych in November 2008 as fellow judges for a fudge contest as part of the 25th anniversary tribute to the film "A Christmas Story" held in Hammond, Ind.

(Author's Collection)

Here are just a few more of my favorite ladies, including kind and creative Mindy Suich, who surprised me for my August 2007 37th birthday with a custom created bobble head likeness of myself. And this January 1999 photo of my mom (middle) with her twin sister Patty (left) and their older sister Ruby (right) has always been a holiday classic. On the subject of red, here I am with my mom and Radio One Communications on air personality Laura Walszuko, hosting the May 2009 American Heart Association "Go Red" Luncheon. And for a "clean sweep," I've also included syndicated newspaper household hints columnist Heloise, shown with me, feather dusters in hand, in Indianapolis, Ind. in January 2003.

(Photo by Michael Berkos)

Here I am with Martha Stewart in the historic Walnut Room of Macy's department store on State Street in Chicago in this November 2007 photo, chatting about holiday decoration ideas.

(Author's Collection)

Here are two photos that both rank as "sweet treats." My mom is playing "Hostess" and beaming with good reason as she displays one of her recipe specialties: Mock Hostess Ho-Ho Cake, which was featured in my second cookbook. And everyone in our small town knows Lorraine "Blondie" Wappel and her sunny personality.

What a wonderful reunion I had, along with my parents, in March 2009 when we visited cousin Bernie and her daughters Sherry and Mickey at her home just over the bay from Tampa, Fla. We came bearing gifts of mom's homemade jams, my dad's custom created birdhouses and my cookbooks, see photo on page 251.

Mary Tyler Moore is as gracious and kind as you might expect. This photo is from March 1997 in Chicago while she was here to sign copies of her new autobiography.

She's a lady of many entertaining stage talents, but most of all, I think of Lily Tomlin, with me here in May 2007, as a good friend.

(Photo by Michael Berkos)

What a way to spend Mother's Day Weekend May 2007, catching up backstage with Joan Rivers following her show in Joliet, Ill. She said she wanted to give me a recipe for my next cookbook. But the only recipe she said she knows is for toast, "and sometimes I even burn that," she explained.

(Author's Collection)

As it turns out, two is also just as fun as "Three's Company," as long as you're swapping favorite recipes with actress Joyce DeWitt, who also hails from Indiana, as well as being a graduate of Ball State University. This was shot at Chicago's Navy Pier in June 2009.

(Photo by Michael Berkos)

What does Debbie Reynolds usually make for dinner? Reservations. But that doesn't mean this busy gal doesn't enjoy a good cookbook, especially if it features recipes from her friends like Phyllis Diller and Jim Nabors.

(Photo by Michael Berkos)

It's a glorious sight, with every reason to smile, when you have beautiful summer weather, inviting outdoor surroundings and a hot grill ready to cook up a feast for awaiting guests.

(Photo by Robert Wray)

This is a very natural and familiar photo scene, sharing a smile with my parents at an social event while representing my newspaper, in this case, at the January 2009 unveiling of the new hotel and spa at Blue Chip Casino in Michigan City, Ind.

Old fashioned orange chiffon cupcakes net top contest honors

November 18, 2009

For the third year, I served as one of the celebrity judges at the annual intramural bake-off at Purdue University Calumet last week.

This year, it's Bridget Marczewski, 22, of Highland, Ind. who now holds the title of "best Boilermaker baker," after her late Grandmother Eleanor's family recipe for Orange Chiffon Cupcakes with Orange-Scented Buttercream Icing netted the top prize.

Bridget, the daughter of Karen and Joe Marczewski, was one of three student finalists at last week's competition. The sweet finalists also include a pumpkin cupcake and apple cinnamon cupcake.

But it's Bridget's orange-inspired cupcake, which she presented on her grandmother's beloved Waterford Crystal cake plate, which will now be a standing menu item in the PUC cafeteria for the next year. As readers might recall, in prior contest years, it was a brownie recipe and a cookie contest on the PUC campus that was used to crown previous kitchen champs.

I'm sharing this winning recipe today.

Bridget Marczewski, daughter of Karen and Joe Marczewski of Highland, Ind., is shown holding her grandmother's "empty" Waterford cake plate. Her grandmother's recipe for an orange chiffon cupcake with buttercream icing earned her the top honors for the 2009 Purdue University Calumet Intramural Bake-Off on Nov. 9, 2009.

ELEANOR'S ORANGE CHIFFON CUPCAKES INGREDIENTS:

CUPCAKE BATTER:

2 large egg whites

1/3 cup sugar

2 cups sifted cake flour
(equally 2 cups AFTER sifted)

3/4 cup granulated sugar

1/4 cup vanilla-infused sugar
(made by mixing 1 tablespoon vanilla to 2
cups white granulated sugar and allowing to
absorb flavor for at least one day)

2 teaspoons baking powder

1/2 teaspoon salt

1 tablespoon orange liqueur (or extract)

1 cup half and half

1/2 cup canola oil

2 large egg yolks

2 teaspoons finely grated orange zest

ICING:

4 1/2 cups confectioners' sugar

1 1/2 cups unsalted butter

1 tablespoon vanilla extract

3 to 4 tablespoons whipping cream

1 tablespoon finely grated orange zest

2 tablespoons fresh squeezed orange juice

Orange sugar or sprinkles for garnish
(optional)

Eleanor's Orange Chiffon Cupcakes with Orange-Scented Buttercream Icing

- Preheat oven to 350 degrees.

- Line 2 (regular size) 12-cup cupcake tins with liners. Set aside.

- In a medium bowl, beat egg whites to soft peaks with electric mixer.

- Slowly add 1/3 cup of sugar and beat to stiff peaks. Set aside.

- In a large bowl, sift together the cake flour, sugars, baking powder and salt.

- Add remaining ingredients and beat until combined (about 1 minute).

- Fold egg whites in to the batter being careful not to deflate the egg whites.

- Spoon mixture, a little over half full, into each cupcake liner.

- Bake for approximately 18 minutes or until tests done.

- Allow cupcakes to cool in pan for about 5 minutes then remove to a wire rack.

- While cupcakes bake, prepare icing by using an electric mixture on medium speed to combine sugar and butter.

- Add vanilla, orange zest, orange juice and whipping cream and beat on medium speed for 2 minutes, until light and fluffy.

- Ice cupcakes and garnish with sugars if desired.

- Makes 24 cupcakes.

Colonel Sanders' Thanksgiving Day pecan pie a rare find

November 25, 2009

On the way home from visiting Dolly Parton at her Dollywood theme park in Tennessee last spring, my mother, Peggy, and I made a quick detour to tiny Corbin, Kentucky, to see the original eatery where Col. Harland Sanders began selling and marketing his famed Kentucky Fried Chicken.

Sanders, who died at age 90 in 1980, was actually born and raised as a Hoosier in Henryville, Ind.

During our travels, Sanders just happened to be back in the news making headlines, which partly prompted our curiosity.

Just a few weeks early, reports had gone out over the wire serves that the Colonel's secret flavor recipe "of 11 herbs and spices" to create his famous "finger lickin' good chicken" had just been returned to the KFC Louisville corporate headquarters to be housed in a "more secure, computerized vault."

As a closely guarded trade secret, today portions of the secret spice mix are actually made at different locations based around the United States, and the only complete, handwritten copy of the recipe is kept in this new vault.

Back on Sept. 9, 2008, the one complete copy of the recipe had been temporarily moved to an undisclosed location under extremely tight security while KFC revamped the security at its headquarters.

So as the securing of the recipe was causing buzz among the media, KFC disclosed the following details about the recipe and its security arrangements:

● The recipe, which includes exact amounts of each component, is written in pencil on a single sheet of notebook paper and signed by Sanders.

● The recipe was previously locked in a filing cabinet with two separate combination locks. The cabinet also included vials of each of the 11 herbs and spices used.

● Only two executives ever have access to the recipe at any one time and KFC refuses to disclose the names and titles of either executive.

● One of the two executives also told the Associated Press that no one has ever come close to guessing the contents of the secret recipe, adding that the actual recipe "would include some surprises."

My mom and her family are originally from Jasper County, Ind. around the Wheatfield and Rensselaer area, and growing up, we had often eaten at the Kentucky Fried Chicken in Rensselaer, Ind. while visiting my mom's mother, Grandma Green, or visiting my sister Pam while she attended St. Joseph's Catholic College. The restaurant, opened in 1971 by Harold and Harriet Evers, was the first restaurant franchise to open in this part of the Hoosier state. Even today, it still features lots of memorabilia and photos of the Evers with Colonel Sanders.

As for our visit to the Sanders' Cafe, it's free to tour and still includes a working KFC for dining. But the best part is walking through the Colonel's office and first kitchen, which includes all the original dishes, pots, cutting board and furnishings.

Even though I can't share the Colonel's recipe for his original fried chicken, we did get a copy of his favorite pecan pie recipe, just in time my mom and readers to make for Thanksgiving Day dinner.

Enjoy and Happy Thanksgiving!

Colonel Sanders' Pecan Pie

INGREDIENTS:

4 eggs, slightly beaten

1 cup golden corn syrup
(The Colonel prefers Karo brand.)

1/3 cup sugar

Pinch of salt

1 tablespoon lemon juice or vinegar

4 tablespoons room temperature butter

2 teaspoons vanilla

2/3 cup pecan halves

1 unbaked 9-inch pie shell

- Preheat oven to 325/350 degrees (depending if your oven bakes hot or slightly cooler than indicated).

- Pour the pecan halves in the unbaked pie shell.

- In a large mixing bowl, mix together all the remaining ingredients and pour over pecans in pie shell.

- Bake for 35 minutes or until golden.

- Makes 10 serving slices.

Here I am with my mom outside the famed Sanders Cafe in Corbin, Ky. in this April 2009 file photo. Colonel Harland Sanders, the man who started the Kentucky Fried Chicken restaurant franchise, developed his "secret ingredient" recipe for fried chicken in this tiny roadside cafe.

Time to announce winners of WiseWay holiday recipe contest

December 2, 2009

It's time to start planning holiday baking.

And as announced last month, it's also time to reveal the winners for the 2009 Holiday Baking and Caring Contest benefiting The Caring Place for Victims of Domestic Violence.

I've been working with The Caring Place and WiseWay grocery stores to help raise money with this fun recipe contest for all types of holiday goodies.

And after plenty of sorting, debating, cooking and baking, we're ready to announce the winning recipes at this Saturday's party event and cooking demo at 1 p.m. at WiseWay Foods on U.S. 30 in Valparaiso, Ind.

There will be a seating area at Saturday's WiseWay event and guests will sample some of the winning recipes before they are published in The Times the following week.

As for this week's showcased recipe, my congratulations to the winners of this year's Downtown Hammond Council's A Christmas Story Fudge Recipe Contest, held Nov. 21. As for the overall winning honors, top prize went to Kristi Perez of Hammond for her versatile Either/Or Chocolate Walnut or Chocolate Peanut Butter Fudge.

Either/Or Chocolate Walnut or Chocolate Peanut Butter Fudge

● Combine marshmallow cream, sugar, milk and butter in a saucepan and bring to a full boil, stirring constantly until sugar is dissolved.

● Continue cooking over medium heat, stirring constantly while boiling for a full 5 minutes.

● Remove from heat and add in chocolate chips, stirring until smooth and evenly blended before folding in walnuts. (BUT, If making chocolate peanut butter fudge recipe, rather than folding in walnuts, after step of stirring in chocolate chips, allow fudge to set 15 minutes then blend in peanut butter before next step of spreading in pan.) Pour into a glass pan of desired depth to create the thickness of fudge according to preference.)

● Allow to set and firm in refrigerator for at least 2 hours.

● Makes 3 pounds of fudge.

INGREDIENTS:

1 (7-ounce) jar marshmallow cream

1-1/2 cups granulated sugar

2/3 cup evaporated milk

1/4 cup butter

1 (12-ounce) package semi-sweet chocolate chips

1/2 cup chopped walnuts OR 1/2 cup creamy peanut butter

Holiday library party event includes salute to Christmases past

December 9, 2009

If you read my entertainment column in today's newspaper, you can see just a few examples of all the wonderful holiday memories that return to all of us this time of year, in addition to all of the holiday "have-to" lists, from shopping and cleaning to Christmas cards.

This week, I'd like to invite readers to join myself, and my parents, Chester and Peggy, for a wonderful holiday Christmas party event saluting "Christmases from the Past."

This 2009 From the Farm Christmas Party is at noon Dec. 19 at the beautiful Lowell Public Library, in Lowell, Ind. Join the fun for great holiday last minute ideas, recipes to sample as part of a "light lunch" and a selection of delicious refreshments, along with wonderful decorations. And my gift to readers is more than $700 in free drawing prizes.

Seating is limited to 75 guests and reservations must be made in advance by calling the library by 7 p.m. Dec. 17. There is a $3 "at the door" fee to attend for party preparations.

Among the desserts served at the party will be samples from Saturday's announced winning recipes from the WiseWay Baking Contest that benefited The Caring Place.

My congrats to our winners Cathy Kallok, of Griffith, Ind. for her brownie cups (see recipe photo in color photo section page XI), and Valparaiso, Ind. cooks Lydia Kreiger, for her chocolate clusters and LaVonne Silhavy for her yummy wreaths.

LaVonne's wreath recipe made me particualarly nostaglic, since my dear friend Irene Jakubowski, who passed away in the spring of 2008, would always make this same recipe for her holiday cookie platters every Christmas.

Dreamy Creamy
Peanut Butter Brownie Delights

- Heat oven to 350 degrees.

- Prepare brownie batter as directed on package, using either 1 or 2 eggs as directed and required amounts of water and oil.

- Spoon batter into 20 paper-lined muffin tins or cupcake pan.

BROWNIE DELIGHTS INGREDIENTS:

1 (20-ounce) package brownie mix

1 or 2 eggs (as directed)

1/3 cup oil (or as directed)

1 (8-ounce) package cream cheese, softened

1/3 cup sugar

1 egg

1/4 cup creamy peanut butter

1/2 teaspoon vanilla

20 maraschino cherries

CHOCOLATE GLAZE:

1/2 of a (4-ounce) carton of frozen whipped topping

3 squares semi-sweet baking chocolate

- In a small bowl, beat cream cheese with sugar, 1 egg, peanut butter and vanilla with mixer until blended.

- Spoon 1 rounded tablespoon into center of batter in each cup, pressing lightly into batter.

- Bake 30 minutes or until centers are set. Cool.

- Microwave frozen topping with baking chocolate for 2 minutes, stirring at least once to create a blended, shiny glaze. Let stand 15 minutes to thicken slightly.

- Glaze brownie cups with a dollop of chocolate glaze and top with maraschino cherry.

- Makes 20 dessert cups.

Easy Chocolate Clusters

- In a slow cooker, combine candy coating, chocolate chips and German chocolate.

- Cover and cook on high for 1 hour.

- Reduce heat to low; cover and cook 1 hour longer or until melted, stirring every 15 minutes.

- Add peanuts; mix well.

- Drop by teaspoonsful onto waxed paper. Let stand until set, usually about 20 minutes.

- Store at room temperature.

- Makes 3 -1/2 dozen.

CHOCOLATE CLUSTERS INGREDIENTS:

2 pounds white chocolate candy coating, broken into small pieces

2 cups semisweet chocolate chips

1 (4-ounce) package German sweet chocolate

1 (24-ounce) jar dry roasted peanuts

Classic Edible Wreaths

- Spray waxed paper with cooking spray. Set aside.

- Combine margarine or butter with marshmallows and cocoa and microwave for 2 minutes.

- Blend and add coloring, stirring until smooth and combined.

- Immediately add to cornflakes in a large bowl; mix until evenly combined.

- Keeping hands wet or sprayed lightly with cooking spray, drop mounds of the mix on waxed paper; make center hole (if you wish or leave in little leaf clumps) and add 3 candies to resemble berries.

- Allow to dry slightly and set.

- Makes 12 to 20 wreaths, depending on desired size.

EDIBLE WREATHS INGREDIENTS:

2 heaping teaspoons cocoa powder

1 (10-ounce) bag marshmallows

1 to 2 teaspoons green food coloring

4-1/2 cups cornflakes

1 tablespoon margarine or butter

80 red mini candy-coated chocolates or cinnamon red-hot candies

Chocolate cake recipe a reason to celebrate

January 20, 2010

Even though I'm not indulging in many sweet temptations these days while following Seattle Sutton's meal plan as one of the contestants in the 2010 Slim Down Challenge, at least I can still write about some delicious observations.

Over the weekend, I attended an 80th birthday party celebration for Shirley Porch of St. John, Ind. who is the mother of Sue Bero, who has been a correspondent for The Times for 15 years. She is also the wife of one of my former features editors, Bill Bero.

I'm always grateful for the support and friendship of the Beros, as the following story illustrates.

When this farm column was first launched in May 2002, it did not have an instant readership.

Readers might recall that From the Farm was launched as a new feature for the food cover in the space previously occupied by the column "Ask Aunt Maxine," and later "Farm Fare," which was written by Mary Vanderlin Ewen.

I still recall how my food editor at the time, Katie Karnopp, received a call from bookstore publicist Jeanne Leurs, who worked for Barnes & Noble in Hobart, Ind. at the time.

Jeanne was interested in launching a monthly Martha Stewart-affiliated cookbook and craft event at her store called "What's Cooking ... It's a Good Thing." She asked Katie if our Times contributing food writer Jane Dunne, whose column "At Table" also appeared each week on the food cover, would be interested in hosting the event. Since Jane and her husband divided their time between a busy schedule between Chicago and Northwest Indiana, Katie suggested my name as an alternative to serve as host. (It most likely helped that

Sue and Bill Bero visiting our farm in this September 1999 photo paying homage to the classic farmer and wife image portrayed in the painting "American Gothic."

I happened to be sitting right next to Katie at the time.)

The first free bookstore reader event was in September 2002 and the recipe sampling I featured was my mom Peggy's homemade crabapple jelly (that recipe is featured in my first cookbook from 2004) served on toast squares. Six people attended that event, two of which were my parents, along with Bill and Sue Bero and one more kind couple.

It's true that persistence and a little promotion really pays off.

By May 2003, I was celebrating the one year anniversary of "From the Farm" with Jeanne and Barnes & Noble hosting a reader party which attracted more than 250 people jamming the store!

Of course, we served cake at the celebration.

After much urging, I have finally persuaded Sue Bero to share her "from scratch" recipe for a delicious homemade, moist chocolate cake. She served this cake at her mother's party over the weekend and has finely agreed to share it with readers.

The recipe is more than 50 years old and comes from her family's dear neighbor from the days of their old South Holland, Ill. neighborhood. Mrs. June Tinker, who has now passed, was always proud of this homemade chocolate cake recipe, which was always the hit at any party or gathering.

Using the recipe from our dairy farmer neighbor Donna Dolezal for her rich "Chocolate Buttercream Frosting" (which includes a splash of hot black coffee) for icing, this cake is great. That recipe is featured in my second cookbook "More From the Farm" (2007 Pediment Press), along with another great option, "Yummy Choco-Mint Frosting."

Mrs. Tinker's Moist Homemade Chocolate Cake

- In a large mixing bowl, add boiling water to butter and chocolate.

- Whisk to blend and then add sugar and combine.

- Add one egg at a time to cake batter and beat until smooth.

- Add sour cream and remaining dry ingredients.

- Pour cake batter into a greased and floured 9-inch-by-13-inch cake pan or two 9-inch greased and floured layer cake pans.

- Bake at 350 degrees for 40 to 45 minutes or until cake tests done.

- Frost with a favorite frosting and decorate as desired.

- Makes 8 to 14 serving slices, dependent on which cake design is preferred, single or double layer.

INGREDIENTS:

1 cup boiling water
1/4 pound butter
4 squares unsweetened baking chocolate
2 eggs
2 cups sugar
2 cups flour
1 cup or (8-ounce) carton sour cream
2 teaspoons baking soda

Homemakers of yesterday always had chore days

January 27, 2010

Growing up at the farm, I remember walking from our ranch house, across the cornfields to the big white farmhouse where Grandma Potempa lived and how she, along with Auntie Lilly (who also lived there) always had their "set days" for all of the weekly household chores.

For example, Monday was always laundry day and Tuesday would be ironing day, followed by Wednesday, which was washing the floors, dry-mopping the hardwood floors and dusting the furniture. Thursdays, might be yardwork or gardening, depending on the season, and Fridays would be shopping day and cooking and baking for the weekend.

Today, I think it's quite rare for working women to have such a schedule.

Even my mom's work schedule varies quite a bit now that she's later in life.

However Monday is still her laundry day and Friday is still her grocery shopping day.

As for ironing, it still ranks as one of my Mom's least favorite tasks.

She's always saying how grateful she is for "today's more modern fabrics," many of which are permanent press and boast as "wrinkle-free."

Her older sister, my Aunt Ruby, also observed strict weekly housekeeping duties as well.

But even she has relaxed some of her usual routines.

However, my dad's sister, Auntie Wanda, who lives with Uncle Bob in Chicago, still has her rigid schedule each week for her housework.

Monday is laundry day. Tuesday is reserved for all the ironing, including all undershirts and bed linens. Wednesday is all the inside cleaning and dusting, including doing all the floors and vacuuming. Thursday is baking day and cooking for the weekend. And Friday is always the laundry day for all the bed linens and changing all the towels and linens. Saturday is always Aunt Wanda's shopping day, since that would traditionally be the day when Uncle Bob would be home to drive her to Archer Avenue to do her marketing and then to her standing weekly beauty shop appointment.

It's nice to know that there are traditional, standing observed practices adhered to in today's busy, erratic society of constant changes.

And of course, of all of Auntie Wanda's "have-to" task days, it's always best to stop by on baking day.

Today's recipe for her old fashioned nut cups is an easy and tasty baking idea on a cold, winter day.

I've been after this recipe for a while, and since she just baked these recently, I had her jot down her recipe to share with readers.

Aunt Wanda's Pecan Delight Nut Cups

- Combine dough ingredients and mix and work together as though making a pie crust.

- Form into a large ball, wrap in plastic wrap and chill for 1/2 hour.

- Meanwhile, make the filling by combining all filling ingredients together and mixing well.

- Remove the chilled dough and form into 24 tiny round balls, about the size of a half a walnut shell.

- Press each of the balls into the sprayed muffin tins, to from little pie shells.

- Fill the centers of each tiny shell with the nut filling.

- Bake in a 350 degree oven for 1/2 hour.

- Cool nut cups completely and then sprinkle with a light dusting of powdered sugar.

- Makes 24 nut cups.

INGREDIENTS:

(2 mini-muffin tins required)

SHELL CRUST:

1/4 pound butter

1 (3-ounce) package cream cheese, softened

1 cup sifted flour

FILLING:

1 whole egg

3/4 cup brown sugar

1/4 teaspoon salt

1/2 teaspoon vanilla

2 tablespoons butter, softened

1 cup finely chopped pecans, or walnuts, if preferred or a mix

This October 1978 snapshot is exactly how I always think of Aunt Wanda and Uncle Bob, including their many weekend visits from their home in Chicago to the farm.

Grandma Green always ready to serve up something sweet

February 24, 2010

My mom is much like her mom, my Grandma Green.

Like her own mom, who passed away at the end of the summer in 1988 just as I was starting my first year at Valparaiso University, my mom always is quick to serve up something special to guests.

Growing up, I remember Grandma Green would visit us at the farm, about once a week on a weekday, in her green 1969 two-door Oldsmobile Cutlass. That was Grandma Green's last car, which then became my first car and the automobile I first learned to drive in. (I included some great color photos of this car in my second cookbook). She would always have just come from shopping at the one and only little grocery store in our town and like my older brothers and sisters, I was always eager to see what "surprise" she would be bringing.

It really wasn't much of a surprise.

It was always one of two things.

If we were lucky, it would be a large bag of M&M candies.

If we were less lucky, it would be a bag of those overly-sweet iridescent orange Circus Peanuts marshmallow confections.

And on Sundays, it was our turn to ride along with mom for her weekly visit to Grandma Green at her little white house in Rensselaer, Ind., which is about 45 minutes from the farm.

Grandma Green, who grew some of the most beautiful rose bushes I've ever seen, always had a pot of coffee ready and sandwiches and sweets to serve during our visit, which was just in time for supper.

The one part of the visit we didn't like was having to face her mean, fat white toy poodle Frosty.

Long widowed, Grandma Green lived alone and this dog, which was already older by the time I met him face to face, was very protective of her and did NOT like children. It didn't make matters any better that I had once been accused of pinching Frosty's nose. (I was only age 3 or 4 at the time, and I guess that black button nose probably looked like something that should be pinched?)

At least for those Sunday visits, there was always a candy dish of Hershey's Chocolate Kisses to look forward to, along with the other goodies Grandma Green would serve. The other plus was getting to watch Grandma Green's big screen color console TV set for our favorite Sunday night shows, like "The Wonderful World of Disney" and "The Hardy Boys and Nancy Drew."

Since I ran a recipe for Grandma Green's Favorite Peanut Butter Bon Bons in my second cookbook, I decided to run another bon bon recipe I know she would also have loved.

This easy recipe comes from Chris Hovan, of Elkhart, Ind., one of my Valparaiso University students who prepared it in mere minutes for his demonstrative speech in my public speaking class this semester.

Easy Assorted Dessert Bon Bons

- Using a large freezer bag (or a food processor can be used), crush whole cookies, including the white cream center, until they are ground into a fine power.

- Set aside 1 cup of the crushed cookies to use in a later step.

- In a large mixing bowl, combine the crushed cookies with the butter and cream cheese, mixing well.

- On a tray lined with wax paper, roll the cookie mixture into tiny 1-inch diameter balls.

- In a separate microwave-safe bowl, melt the chocolate chips.

- Using a small spoon or tongs, coat the balls in the chocolate and return to the tray.

INGREDIENTS:

1 (16-ounce) package of chocolate sandwich cookies (divided use)

1 (8-ounce) package cream cheese, softened

1 tablespoon softened butter

1 (23-ounce) package of milk chocolate or white chocolate chips

Garnish with white coconut flakes or toasted coconut or cupcake candy sprinkles (optional)

- Before chocolate sets, sprinkle with the remaining crushed chocolate sandwich cookies as a garnish or if desired, the coconut or candy sprinkles to create an attracted selection of bon bons.

- Chill for 20 minutes. Should be stored in airtight container in a cool place or refrigerate.

- Can be served in tiny candy paper cups if desired for an elegant presentation.

- Makes 4 dozen.

This 1981 Green Family holiday photo is one my mother loves. It includes her, along with her twin sister Patty, their older sister Ruby and brothers Arthur (Sonny) and Walter Jr. (Junior) gathered around their mom, my Grandma Green, who is holding her beloved toy poodle Frosty. Grandpa Green (Walter Green Sr.) (shown in inset photo) died November 1938 at the young age of 34.

March arriving with sheepish sweet tooth for bread pudding

March 3, 2010

As the saying goes, when it comes to weather predictions, the month of March either arrives like a lamb and goes out like a lion or vice versa.

I'm not sure how to describe this week's March arrival weather.

But for the sake of hoping this long winter is nearing an end, I'm going to say March arrived like a lamb.

"You know how the weather expression goes," sheep farmer Barbara Kloese reminded me in March 1996 when I interviewed her for a story.

The lion and lamb proverb used for centuries to predict March's weather patterns originated from livestock farmers like the Kloeses, who at the time of my interview, were raising more than 30 sheep on their Union Township farm along U.S. 30 near Valparaiso.

March is traditionally when lambs are born.

"This is a time when we hope for milder weather, since lambs are delicate when they're born," Charles Kloese told me.

"Lambs only have about an inch of wool when they're first born."

Considering the weather outlook for later this month, any newborn lambs may need scarves and winter coats before the end of March.

For this week's recipes, I convinced Amy and Ted Bauer, family farm friends who raise more than 50 heads of sheep at their farm in Monterey, Ind., to share a recipe favorite I've been after for a long time.

The Bauers, who have four children, are good friends with my oldest sister Carol and her husband Bill, whose farm is just a stone's throw away from the Bauer Family.

Bread pudding has always been one of my dessert favorites.

Even on my Seattle Sutton meal plan that's been my weight-loss menu base for the past eight weeks, Seattle Sutton will occasionally include a tiny square of her famous pineapple bread pudding in the dessert compartment of my provided meal.

Amy Bauer's bread pudding recipe is more than 25 years old and it gets more delicious every year.

One of my oldest sister Carol's twin boys, nephew Bobby, has his hands full, trying to work with a wily sheep in this 1991 photo at the Pulaski County Fair.

PUDDING INGREDIENTS:

1/4 cup butter or margarine

1 loaf of cinnamon swirl bread, cubed

7 eggs

1/2 cup granulated sugar

1 teaspoon cornstarch

1/8 teaspoon salt

6 cups milk

1/2 teaspoon vanilla

Amy Bauer's Bread Pudding with Vanilla Sauce

- To make pudding, spread butter or margarine in the bottom of a 9-inch-by-13-inch baking pan.

- Spread the bread cubes along bottom of the pan.

- Using an electric mixer, beat eggs and add in sugar, cornstarch and salt.

- Add in milk and vanilla. Pour milk and egg mixture or bread layer.

- Bake in 350-degree oven for 1 hour.

- Pudding is done when a butter knife inserted in center comes out clean. Cool.

- While pudding is baking, make sauce by combining sugar, 1/2 cup water, and butter or margarine in a saucepan and cooking until boiling.

- In a small bowl, combine 1/4 cup water with cornstarch, mixing until clear and smooth, then add to boiling mixture.

- Remove from heat and add salt and vanilla.

VANILLA SAUCE INGREDIENTS:

1/2 cup granulated sugar

1/2 cup plus 1/4 cup water (divided use)

1/4 cup margarine or butter

1 tablespoon cornstarch

1/4 teaspoon salt

1 teaspoon vanilla

- Mix well and serve 1 to 2 tablespoons of sauce over each square of bread pudding served.

- Makes 16 servings.

Amy and Ted Bauer are shown in this 2009 family photo with their two youngest daughters, Jackie and Karlie.

March going out like an lamb, not like a lion

March 31, 2010

I always say my interest in cooking and preserving family memories comes from the traditions started by my Grandma Potempa.

No one worked harder than she did, coming from Poland to America as a teenager to start a new life, first in Chicago with Grandpa, and then moving to a small farm in Indiana where they raised nine children.

My dad, now 80, is the youngest of the children.

My grandparents raised everything on their farm from pigs and chickens to cows and horses on our family farm.

The only four-legged barnyard faces missing were sheep.

That changed the day Grandma Mary Potempa found a little lamb.

Bo-Bo joined the family farm as a gift from my Uncle Joey and Auntie Judy. They already had moved from the farm to Chicago for work. One day, their friend who worked at the Chicago stockyards told my aunt and uncle about a tiny lamb that had been born right in the middle of the unloading of the flocks from the trains to the stockyards. While the mother was led off with the rest of the sheep to the slaughter, the men took pity on the lamb left behind. Knowing Uncle Joey and Auntie Judy traveled to a family farm in Indiana on weekends to visit Grandma Potempa, the friend asked if they'd be willing to take the lamb to rural safety.

Bo-Bo was a baby lamb, shown here in a June 14, 1955 photo complete with bell and bottle. That's my cousin Ronny, feeding this eager fuzzy friend.

Grandma, who bottle-fed the tiny lamb, from that day on had a constant companion who followed her everywhere, just like the familiar nursery rhyme.

However, Bo-Bo followed around Grandma Potempa a little too much, including getting into her flower beds and vegetable gardens, which didn't make her always very happy.

Something that did make Grandma Potempa happy was baking and she was the best at this daily chore.

She began every day making many loaves of bread to feed her large family.

And on special ocassions, she would make the tiny little fruit filled cookies which are still my favorite today.

"Kolachky" are simple, basic pastries my late Polish grandmother made by the dozens during her days on the farm. They are the size of a small cookie and topped with a fruit filling, traditionally prune, poppyseed or apricot. Strawberry and a farmer's cheese or cream-cheese filling (a simple mix of cream cheese, cornstarch, powdered sugar and vanilla) also are popular.

This particular European recipe worked well on a farm because the ingredients are basic, there's always plenty of fruit preserves in the cellar (which tends to thicken and become still the longer the jam stays in the cellar, making it ideal for baking with) and most of all, they stay fresh for days in the pantry in any season since the dough is incredibly moist and flaky.

I've shared recipes for this fruit-filled Polish cookies in past columns, including a printed recipe version in both my first cookbooks in 2004.

But I've never shared my Grandma Potempa's recipe.

Thankfully, it was preserved by my dad's sisters, my Auntie Judy and my Auntie Wanda.

Grandma Potempa's Kolachky

- In a large bowl, mix all ingredients together.

- Roll into small balls and press flat, forming a dent in the center of each cookie.

- Fill centers with fruit fillings as desired.

- Bake on cookie sheets in 350 degree oven for 13 to 18 minutes, until golden. Do not over-bake.

- Remove and cool COMPLETELY, before dusting with powdered sugar.

- Makes 2 to 3 dozen.

INGREDIENTS:

2 cups all-purpose flour

1/2 cup granulated sugar

1/4 pound sweet butter

1/4 pound unsalted butter (or regular margarine)

2 egg yolks

1 teaspoon vanilla

Favorite fruit jams or fruit pastry fillings

Powdered sugar for Garnish

Small town elementary school teachers left a life-lasting educational impact

April 14, 2010

Next weekend is the annual alumni banquet gathering for our town's high school, which no longer stands, but the wonderful memories remain.

Best of all, it's always a chance to seem some of the teachers from my elementary days.

I've written in previous columns and books about just how important these teacher were to guiding me into my career as a writer.

An education is an amazing thread that sews together many lives and experiences during our classroom journey.

And today's recipe has an even longer lasting connection.

This no-bake cookie recipe is one which many people I'm sure already have.

But what makes it so special for me is because I can remember making it in my kindergarten class when my first teacher, Lois Haring helped us make these sweet treats as a classroom project.

Isn't it amazing how something which seemed so minor and everyday 35 years ago can leave such a lasting impact.

My class of students was particularly special for Mrs. Haring, because she had just graduated from college and we were her first classroom assignment.

Every year, I see Mrs. Haring at our annual school banquet gathering and she still looks the same after 35 years.

She just retired from teaching last year. But her lasting educational impression will continue with the many classrooms of students she guided, such as myself.

Mrs. Haring's
Easy No-Bake Cookies

- Heat sugar, cocoa, milk and butter to a boil and boil for just 1 minute.

- Remove from heat and add peanut butter, vanilla and oats.

- Drop by teaspoonfuls on wax paper and allow to set-up for 1 hour.

- Makes 3 dozen.

INGREDIENTS:

2 cups sugar
1/3 cup cocoa
1/2 cup milk
1 stick butter
1/2 cup peanut butter
1 teaspoon vanilla
3 1/2 cups oats

Polish immigrant inspiration for cabin dining

March 7, 2007

COLORADO -- Columnist Philip Potempa is reporting from Vail this week.

While visiting my friend Jim Rusnak this week in Colorado, one of the highlights I wanted to visit high up in the mountains of Vail came from his recommendation.

Jim, a former sports writer for The Times who moved to Colorado in 2001, told me about Beano's Cabin, a restaurant tucked away in the Beaver Creek Resort that is accessible to guests only by sleigh.

However, today's modern sleighs are not drawn by horse, but rather by Snowcats (a heavy snow tractor with tracts instead of wheels).

There are lots of very tame porcupines, who surround the cabin eatery every night to greet unsuspecting guests!

In addition to late President Gerald Ford (who has the Vail Post Office renamed after him) and Betty Ford, Ross Perot, Bill Clinton (minus Hillary Rodham Clinton), President George Bush and Barbara Bush and Dan and Marilyn Quayle have all enjoyed duck, buffalo, elk, boar, salmon and other wild game specialties.

But when it comes to wild game, I'm most amazed at how many porcupines there are in Colorado. I'd describe them here as being as common as raccoons and opossums back in Indiana. However, when it comes to damage control, itís not the prickly quills people here worry about. Instead, itís the sharp claws the porcupines have and use to pull away the bark from pine trees searching for the destructive pine beetles underneath.

When it comes to deciding which is worse -- porcupines peeling away the pine bark or the beetles eating away underneath -- it seems an even call. The end result is still the same: lots of orange, dried-up pine trees lining ski slopes and landscapes.

As far as Who are some of the famous folks spotted skiing the slopes of Vail this season? Actress Rebecca De Mornay (who dated Tom Cruise after they filmed the 1983

movie "Risky Business" together), Kelsey Grammer, who has a winter home at Beaver Creek Resort, actress Minnie Driver and a messy-haired Richard Dean Anderson of "MacGyver" fame.

What fascinated me most about dining at this little cabin restaurant was its history, named for Frank Bienkowski, a Polish immigrant from Chicago who came to the Vail area in

1919 and built his cabin in an area that eventually would become landlocked by National Parks property.

Frank, just like my own Grandpa Frank Potempa, was a Polish farmer. He grew iceberg lettuce and cabbage. Today, his cabin still stands and has been expanded to accommodate diners who enjoy top-notch cuisine from English chef Steven Topple, who was kind enough to share today's recipe with readers. I realize today's recipe is French and not Polish, but I requested it because I'm a fan of strawberries and I rarely get to run breakfast recipes in this space.

Strawberry Stuffed French Toast

● In a small saucepan, add water with vanilla and white sugar and bring to a boil, before reducing heat to simmer, stirring until a smooth syrup is created. Set aside.

● Heat a nonstick pan.

● While pan is heating, place the bread slices on a sheet tray. Remove hulls from strawberries and slice lengthwise, reserving a few strawberries for the sauce. Place slices on top of each bread slice. Place another slice of bread on top.

● Cut reserved strawberries into quarters and add to the saucepan with syrup; continue to cook over medium heat until sauce turns pink and sticks to back of spoon. Remove from heat to cool slightly and thicken.

● Whip cream with sugar until peaks form; refrigerate to chill slightly.

● Add the butter to heated pan.

● Whisk eggs with milk and carefully dip each of the stuffed French toasts into the egg mixture and place into the heated pan with butter. Turn French toast over on either sides after 2 minutes, until golden brown. Remove from pan and cut diagonally.

● Place French toast on heated plates and top with strawberry sauce and whipped cream, garnishing with sprig of mint.

● Makes 4 servings.

● SOURCE: Chef Steven M. Topple's "So You Want to Impress Cookbook" (Authorhouse Press, 2005, $12) and Beano's Cabin, Beaver Creek Resort, Vail, Colo.

INGREDIENTS:

2 cups water
1 teaspoon vanilla extract
1/2 cup very fine white sugar
8 slices white bread, crust removed
2 pints fresh strawberries, divided use
2 cups heavy whipping cream
1 tablespoon powdered sugar
1 ounce soft butter
6 eggs, cracked and beaten
1 ounce milk
4 sprigs mint

Field strawberries gone, but recipe's still great

June 20, 2007

It's not easy being a farmer these days.

I'm fortunate my family long retired from field days.

But all of our neighbors and friends are farmers and still have weather worries, so we, too, still share the same concerns for the crops, even though we rent out most of our fields.

We received nearly an inch of badly needed rain over the weekend.

And even though once the skies opened up to downpours and it almost once again washed away our town's annual Mint Festival parade, we managed to roll down the street, despite a few puddles.

On the subject of farm frustrations, I've called around and it seems not only are the June berries of strawberry season gone, but even the smaller jam berries that always bless the plants during the final pickings.

However, today's quick-and-easy recipe for Strawberries and Creme Refrigerator Jam only requires a quart of berries, which is easy enough to find in most stores.

This delicious recipe, which has just a hint of vanilla, remains as a "soft-set" jam and is out of this world when spread by spoon on warm toast or slathered across the top of a crusty English muffin.

Strawberries and Creme Refrigerator Jam

INGREDIENTS:

1 quart strawberries (EXACTLY 2 cups mashed strawberries, leaving some chunks and liquid)

4 cups sugar

1 (3-ounce) foil pouch liquid fruit pectin

2 tablespoons lemon juice

1 tablespoon vanilla extract

- Combine the mashed strawberries with the sugar and vanilla and allow to stand for 10 minutes for sugar to dissolve.

- Meanwhile, mix 1 foil pouch fruit pectin liquid with 2 tablespoons lemon juice.

- After the 10 minutes, stir pectin into fruit, stirring constantly until sugar dissolves. (A few sugar bits might remain.)

- Pour jam into six freezer-safe 1-cup glass jars, with rings and flat lids, allowing 1/2-inch space at the top of each jar for expansion in freezer.

- Allow filled jam jars to soft set for 24 hours by chilling in refrigerator.

- Jam should then be refrigerated and used within one month or if placed in a freezer, it will keep for up to one year.

- Makes 6 cups.

Town's nurse will be greatly missed

September 5, 2007

It takes a very special kind of person to be a nurse.

And in our small town, I always thought Doris Boisvert was the perfect example of what a nurse should be like.

Doris, who was 81, passed away on Friday and her funeral is today at our small Catholic church.

She always had a smile and a recommendation whenever anyone voiced a health concern and needed a little direction (and, at times, that "direction" might mean her smile would disappear and she would say "Get to the doctor right away!").

Doris was born in Calumet City, Ill. where she married her husband Leo (who also just passed away a couple years ago) on Sept. 7, 1946.

In fact, Doris would tell me at church that one of the things she enjoyed was when her sister Marjorie of Hammond would clip out this weekly "From the Farm" column feature and mail it to her.

I wrote about Doris and her family for a recipe feature in 1993 and one of the proudest parts of her interview with me was when she said: "I have seven daughters who all work as either nurses or are in the medical field, as well as three daughter-in-laws and two grand-daughters."

As I mentioned earlier, it takes a very special kind of person to be a nurse.

Doris became a nurse in 1947 and for more than 32 years she worked at the large Catholic nursing home in our town, "Little Company of Mary," which is now called "Holy Cross Care Center" and where Doris was cared for recently while on the mend from a fall.

Doris' Syrian Nutmeg Coffee Cake

- Heat oven to 350 degrees.

- Blend sugar, flour and shortening into crumbs.

- Put 1/3 of the crumb mixture into a greased 8-inch-square cake pan.

- Add remaining ingredients EXCEPT nuts to the remaining crumb mixture in mixing bowl.

- Mix well and pour over crumbs in cake pan.

- Sprinkle with nuts and bake for 55 minutes or until tests done.

- Makes 9 servings.

INGREDIENTS:

2 cups brown sugar
2 cups sifted flour
1/2 cup shortening
1 egg
1 teaspoon nutmeg
1 cup sour cream
1 teaspoon baking soda
1/2 cup chopped nuts

Sister's breakfast casserole great for holidays

December 19, 2007

While in Florida over the weekend with my sister Pam and our parents to visit Auntie Lottie and Auntie Loretta at their homes near Sarasota, my sister reminded me of a great recipe.

During the Thanksgiving weekend, while she was at the farm, she whipped up a recipe for an easy and delicious breakfast casserole.

It's so flaky and light (because of a top and bottom crust made of baked crescent rolls), it reminds me of the texture of the yummy recipe for Mrs. Herring's Chicken Pot-Pie once served at Marshall Field's Walnut Room restaurant in Chicago.

With Christmas less than a week away, I agreed this would be an ideal time to share my sister's recipe with readers, many who might be having guests staying over for the holidays.

While I had a nice visit traveling and catching up with my older sister, my dad also had a great time catching up with and seeing his own two older sisters. Auntie Loretta, who is my godmother, is now 80; Auntie Lottie is 84.

And, of course, escaping the blast of cold and snow that came over the weekend while enjoying the 80 degree temps of the Sunshine State was our early Christmas gift.

Despite the harsh weather reports, my dad said he would still rather be home outdoors shoveling snow, a hobby he enjoys. (Meanwhile, this comment annoyed my mother who gave him a few mean looks whenever he reminded us that he was homesick.)

But, by the end of our travels, we all agreed, weather or not: there's still no place like home.

And with Christmas just around the corner, I couldn't resist sharing this traditional recipe for a festive holiday juice-based punch in this week's column, ideal to welcome the arrival of Christmas morning.

Rounding out today's column's recipe selection is another recipe comes from my sister Pam. My sister loves to make these for a "quick energy" snack to take with her when she's riding her bicycle on the weekends.

Merry Christmas from my family to all our readers!

INGREDIENTS:

1 (8 oz package) fresh sliced mushrooms

1-1/3 cup of chopped sweet onion

1/2 cup of diced ham or 1/2 pound bacon

6 eggs

3/4 to 1 cup of shredded cheddar or cheddar and Colby cheese (divided use)

1 (10 ounce) package crescent rolls

2 tablespoons butter or margarine

1/2 teaspoon garlic powder

Salt and pepper to taste

Pam's Breakfast Pot-Pie Casserole

● Preheat oven to 375 degrees. Saute mushrooms, onions and garlic powder in butter or margarine. Add diced ham or one-inch pieces of bacon when onions become opaque. Saute for another 1-2 minutes. Drain and pat dry with a paper towel.

● In a small bowl, beat eggs and pepper together and add to mixture above. Scramble eggs but make sure to leave them slightly wet. Do not overcook the eggs.

● Place one half of the package of crescent rolls in the bottom of an 8-inch square baking dish. You will need to stretch the crescent rolls to cover the whole bottom of the dish or even roll them out on a lightly floured surface.

● Spread some of the egg on the bottom crescent layer, and then a layer of the mushroom-onion-meat mixture on top of eggs and then sprinkle some cheese into the dish. Repeat steps, ending with spreading shredded cheese on top.

● Take the other half package of the crescent rolls and stretch/roll out and place on top of the cheese. You will need to stretch the crescent rolls to cover top completely. Sprinkle top generously with black pepper.

● Bake in 375-degree oven for 15 minutes or until top layer of crescent rolls is lightly brown.

● Note: This warms up nicely the next day in the microwave.

● Serves 9.

Christmas Morning Brunch Punch

● Mix all ingredients in a large punch bowl.

● Add an ice ring made of frozen water or juice to keep chilled while serving.

● Makes 20 servings.

BRUNCH PUNCH INGREDIENTS:

1 large (46 ounce) can orange-grapefruit juice

1 large (46 ounce) can pineapple juice

2 cups cranberry juice

1 liter lemon-lime soda

1 liter ginger ale

Pam's Easy Energy Graham Cracker Treats

● Spray a cookie sheet or jelly roll pan with non-stick cooking spray.

● Break crackers apart at seams and spread evenly to make one layer covering across entire pan.

● In a small saucepan over low flame, melt butter and add sugar, stirring to bring to boil, always stirring while cooking.

● Remove caramel sauce from stove and immediately spoon over cracker layer using back of spoon to cover consistently.

● Top with banana chips and nuts and then bake for 10 minutes at 325 degrees.

● Remove from oven, and let stand for 5 minutes, allowing topping to set.

● Immediately remove from pan, using a fork to assure, even small squares for serving. Store in a sealed container or plastic bag.

● Makes 24 squares.

GRAHAM CRACKER INGREDIENTS:

1 (14.4 ounce) box Graham crackers

1 cup butter

1/2 cup brown sugar

1 1/2 cups dried banana chips, crushed (optional)

1 1/2 cups chopped pecans or nuts of choice

Prison recipe inspires tin cup creativity and a tribute to Dillinger's favorite actor Clark Gable

June 25, 2008

I know spring is gone and summer is officially here when I'm busy helping my parents bottle our dandelion wine at the farm.

This week, we finished bottling the final half-dozen bottles, resulting in two cases (24 bottles) now stored in the cellar.

We use the old recipe from my Uncle Swede and Auntie Lottie, which was featured in this column back in 2002 and appears in my first "From the Farm" cookbook from 2004.

Our recent wine-bottling duties resulted in a funny moment recently while I was teaching one of my college classes at prison.

As many readers know, for the last seven years, I've spent my early Friday mornings as a part-time adjunct professor for Purdue North Central teaching public speaking at the Michigan City State Prison and Westville Correctional Facility.

I've always been fascinated by a special culinary arts program at Westville, run for the past 12 years by Ron Edwards of Valparaiso. Inmates are taught both basics and advanced methods of food preparation and serving techniques in a neat little kitchen and mock restaurant dining room in the education building, preparing inmates for future careers in food service.

Of course, the students have limited access to sharp objects and all fresh fruit, sugar, yeast and juices must be kept under lock and key (otherwise there's a risk that homemade fermented wine could be manufactured, which the inmates call "hooch").

When the students asked why I was late for class one day, I casually mentioned what chore I had been helping my parents to finish, which resulted in a sea of wide eyes and smiles. I quickly changed the subject.

So if readers happen to drive past inmate crews this summer working along the highways with mowing crews, and the men in orange are stuffing yellow dandelions in their pockets, you now know the reason why.

Today, I'm once again showcasing some recipe talent from behind the big wall.

Imagine the surprise and table conversation when you serve this easy muffin recipe and divulge the secret of its origin to your family and guests.

It comes courtesy of Larry Dennis, inmate No. 170216 of Fort Wayne, who turns 30 next month and is serving time for burglary and scheduled to be released in late 2009.

And I'm told filming has finally wrapped up for the shooting of Universal Pictures' film "Public Enemies," starring actor Johnny Depp as gangster John Dillinger.

The movie, which I have a featured role in playing a newspaper reporter interviewing Depp as Dillinger, was shot around Northwest Indiana, as well as in Chicago, Aurora, Ill. and Wisconsin.

Dillinger loved going to the horse track and to the movies, which is why he spent his final fateful evening in the comfort of the air-conditioned Biograph, watching Clark Gable as a mobster and Myrna Loy as his moll opposite good guy William Powell in the 1934 film "Manhattan Melodrama."

Last week, during an appearance on David Letterman's talk show, Depp listed Powell and Humphrey Bogart as his two favorite all-time actors.

Dillinger, who is said to have thought of himself as a modern-day Robin Hood, credited tough-guy Gable as one of his favorite actors.

As a bonus to our prison muffin recipe, here's an original 1935 recipe from Hollywood legend Gable, who died at age 59 in 1960, which Dillinger would also have loved.

If he lived just a few months longer, he would have seen them printed in a special recipe booklet "Let the Stars Show You" featuring the top box office stars of MGM Studios.

As for the release of "Public Enemies," and my first chance acting on the big screen, the movie would hit theaters until next year on July 1, 2009.

Prison Tin Cup Muffins
No. 170216

● Using a paddle or spoon, cream together sugar, shortening and salt or, even better, if you have access to an electric mixer, set to second speed and cream these ingredients together until smooth.

● Add the eggs gradually, while continuing to mix at same speed for 2 minutes.

● Add flour, baking powder and spices, along with about 2/3 of the milk and mix until smooth.

● Fold in apples and raisins to the batter.

● Grease muffin tins and fill each tin about 3/4 full and bake at 400 degrees for 10 to 12 minutes until golden brown or muffins test done with a toothpick.

● Makes 1 dozen.

INGREDIENTS:

1 cup white sugar
1/2 cup shortening
1/2 teaspoon salt
2 eggs
1 heaping cup all-purpose flour
3 teaspoons baking powder
1 teaspoon cinnamon
1/2 teaspoon nutmeg
1/2 cup milk (divided use)
1 cup peeled, diced apples or about 3 medium apples
1/2 cup raisins

Clark Gable's Griddle
Blueberry Breakfast Cakes with Maple Syrup

- Combine Bisquick mix, milk and eggs.

- For a slightly thinner pancake, add 1 1/2 cups of milk instead of one cup.

- Fold in berries.

- Heat a greased griddle or frying pan.

- Pour about 1/4 cup of batter per pancake and cook until edges are firm and then turn and heat until golden.

- Serve with fresh maple syrup.

- Makes 14 griddle cakes.

INGREDIENTS:

2 cups Bisquick mix

1 cup milk

2 eggs, beaten

1 cup of blueberries, rinsed and dried

Curiosity seekers gather outside of the Biograph movie theater in Chicago following the 1934 capture and shooting of Public Enemy No. 1 John Dillinger.

VHS students win top honors with apple strudel

June 3, 2009

As many Porter County readers might have read in Friday's newspaper, Valparaiso High School students in the food and consumer science classes competed Friday in their own version of Food Network's popular "Iron Chef" competition.

Teacher Debbie Shaffer organized the timed contest and asked teams of students in her nutrition and wellness class to create their own recipes, write shopping lists and plan menus that were based on apples as a key ingredient. They had to prepare and serve an appetizer, entree and dessert.

(Shaffer suggested the students select peaches as their key ingredient, but the students wanted to build their recipes and menus around apples.)

I joined Valparaiso High School assistant principal Kathy Spears, formerly a VHS home economics teacher for two decades, and Olga Granat, a VHS instructional technology teacher for 15 years, on the judging panel for the taste-testing and to name the winning team.

The grand prize of extra credit -- and my autographed "More From the Farm" cookbooks -- went to the team that made an apple- and brown sugar-glazed chicken breast , with an apple compote appetizer, and a flaky apple strudel for dessert, the recipe for the latter is included today.

Here I am with Valparaiso High School teacher Debbie Shaffer (left) and the winning students following their fun cooking competition at their school on May 29, 2009.

The winning team of challengers consisted of Ashley Panozzo, 17, Brandon Pylipow, 18, Emily Guzek, 17 and Ron Wilhelm, 17, all of Valparaiso, Ind.

What was equally fascinating about spending the day back in high school was the chance to meet and greet so many teachers. One of Shaffer's department counterparts, Mary Kay Stemple, of Valparaiso, retired Friday after 37 years of teaching home economics. I've been out of high school for two decades and times have certainly changed. It's no longer called home economics. Today, it's called Family and Consumer Science class. And while it used to be the boys took shop/industrial arts classes and the girls only took home ec, now it's an equal opportunity experience.

My congrats to Shaffer and her classroom of winners. Enjoy the summer vacation!

Viking Apple Strudel

- Thaw pastry 20 minutes.

- In a cup, combine egg and water; set aside.

- Preheat oven to 375 degrees. Grease a 15-by-10-inch jellyroll pan.

- On a lightly floured surface, roll out pastry sheet into a 15-by-10-inch rectangle.

- Place on the prepared jellyroll pan.

- In a large bowl, combine sugar, flour, cinnamon and nutmeg.

- Add apples and raisins and toss to coat.

- Spread a strip of the filling down one of the long 15-inch sides of the pastry, allowing a 1-inch margin from the edge of pastry.

FILLED PASTRY INGREDIENTS:

1 sheet frozen puff pastry

1 egg

1 teaspoon water

2 tablespoons sugar

1 tablespoon all-purpose flour

1/3 teaspoon ground cinnamon

Dash of nutmeg

3 cups sliced apples or 2 large cooking apples, peeled, cored and thinly sliced

2 tablespoons raisins

- Brush edges of the pastry with egg and water mixture and roll up up pastry starting from the filling side and rolling dough length wise so filling is contained in the pastry layers.

- Place in the middle of the jellyroll pan seam side down and brush outside of pastry with remaining egg mixture.

- Cut several diagonal slits across the pastry, about 2 inches apart on top.

ICING GLAZE INGREDIENTS:

2 to 3 tablespoons milk

1 cup confectioners sugar

1 tablespoon butter, softened

1/2 teaspoon vanilla extract

- Bake 35 minutes or until golden.

- Cool on pan placed on a wire rack about 30 minutes.

- Combine all ingredients to make icing. Drizzle across warm pastry.

- Makes 6 servings.

Time for Hammond's festival and pie main event

September 16, 2009

During the three years I've judged the Downtown Hammond, Ind. Bizarre Bazaar-Festival's annual Pie Baking Contest, I've given top honors to a pineapple pie, a mincemeat pie and a chocolate-peanut butter "monkey" pie.

This Saturday, a new pie will garner all the praise and awards.

Today I am sharing a great recipe I've been saving since I received it last September from Julie Masterson, the gracious and always smiling wife of our newspaper's publisher Bill Masterson. (To be fair, Bill smiles quite a bit as well, and is equally gracious.)

Julie sent a large basket of these warm, melt-in-your-mouth muffins down to the farm last year as a "thank you" for a brimming basket of vegetables from my parents. She sent a delicious loaf of her famed zucchini bread this year.

Julie's note enclosed with the muffins was equally short and sweet: "I do love these muffins and we get a craving every once in awhile to make them."

Julie's Favorite French Breakfast Puff Muffins

- Cream together shortening, sugar and egg.

- In a separate bowl, combine flour, baking powder, salt and nutmeg.

- Stir the flour mixture into the shortening mixture alternately, with the milk.

- Spoon dough into greased muffin cups so each tin is two-thirds full.

- Bake at 350 degrees for 20-25 minutes.

- Blend sugar and cinnamon in a small bowl.

- Remove warm muffins from muffin tin and roll first into butter, then cinnamon sugar.

- Makes 1 dozen muffins.

INGREDIENTS:

1/3 cup shortening

1/2 cup sugar

1 egg

1 1/2 cups flour

1 1/2 teaspoon baking powder

1/2 teaspoon salt

1/4 teaspoon nutmeg

1/2 cup milk

6 tablespoons butter, melted

1/2 cup sugar

1 teaspoon cinnamon

Christmas memories are still as bright as ever

December 23, 2009

A wonderful early Christmas gift arrived at the front counter of the newspaper office last week.

Reader Bette Saxsma, of Griffith, Ind. met me at a book signing event in Highland, Ind. earlier this year and told me all about her Dutch family's holiday baking tradition of making a flaky rich almond filling pastry roll called "Banket."

All of the ingredients in this sweet treat are basic and the steps are easy to follow.

Bette stopped by The Times office not only to drop off her family's age-old Dutch recipe for me to share with readers this week, but also a generous tray of the pastry, still warm from the oven, to sample and take home to my parents at the farm. She was hopeful that I might print and preserve this great family recipe in my column and future cookbook so it will live on for many future generations to enjoy.

When I think of favorite holiday memories, I always think of a less hectic and more relaxed decade of the late 1970s when sister Pam, who is just four years older, would grab the thick annual holiday department store catalogues (we called them "wish books"). We'd marked page after page of toys we hoped we would find under the tree on Christmas Day.

I know it dates myself (and my siblings as well) by listing what some of our most memorable gifts were from Christmas 1977, but Santa brought me Kermit the Frog and Miss Piggy puppets and a Mr. Magoo board game, while my sister Pam got two "Charlie's Angels" dolls -- Farrah Fawcett-Majors and Kate Jackson. My older brother David (who's eight years older than me) received a new stereo record player and a "Jaws" game.

This latter shark game was one of the most entertaining gifts of our holiday. And imagine this, it didn't even need batteries. Players used plastic hooks to carefully fish "items," such as old tires, oil drums and fish skeletons, out of the rubberband-hinged jaws of the great white without causing the mouth to snap shut!

When I'm asked to share a few favorite family memories from Christmas celebrations of the past, it's always tough to narrow down which stories to share.

Most of all, I always feel so blessed and grateful while looking through old family Christmas albums that I find many of the smiling faces in the photos are still around and smiling during the same family holiday gatherings.

My parents Chester and Peggy and my older brothers David and Tom and my older sisters Pam and Carol were all together with me at our family farm for Christmas 2009.

Although all my grandparents and many of my aunts and uncles and a few cousins and a nephew have passed on, their spirits live on at Christmas and all year round.

One of the things I love the most about remembering our past Christmas moments, and something reflected in all of the photos snapped each year, is our family Christmas tree.

While growing up, it was always an anticipated event to go with my parents to the next tiny town, Toto, Ind., to the Christmas tree farm to select just the right Christmas tree.

And once it was in the water stand and the branches began to unfold, the entire living room filled with a fragrant pine aroma as the sound of the tiny attached pine cones began "cracking" as they opened up in the heated indoors. Once decorated, it was hard to even spot a pine cone since the branches were always so heavily laden with glittery garland and glitzy tinsel icicles, a staple of most Christmas trees of the 1960s and 1970s.

From the time my parents were married in 1953, there has always been a Nativity scene displayed right in front of the Christmas tree. And for as long as I can recall, it's always been the same manger scene set, which in Christmas 2009 is right where it belongs prominently in front of this year's tree in my parents' living room.

One of the primary differences about today's Christmas giving, as opposed to the Christmas gifts I recall from my youth being so treasured all during the 1970s, is a reference to the amount of gifts that appeared under our Christmas trees decades ago.

Today, it seems children - my own nieces and nephews and all of the grandchildren and great-grandchildren of our family as well - receive so many more gifts and toys than ever before.

I selected a few of my own family Christmas photos from our albums to share and as I gave all of the photos a careful look, I noticed that each year, we only received a few toy gifts, which were all items that we would "really want."

Myself, my sister Pam, who is four years older than me, and my brother David, who is eight years older, all look happy in our Christmas setting photos with our few gifts from Santa Claus. My oldest brother and sister, Tom and Carol, seem to always be the ones snapping the photos of us with our gifts, and therefore not featured in these later photos from my youth.

Traditional Banket Dutch Pastry

- Mix all of the dough ingredients together, using a mixer, to make the dough and store in refrigerator overnight.

- The next day, divide the dough into 8 parts.

- Flour a surface and roll each part into 12-inch by 10-inch rectangles.

- Try not to handle dough too much, because the warmth of hands will make the outcome less flaky.

- Spread the filling on the bottom part of the rectangle.

- Roll up each pastry lengthwise to make a roll and place on a greased jellyroll pan.

- Brush tops of each completed roll with egg whites and sprinkle with sugar.

- Bake at 400 degrees for 30 minutes. Up to 4 of these rolls can be baked on one jellyroll pan at a time.

- Unbaked rolls can be frozen and baked later.

- Makes 8 pastries.

INGREDIENTS:

DOUGH:

1/2 pound butter
1/2 pound margarine
4 cups flour
Pinch of salt
1 cup water

FILLING:

1 pound grated almond paste
1-1/2 cups granulated sugar
3 slightly beaten eggs
1 teaspoon lemon juice

'Alice in Wonderland' my theme for this year's Lake County Library Literary Tea

April 7, 2010

Easter Sunday is a time of year when many people traditionally think of elegant and impressive new hats showcased at Sunday church services.

I'm hoping I'll see lots of hats this month when I help host an afternoon tea fund-raiser for the Lake County Public Library's annual literary event.

The last time I was asked to speak at this event was in April 2006 and all 150 seats sold out very quickly.

That year, I spoke about legendary newspaper columnist Hedda Hopper, who made hats her own legendary trademark. I shared part of a collection from Hopper's own estate, including a display of her hats, clothes, jewelry, correspondence (some representing her catty side) and rare photographs.

I even brought of Hedda's personally owned multi-flowered wide-brimmed hats to display.

For this year, my theme is "Alice in Wonderland."

Afterall, it's not just a favorite storybook by Lewis Carroll.

Now, it's also hit new 3-D movie by Walt Disney Pictures directed by Tim Burton and starring Johnny Depp as the Mad Hatter.

I'm "filled to the brim" having fun on the Mad Hatter's Tea Cup ride at Walt Disney World Paris in this August 2000 photo.

I still feel lucky that I got to do a scene with Depp in his last big motion picture "Public Enemies" for Universal Pictures, which had him starring as gangster John Dillinger and I played a newspaper reporter interviewing him for my scene.

And as it so happens, I was wearing a very special hat in my scene. It was a rare fedora that had once belonged to gossip columnist great Walter Winchell.

As you might guess, it's a perfect afternoon gathering for all of the Red Hat Societies represented in our readership area.

My parents will be joining me for the afternoon and our tea table will feature a special "Alice in Wonderland" tea pot and matching tea cups and saucers.

In fact, I'm donating a special "Alice in Wonderland" tea pot and matching tea cup and saucer set I brought back with me earlier this month from my visit to Walt Disney World in Florida, as a give-away.

I hope to see you at this "mad" tea party for a good cause!

As for today's tea-perfect recipe, it's for a favorite tea cranberry scone recipe from Hannah Mattison, from Rock Island, Ill., one of my Valparaiso University students.

She recently made this recipe for her demonstration speech for the public speaking class I teach. She said she first sampled it at The Old Ivy Bake Shoppe in Fort Madison, Iowa.

Hannah's Favorite Cranberry Tea Scones

● In a large bowl, combine flour, baking powder, lemon peel, salt and sugar.

● Add the chilled butter and using a knife or pastry blender, cut into flour mixture to make a "course meal texture." (This is an important step, because those tiny chilled butter pieces in the dough melt during the baking process to create steam and a final flaky texture when baked.)

● In another bowl, combine pecans and cranberries. Fold into dough.

● Add in cream, egg and lemon juice.

● Turn dough onto a floured surface and combine just slightly with hand but do not overwork. Form into a ball.

● Split dough in half and make two 6-inch flat discs of dough. Cut dough into small triangle wedges, about 16 to 20 smaller scones or 12 large ones, if desired.

● Place scones on greased cookie sheets. Since dough will expand, do not over-crowd when baking.

● Bake in 400 degree oven for 12 to 14 minutes, or until golden. Do NOT over-bake.

● While scones are baking, combine glaze ingredients and heat slightly to dissolve sugar.

● Remove scones from oven and apply glaze to hot scones to set up.

● A few sprinkles of fancy large granual sugars can also be add to the tops of the just-glazed scones at this time, if desired.

● Makes 12 to 20 scones.

INGREDIENTS:

DOUGH:

3 cups flour

1 1/2 tablespoons baking powder

1 tablespoon dried lemon peel

1 teaspoon salt

1 cup granulated sugar

1 1/2 sticks COLD unsalted butter, cut in pieces

1/2 cups chopped pecans (optional)

1 cup dried cranberries

3/4 cup light cream

1 egg

1 tablespoon lemon juice

GLAZE:

2 tablespoons granulated sugar

1 teaspoon lemon juice

Thoughts and prayers helping father with recovery

April 11, 2007

Thank you for the e-mails, cards and voicemails I received from readers last week regarding my father's open-heart surgery on Monday.

After six hours in the operating room at University of Chicago Hospital attended by its heart-care specialists, especially his surgeon Dr. Valluvan Jeevanandam, my father came through the bypass surgery, and his surgery team was even able to repair his leaking heart valve rather than having to replace it. He now remains in the IC unit and has the constant care of a private nurse at his side.

We are hopeful and confident he will continue to improve each day and be moved to a room later this week.

Meanwhile, my mom and my siblings have been at the hospital every day.

When selecting a recipe for today, I decided to share the one for roast lamb I prepared for Easter dinner for my dad, since his strict dietary restrictions from prior surgery prevented his having all the things he would normally have for the holiday, like ham, sausage, sauerkraut, boiled eggs and other foods heavy in fat and salt.

Though my father loves lamb, I have to admit it's not a dish we traditionally prepare. My dad's eldest brother, my Uncle Joe, who died in 1995, hated lamb, even though my Aunt Rose loved it. Uncle Joe always talked about how when he was in the Army, he was always served "tough Mutton."

Today's recipe is a slight variation of one from the mother of Jeff Precourt (a friend at The Times who works in the advertising department). When I prepared it, I made a few minor changes for my own family's tastes and it came out to perfection.

Mrs. Precourt's Mediterranean Roast Lamb

- Heat oven to 325 degrees.

- In a large covered baking dish, splash a little olive oil on the bottom and rub the rest over entire roast.

- Sprinkle all the seasonings over roast, topping with fresh rosemary. Do NOT add any water.

- Arrange vegetables around roast. Insert a meat thermometer in thickest part of roast. Cover and slow roast for 2-1/2 hours. Remove cover for final 45 minutes.

- Once roast has reached an internal temperature of 175 degrees, remove from oven.

- Makes 6 to 8 servings.

INGREDIENTS:

1 (4-pound) boneless lamb roast

4 tablespoons olive oil

2 tablespoons minced, fresh garlic

1 large bunch fresh rosemary

Generous sprinkling original blend Mrs. Dash

7 to 8 fingerling potatoes, sliced

3 chopped carrots, sliced

1 medium onion, chopped

You're invited to fifth anniversary farm party

April 25, 2007

This Friday marks the fifth anniversary of this weekly "From the Farm" column feature.

I can't believe it's already been five years of sharing my family, our favorite recipes and a bounty of stories about rural life and interesting people.

As announced last month, we're celebrating this fifth anniversary of "From the Farm" with a second cookbook -"More Recipes From the Farm: Family Recipes and Memories of a Lifetime" (Pediment Press, 2007, $29.95).

This follow-up to my original "From the Farm" cookbook in 2004 is just one reason why I'm smiling and counting my many blessings.

I hope you will join me fro 1 to 3 p.m. Saturday, May 12, which is Mother's Day weekend, as my guest at a farm party along with all my family and friends.

I guarantee it will be unlike anything you've ever seen or experienced before.

And if you attended the May 2004 farm party that unveiled my first cookbook, you already know about the fun and surprises in store.

Fresh-cut flowers, fresh lemonade, sheet cake, bales of straw and scores of decorations for the afternoon will set the scene.

I'm lucky the nice people at Borders in Merrillville in Westfield Southlake Mall are letting me transform their store into a facsimile of our farm, rather than running the other way when they see me back up with a farm truck filled with everything but the farm's kitchen sink!

In addition to officially unveiling this second cookbook, we'll also give away more than $3,000 in prizes for the afternoon's free drawing.

Debbie Wappel is shown visiting family farm friend Ruth Hankey at her home in Elkhart, Ind. in this March 2002 photo. She turned 91 in 2010.

Best of all, this party promises a relaxing afternoon together and a chance for you, the reader, to meet the friends and family names you read about in this column every week.

And, of course, they'll all be happy to sign the pages inside the new book that feature their recipes and photos.

You'll be happy you decided to join the fun.

As for today's recipe, it's delicious and once again from the file of our farm-wife friend down the road, Debbie Wappel.

She brought my parents a warm casserole dish filled with these hearty chicken-and-potato dumplings, and we enjoyed them for two much-appreciated suppertime meals.

Quick and Delicious Chicken-and-Potato Dumplings

● To make dumplings, in a small bowl, combine all ingredients. For a lighter and fluffier dumpling, refrigerate dumpling dough overnight. For a more dense dumpling, mix dough and drop into chicken-and-sauce mixture immediately, once sauce has come to a simmer.

● Boil 1 pound of chicken breasts in 6 cups water, until tender, reserving broth.

● SautÈ onion and garlic in oil for 3 to 4 minutes or until onion is tender.

● Place sautÈed mixture and reserved boiling broth in a large 8-quart pot, along with deboned and chopped chicken meat, celery, carrots and sage. Bring mixture to a boil, reduce heat and cover and simmer for 10 to 15 minutes or until vegetables are tender.

● Once sauce and chicken mixture begins to simmer, drop heaping teaspoons of the dumpling dough into the pot to cook with the liquid and chicken. When all the dumplings are in the pot, cover and simmer for 20 minutes or until a toothpick inserted into the dumplings comes out clean. Do not lift cover while dumplings are cooking. Since dumplings are being served with the chicken, the sauce will and should be left thinner, rather than thick.

● Makes 6 servings.

INGREDIENTS:

DUMPLINGS:

1 (8-ounce) box buttermilk biscuit mix

1 cup cold mashed potatoes, with a little milk added for smoothness

1/4 cup milk

1 tablespoon dried or fresh chopped parsley

1/4 teaspoon black pepper

CHICKEN AND SAUCE:

1/4 cup onion

2 garlic cloves, minced

1 tablespoon vegetable oil

6 cups chicken broth (reserved from boiling chicken)

2 cups cubed chicken breast meat

2 celery ribs, chopped

2 medium carrots, chopped

1/4 teaspoon dried sage leaves

1 tablespoon chicken bouillon

Indy weekend filled with memories old and new

May 30, 2007

My holiday weekend in Indianapolis for the Indy 500 Race gave me a chance to catch up with friends.

On my way home on Monday, I stopped in Monticello to visit good family friend Irene Jakubowski and have dinner with her at the always-good Skyroom Restaurant overlooking the boardwalk at Indiana Beach amusement park.

Not only was the menu great, but so were the memories shared by Irene, who will turn 85 in August 2007.

She's often talked to me about her parents taking her and her brother and sister to the 1933 World's Fair in Chicago when she was just 10.

Even though her father was a shoe cobbler, she and her siblings still were made to wear shoes that were slightly bigger than their feet (stuffed with newspaper in toes) so they could grow into the "clodhoppers."

Irene's two most vivid memories of the fair are very different.

One is seeing a Morton Salt sponsored exhibit in one of the pavilions that featured a real-life little girl with a large umbrella walking under real showers of salt, just like on the brand's packaging.

The other memory is of her eyes being covered when they walked past the billowing banners in front of the showcase entertainment stage advertising exotic fan dancer Sally Rand, who would later be infamously

Irene Jakubowski's smiling face is an image in my mind that will last forever. Here she is with my parents in September 1996, after having just moved into her new home in Monticello, Ind.

arrested for lewd charges for a Lady Godiva publicity stunt at the fair.

Since Irene makes a great traditional lasagna recipe, I brought her a copy of my Indy friend Amy Scamerhorn's meatless and more calorie-conscious alternative. I know readers will enjoy it as well.

Amy's Quick and Skinny Lasagna

- Heat oven to 350 degrees and spray a 13-inch-by-9-inch pan with nonstick cooking spray.

- Mix ricotta, cottage cheese, parsley and garlic, set aside.

- Pour 1 cup sauce in bottom of pan and then arrange 1/3 of the noodles in the pan so they touch, but don't overlap.

- Spread half of the combined cheese mixture over noodles and top with 1/2 of the mozzarella, olives and mushrooms.

- Top this layer with 1 cup of sauce and another 1/3 of the noodles and the remainder of the cheese mixture and mozzarella.

- Add another cup of the sauce, another layer of noodles and then the remainder of the sauce.

- Top with Parmesan cheese and bake tightly covered with

INGREDIENTS:

2 cups lowfat ricotta cheese

1 cup lowfat cottage cheese

2 tablespoons dried parsley

1 teaspoon chopped garlic

4 cups favorite spaghetti sauce, divided use

12 to 15 uncooked lasagna noodles

4 ounces shredded part-skim mozzarella, divided use

1 (14-ounce) can black olives, drained, divided use (optional)

1 (8-ounce) can mushrooms, drained, divided use (optional)

1/4 cup grated Parmesan cheese

foil for 60 minutes.

- Note: This lasagna can be prepared in advance, refrigerated and then just add 15 more minutes to baking time.

- Makes 12 to 14 servings.

Amy Scamerhorn has followed in her mom and aunt's footsteps, loving to cook and bake. Here she is helping prepare the Thanksgiving table at her family's farm home in November 2009.

Tune in TVs at 9 tonight for Phil grilling fun

June 6, 2007

The grilling season is in full swing, so all this month I'm helping our local PBS station in Merrillville, Lakeshore Television Channel 56, with some fun barbecue segments on the 9 p.m. Lakeshore News Tonight newscasts on Wednesday and Fridays.

So tonight, you'll definitely want to tune in to Channel 56 for some fun and surprises.

I'll admit I'm not as much of an avid grill guy as many other people. At the farm, the only time we pull out the grill is in the summer for our four basic holiday family barbecues: Memorial Day, Father's Day, Fourth of July and Labor Day.

So, I've invited some local notable friends of mine to help me with some of the segments.

Tonight, it's Mary Beth Schultz of Valparaiso in the spotlight. It's her zipped-up whole grilled chicken recipe you see below that we'll be whipping up on air.

Of course, Mary Beth is most famous for her quiche recipe that netted her a trip to the 2006 Pillsbury National Bake-Off in Orlando, Fla..

My parents and I will be dining on today's beer can chicken recipe tonight at Mary Beth's house as she hosts a dinner party in honor of the segment's launch tonight.

Also on this evening's menu, besides the highlighted chicken, a coconut shrimp appetizer, a baked potato bar featuring crumbled bacon, chives, sour cream, shredded cheddar, fresh cucumber salad, my mom's fresh canned sweet garden from last year's garden bounty and for dessert, homemade strawberry shortcake with whipped cream.

My Friday TV segment is with TV talk show host turned local politician Michael Essany, along with his fiance Christa, grilling up their favorite recipe: "Essany's Italian Grilled Garlic Chicken."

Mary Beth Schultz joined me on one of my summer 2007 "Grill with Phil" cooking segments, whipping up one of the most juicy and delicious roast chicken recipes for a grill that I've tasted.

(Photo by Michael Berkos)

Mary Beth's Beer Can Beneath Chicken

- Empty out 1/2 of the can of beverage of your choice (otherwise, the liquid will bubble over and make a mess on your grill).

- Insert crumbled bay leaves into the half can of beverage.

- A wire rack can be purchased at most department stores or even some bookstores by the cookbook section,but it's not necessary. Position chicken over the half can of beverage with the large body cavity inserted first over the can, so the chicken looks like it's standing on its legs.

- *Whether using a pre-purchased rack for ease or no rack, set the entire chicken on the can (and slip the can/chicken in the wire rack if using one) and place standing up inside an aluminum pie pan to catch the liquid drippings so it doesn't drip onto grill rack and into flames below.

- Before placing prepared chicken onto grill, plug up the neck cavity opening with a small onion or potato or even a piece of apple.

- Spray exterior of the chicken with spray olive oil or cooking spray.

INGREDIENTS:

1 whole (3-4 pound) chicken

1 can of favorite beer or soft drink (even diet drinks are fine)

2 bay leaves, crumbled

Spray olive oil or cooking spray

1 small onion, or small potato or small apple piece

1 teaspoon Italian seasonings

1 teaspoon garlic salt

1 teaspoon Greek seasonings

1/2 cup honey mustard

- Use your favorite rub (Mary Beth likes 1 teaspoon of Italian Seasoning, 1 teaspoon of garlic salt and a teaspoon of Greek Seasoning) and coat thes prayed chicken with these seasonings.

- Place on the grill over medium heat to cook with grill lid closed as much as possible for an hour and a half.

- During the last 1/2 hour, baste entire chicken with honey mustard.

- The secret to the can cooking method has less to do with the type of beverage in the can and more to do with the steaming effect from the inside out, while the outside gets nice and crisp.

- NOTE: If desired, the chicken can be prepared as directed above and baked in a conventional oven at 365 degrees for an hour and half with close to the same results.

- Makes 4 servings.

Essany's Italian Grilled Garlic Chicken

- Rinse chicken breasts and pat dry with paper towel.

- In a medium bowl, combine all coating ingredients and whisk mixture until smooth.

INGREDIENTS:

4 boneless, skinless chicken breasts

1 teaspoon ground red pepper

1 spoon garlic powder

1/2 cup whipped light salad dressing (such as Miracle Whip)

1/2 light Italian dressing

- Coat both sides of each chicken breast and grill each side for 10 minutes or until inside tests done. Caution, do not over-grill so chicken breasts will retain juiciness.

- Serve chicken breasts with green toasted salad and fresh ears of sweet corn for a complete meal.

- Makes 4 servings.

Grill for Father's Day and visit Mint Festival

June 13, 2007

This weekend is our town's 30th annual Mint Festival and I've been asked to redeem my "rain check" from last year's Sunday parade day wash-out.

Yep, last year, I served as celebrity grand marshal for the 29th annual Mint Festival, but I only had the chance to fulfill one day of my honor.

When parade time came, a downpour and a badly needed inch of rain forced the entire parade to be canceled.

North Judson is also on Central Standard Time and the Sunday parade will be at 4 p.m. right down Main Street (where the town officials have already done our annual tradition of painting a green stripe right down the center of the parade route).

Some other highlights include a booksigning of my second cookbook "More From the Farm: Family Recipes and Memories of a Lifetime" (Pediment Press, 2007, $29.95) from 10 a.m. to 1 p.m. Saturday at the town's Civic Center and the annual "Cooking with Mint Contest" at 11 a.m. at the Girl Scout Cabin.

And, of course, my favorite is the annual mint farm tours, where guests get an inside look at the entire process of harvesting mint oil. The tours are at 11 a.m. and 3 p.m. Saturday and 1:30 p.m. Sunday. Another highlight for visitors (besides buying vials of real, raw peppermint oil) are the free rides on our town's antique restored train which takes travelers on a scenic roundtrip to our neighboring towns like LaCrosse and Englis Lake, Ind.

You can watch me tonight at 9 on Lakeshore News Tonight on Merrillville PBS station Channel 56 as I grill ribs and share a favorite barbecue sauce recipe from my new book.

And on Friday, Ron Edwards of Valparaiso, Ind. director of the culinary arts prison program at Westville Correction Center, will be with me for my 9 p.m. TV segment to demonstrate his recipe for "Prison Stripe Seared Hamburgers."

In the meantime, give my friend Amy Scamerhorn's recipe for easy beef marinade for kabobs a try. You won't be disappointed.

And if you're in my town this weekend, remember to visit me at the book signing to say hello or shout my name as I walk the parade route.

Amy's Mouth-watering Beef Marinade

- In the bowl of a food processor or a blender, combine all ingredients, slowly drizzling olive oil.

- Pour the marinade over the cubed beef and toss to coat.

- Place beef in marinade and refrigerate in an airtight container or a sealable plastic bag at least two hours.

- Place marinaded beef (adding additional veggies) on wooden skewers and cook to desired doneness on hot grill.

- Makes 4 servings.

INGREDIENTS:

1-1/2 pounds sirloin steak, cut into cubes

2 teaspoons garlic powder

2 teaspoons paprika

2 teaspoons ground cumin

1 teaspoon salt

1/2 teaspoon black pepper

1/3 cup red-wine vinegar

1/2 cup olive oil

After joining my parents to lead the Sunday afternoon parade as celebrity grand marshall at our small town's 30th Annual Mint Festival on June 17, 2007, we took a break to pose for some photos in downtown North Judson, Ind. to capture the occasion. (Photo by Michael Berkos)

Join me at Porter County Fair pie contest and try Phyllis Diller's great recipe

July 18, 2007

Next Wednesday, July 25, 2007 is the annual Pie Baking Contest at the Porter County Fair in Valparaiso and once again I'll be one of the panel judges.

The check-in for pies is 11 a.m. and, this year, the judging is at noon in the air-conditioned Expo East building.

Once again, my parents will be in the audience watching the judging and I hope plenty of readers make it out to watch or participate in this year's event. You won't be disappointed. Lots of fun and surprises are in store.

Here are some hints and details for this year's competition:

● The categories: apple, blueberry, cherry, peach and miscellaneous fruit.

● For baked product competition: filling, frosting, glazing, pie filling and meringue whether uncooked or cooked are NOT permitted to contain cream cheese, whipped cream, unpasteurized milk or

My funny friend Phyllis Diller is shown clowning around with Dick Clark in this 1985 signed publicity photo for the CBS perennial favorite show special "Circus of the Stars." Clark performed ringmaster duties of this particular installment.

eggs/egg whites (pasteurized eggs or eggs cooked to 160 degrees may be used). Home-canned fruits, vegetables or meats are not permitted in products.

- The pie recipe must accompany each baked pie entered and include ingredient measurements and preparation instructions. The recipe will become property of the Pie Committee. Include your name on the back of the card ONLY.

- Only one entry per category per person.

- No items requiring refrigeration may be entered.

- Contestants should carefully wash their hands and make sure their hands do not have any open cuts before preparing foods.

- Whenever possible, baked products should be transported and stored in chilled coolers at 41 degrees.

- Judges' decisions are final.

- Contestants should pick up pie immediately after contest.

- Miscellaneous fruit category defined as fruit other than cherry, blueberry, peach, apples or combination of fruit such as strawberry/rhubarb, etc.

- Prizes will be awarded.

As for this week's featured recipe, I spent last weekend at a booksigning and judging the Midwest rib cook-off in Lima, Ohio, the hometown of Phyllis Diller, who turned 90 yesterday.

This recipe is from good friend Phyllis' kitchen file and it's a delicious favorite. Despite all of her famed jokes and comedy routines, Phyllis is a wonderful cook!

INGREDIENTS:

Cooking spray
2 large eggplants
Pinch salt
1/2 cup margarine
1 cup onion, minced
1 green pepper, diced
2 teaspoons parsley, minced
1-3/4 cup grated Parmesan cheese, divided use
1 (16-ounce) can stewed tomatoes
1/2 teaspoon salt
1/2 teaspoon black pepper
1/3 cup bread or cracker crumbs
1/3 teaspoon paprika

Phyllis Diller's Parmesan and Eggplant Casserole

- Peel eggplants, dice and mix with salt in a bowl to allow to "sweat" for 15 minutes.

- Melt margarine in a frying pan and cook eggplant, onion, and green pepper for 15 minutes.

- Add parsley and 1/2 cup of the cheese, along with tomatoes to other veggies and allow to simmer 5 more minutes.

- Sprinkle with salt and pepper and pour cooked veggies in a sprayed round glass casserole.

- In a separate bowl, combine crumbs, paprika and remaining cheese and sprinkle over the casserole.

- Bake 25 to 30 minutes.

- Makes 6 servings.

Plenty of great pie opportunities

August 15, 2007

Thank you to all the readers who attended both seatings for my Monday birthday tea event at Annie's Tea Room and Ice Cream Parlor in Crete.

Both seatings were filled to capacity and there were more than 100 people in attendance making it a very special day.

For those readers who were on the seating waiting list and unable to attend, there are more great events in the months to come.

Amateur pie bakers are wanted for the second annual "Pie Baking Contest" which is one of the activities at the Bizarre Bazaar event from 11 a.m. to 6 p.m. Sept. 15, 2007 in downtown Hammond.

On the subject of pie, we've had plenty of quick-growing zucchini to share from our farm garden, compliments of the humid weather.

My mom and dad raved about their friends Ann and Richard Boilini's delicious zucchini casserole that is whipped up in a simple glass pie plate.

I made one over the weekend, and was immediately convinced Ann should share it with Times readers.

Mrs. Ann Bolini's Zucchini Parmesan Cheese Pie

- Heat oven to 350 degrees. Mix together all ingredients, EXCEPT mozzarella cheese, and pour into a 9-inch deep-dish glass pie pan coated with cooking spray.

- Bake uncovered for 30 minutes.

- Remove from oven and cover with the shredded mozzarella cheese. Sprinkle generously with black pepper and return to oven and bake for another 10 to 15 minutes or until cheese is melted and casserole is golden brown.

- Makes 10 servings.

INGREDIENTS:

1 cup biscuit mix
3 cups sliced zucchini
1/2 cup chopped onion
1/2 heaping cup Parmesan cheese
1 teaspoon oregano
Dash black pepper
Dash salt
1 teaspoon original Mrs. Dash
1 teaspoon garlic powder
1/2 cup olive oil
4 eggs, beaten
1-1/2 cups shredded mozzarella cheese

Mark calendars for Crown Point tea

October 3, 2007

Now that it's October, you know the holidays are just around the corner.

It's time to mark calendars for a special holiday tea event I'm hosting with Tiffany's Tea Room in Crown Point, Ind.

The light tea luncheon holiday party will be from 1 to 3 p.m. Sunday, Nov. 11, inside old Crown Point Courthouse, an ideal time before the holiday rush.

Tickets are $25 and, once again, seating is limited.

Doors will open as early at 11 a.m. to allow for inside shopping opportunities.

This tea is "special" for a few reasons.

First of all, it will feature "an old English holiday" theme.

Second of all, if you've never been inside the old Crown Point Courthouse, specifically, the converted huge main floor ballroom, complete with hardwood floors, chandeliers and floor-to-ceiling windows, you're in for a treat.

And thirdly, for each ticketholder who attends, you will be entered in a drawing for a special brass tea tray autographed by Paul Burrell, the man who served as Queen Elizabeth's butler for a decade before he went on to become Princess Diana's personal butler. (I donated a similar-style tea tray Sunday for the Breast Cancer Society's annual charity tea event.)

I'll be giving a talk about some of the inside tidbits Mr. Burrell shared with me in a recent interview about how Royal Family members enjoy their personal tea time. I'll also bring more than $1,000 in free drawing prize giveaways.

As for today's recipe, I've been after my mom for some time to share her recipe for stuffed green peppers. I have a few left in my garden and I've been eager to bake a batch.

Peggy's Stuffed Green Peppers

- Preheat oven to 350 degrees.

- Par boil green peppers for 10-15 minutes, until peppers are flexible, but not soft. Drain.

- While peppers are cooling slightly, mix up all filling ingredients and stuff peppers.

- Place peppers in a Dutch oven (an oven-safe pot or casserole with a lid) and cover with tomato sauce and 2 cups water, lastly, sprinkling with Parmesan cheese.

- Bake covered for 2 hours.

- Makes 8 servings

INGREDIENTS:

8 green peppers

FILLING:

2 pounds ground round chuck

1 cup dried rice (yields 2 cups cooked)

1/2 cup diced onion

Salt and pepper to taste

1/2 teaspoon garlic powder

2 teaspoons dried onion soup mix

1/2 cup catsup

SAUCE:

2 (8 ounce) cans tomato sauce

1/4 cup Parmesan cheese

Rooster was part of family farm

November 14, 2007

First and foremost, thank you to all of the readers and kind guests who attended Sunday's tea event at the Crown Point Courthouse.

What a great way to begin the holiday season.

On the subject of holidays, our farm family will be minus one favorite farm pet this Thanksgiving.

Nope, it's not a turkey.

Oscar the Rooster, who had been with us since 2003, passed away and has gone to that big chicken coop in the sky.

My dad named him, and he began ruling the roost from the get-go after we were given him as a gift from my columnist colleague Molly Woulfe.

He was hatched from one of the eggs raised by school students as a classroom project, and Molly's two sons suggested our farm would make an ideal home for him after the school year had ended.

This is a lasting memory photo taken under the pear tree at our farm in March 2007, when Oscar was still "ruling the roost."

All of our farm neighbors always commented to my parents about how they loved to hear Oscar crowing faithfully, and not just in the morning, but also in the afternoons when he was restless.

And I felt the same way every morning.

Many readers met him when I brought him to the launch party of my first "From the Farm" cookbook in May 2004 at the Barnes and Noble in Merrillville, Ind. He's also featured in some great color photographs in my second "More From the Farm" cookbook.

He also did a great job keeping the farm dogs Lucky and Laddie at bay when they tried to aggravate him to get a rise out of him.

The one thing Oscar didn't like was the concrete lawn ornament rooster in our farm yard.

No matter how many times he happened to encounter it when he'd stray into the garden area, he always fluffed up in defense, growled and charged at it over and over.

In Oscar's honor, the following recipe is just as spicy and flavorful as Oscar's personality.

Marjorie Heckel of Crown Point, Ind. was kind enough to type up a little note with the recipe that follows and mail it to Bill Nangle, our long-time executive editor.

Dated Nov. 4, 2007 she wrote: "Dear Mr. Nangle, My family raves about my skinless barbecue chicken. I thought it would be nice to pass the recipe on to others. I am a semi-retired pianist who worked professionally for years but my second interest has always been cooking good food with less sugar, less white flour and less of the wrong kind of fat."

INGREDIENTS:

1 frying chicken, cut into pieces

1 tablespoon cornstarch

6 tablespoons catsup

6 tablespoons cider vinegar

2 tablespoons lemon juice

4 tablespoons Worcestershire sauce

8 tablespoons water

6 (level) tablespoons dark brown sugar

2 teaspoons paprika

2 teaspoons chili powder

Marjorie's Skinless Oven Barbecued Chicken

- Cut-up and prepare chicken, removing skin. Rinse and pat dry.

- In a small bowl, mix 1 tablespoon cornstarch with 2 tablespoons cold water.

- Add cornstarch thickening to all remaining sauce ingredients.

- Use a roasting pan, lined with foil along bottom and sides of pan. Place the chicken in the pan.

- Heat the combined sauce just slightly and pour over the chicken.

- Cover chicken with foil and bake in a hot oven set to 500 degrees for 15 minutes, then reduce heat to 350 degrees and bake 1 hour and 15 minutes.

- Makes 4 servings.

Ed Sullivan would love this recipe

January 9, 2008

Since I had leftover sauerkraut from New Year's Day (our family eats sauerkraut and cabbage on New Year's each year for good luck), I needed a trusty recipe that called for sauerkraut.

Bev Odlivak, another member of the Griffith Lutheran Church Women's Group, was kind enough to share her clever and easy recipe for "Reuben Sandwich Casserole."

And since St. Patrick's Day is just around the corner, this is a great recipe to clip and save.

Whenever I think of any kind of corned beef sandwiches, I think of the late, great Ed Sullivan, who went to that "really big show" in the sky in 1974 at age 73.

The famed Reuben sandwich, which piles corned beef on rye with some Swiss, sauerkraut and Russian dressing, was created in the 1960s by the legendary New York restaurant Reuben's, especially for the popular CBS variety show host known for rarely cracking a smile.

According to author Carol Stevens, of "Shaboom's Kitchen" online recipe archive, who confirms this story, Sullivan also liked chopped chicken livers on his corned beef sandwich.

Reuben Sandwich Casserole

● Preheat oven to 375 degrees.

● Coat a 9-inch by 9-inch glass square glass baking dish with cooking spray.

● Spread the rye bread with mustard and cut slices into cubes, spreading the bread evenly to line bottom of baking dish.

● Crumble corned beef and spread evenly over the bread. Set aside.

● In a mixing bowl, stir together sauerkraut, tomato soup, water and relish. Spoon mixture over top of bread and corned beef layer. Leave cheese for final minutes of baking time.

● Bake assembled casserole for 25 minutes. Remove from oven and cover with cheese slices and return to oven for about 5 minutes.

● Serve warm in generous slices. Garnish with a drizzle of Russian dressing if desired.

● Makes 6 servings.

INGREDIENTS:

5 slices rye bread

1 tablespoon prepared table mustard

1 (12 ounce) can corned beef

1 (10 ounce) can tomato soup

1 (16 ounce) can sauerkraut, drained

1/4 cup water

3 tablespoons sweet pickle relish

5 thick slices Swiss cheese

Russian dressing for garnish (optional)

Join me at free Crown Point arts event

February 13, 2008

This is the time of year when it's always nice to have something to look forward to, especially in the midst of lingering winter.

I'm pleased the Crown Point Mayor's Office of Special Events has asked me to invite readers to a free program from 6 to 9 p.m. Friday, Feb. 22, in downtown Crown Point, Ind. at the South Shore Arts Center, 138 S. Main St., which is the old, historic People's State Bank.

The event, which will feature plenty of seating, fun and games, refreshments and more than $800 in free drawing prizes, is being held in conjunction with the 4th Friday Arts Program.

I will talk about the life of legendary Rudolph Valentino.

For more information, contact Jennifer M. Bzdil, special events director, for the City of Crown Point Mayor's Office of Special Events.

It is good to have a count of those attending, to help with preparations, so please RSVP.

This indeed is a rare archive photo. In fact, Debbie Reynolds didn't even own a copy and asked me share a print with her. While planning her 1956 Hollywood baby shower while expectant with daughter Carrie Fisher, Debbie made sure to invite both Hedda Hopper (right) and Louella Parsons, rather than risk feeling the wrath of either of the powerful gossip columnists.

As for this week's Valentine's Day recipe, since silent-film era movie star Valentino married his second wife, actress Natacha Rambova, in the Crown Point Courthouse on March 14, 1923, I've decided to share his sought-after recipe for his "secret" spaghetti sauce.

It was gossip columnist Hedda Hopper, who had worked with Valentino early on while she was still working as an actress during the early days of film, who finally revealed his "secret ingredient" to be anchovies, which seem to "melt away" as the sauce simmers.

Rudolph Valentino's "Secret" Spaghetti Sauce

- Heat 1 tablespoon oil in skillet over low flame, and cook mushrooms and onions until soft, adding a little water to pan while cooking so contents don't over-heat. Set aside.

- In a large Dutch oven pot, combine the tomato paste, tomato sauce and whole tomatoes, along with cooked mushrooms and onions, reserving skillet to cook meat. Simmer over a very low flame.

- Add 1 tablespoon of oil to coat skillet and add Italian sausage (depending on grade of Italian sausage, meat may need to be removed from casing and crumbled.) Cook over a medium flame and brown sausage.

- While sausage is cooking, add 1 heaping teaspoon minced, fresh garlic or the equivalent of dry garlic powder, stirring constantly to combine.

- Add the cooked meat, undrained, to the sauce pot, along with oregano and rosemary, continuing to simmer. Add 1/2 cup of red wine to the skillet and heat for a few minutes over a low flame to "de-glaze" the skillet, using a spatula to move the wine around and release all of the bits from the pan. Add this to the sauce.

- Now for Valentino's "secret" ingredient ... add 1/2 can of anchovies, stirring vigorously until combined into sauce. Simmer 10 minutes, taste for flavor and desired taste, and add two more anchovies if desired, repeating this step if desired, until all the fillets are gone.

- Simmer sauce for 30 more minutes and serve with favorite type of spaghetti.

- Makes 12 servings.

INGREDIENTS:

2 tablespoons olive oil (divided use)

1 large onion, diced

1-1/2 cups sliced mushrooms

1 (8 ounce) can tomato paste

1 (8 ounce) can tomato sauce

1 (16 ounce) can whole tomatoes, chopped and undrained

1 pound Italian sausage

1 teaspoon minced garlic

1 tablespoon oregano

1 tablespoon rosemary

1 (2 ounce) can anchovies

My mom and dad always love seeing Debbie Reynolds stage show when she brings it to the Drury Lane Dinner Theaters. This 2002 backstage photo at the now vanished Drury Lane in Evergreen Park, Ill. captures the moment. Debbie collects movie memorabilia and even owns a number of Rudolph Valentino's original costumes.

Spring arrival reminds of Strawberry planting

March 19, 2010

Tomorrow is the first official day of spring.

Even if the weather outside the window might seem gray, damp, rainy and cold, I'm reminded that my Grandma Potempa always said this is the typical weather during the Holy Week leading to Easter Sunday, which we hope will be bright and sunny.

As soon as the spring calendar arrives, I always think of the approach of strawberry season.

As I've mentioned before, I spent 10 years (beginning the summer after my fifth-grade year) making extra money with my two older brothers and two older sisters working at the strawberry farm of our friends and neighboring farmers, the Spenner Family.

And by the end of March and the beginning of April, we'd already begin working after school and on the weekends sorting all the new tiny strawberry plants that would arrive to be prepared for spring planting. We'd sit for hours sorting the tiny plants and dividing them at their crowns and runners, removing any weeds that might have slipped into the bundles.

We'd also help unload and stack wagon-loads of straw bales, which eventually would be scattered in-between the rows of strawberry plants in time for picking late May and June berries.

And of course, lots of hand-weeding, on our hands and knees, combing through the previous year's strawberry fields, to guarantee later compliments by customers during the season, all amazed at "how clean all of the strawberry patches were at Jerry and Dee Spenner's farm."

Today's delicious casserole recipe is from Jerry Spenner's older sister Peggy, 85, who married Jim Stonebraker and who still attends Mass ever week at our church. I remember many times helping Peggy and her sister Helen, who is soon to be 88-years-old, pick strawberries for jam during my decade working for the Spenners.

Earlier this month, Peggy brought this 30-year-old casserole recipe to serve my mom's church ladies group when it was her turn to prepare the luncheon. It's a great way to use up any leftover corned beef (diced very fine) from St. Patrick's Day.

I've tried it with both leftover corned beef, as well as using one of the little square cans of packaged corned beef. Either way, it's very easy. The most difficult part of this casserole was trying to use that darn little provided metal key to open the can of corned beef.

Happy Easter!

And don't forget, mark your calendars to join me for a free program and party at noon Saturday, March 29, welcoming spring and celebrating the grand opening of the new Wanatah Public Library, 114 S. Main St., Wanatah, Ind. Recipe sampling, music, contests, book signing and plenty of prizes. RSVP for your seat right away!

INGREDIENTS:

1 (12 ounce) package of kluski-style dry noodles

1 (12 ounce) can of corned beef or 1-1/2 cups finely diced leftover corned beef

1 (8 ounce) package shredded Cheddar cheese

1/3 cup chopped onion

2 (14.5 ounce) cans cream of mushroom soup

1-1/2 cups milk

Salt and pepper to taste

1 cup breadcrumbs

1 tablespoon butter

Peggy Stonebraker's
Corned Beef Casserole

● Cook noodles in 5 quarts boiling water for 8 minutes and drain.

● In a large bowl, crumble can corned beef or add diced leftover corned beef and add in cheese, onion and top with noodles. Mix well to combine.

● Add in milk and both cans of undiluted soup and desired salt and pepper and mix well and pour contents into a buttered 9-by-13-inch casserole pan.

● In a saute pan, melt 1 tablespoon butter and lightly saute bread crumbs to toast and sprinkle evenly over casserole.

● Cover casserole with foil and bake in 350 degree oven for 1 hour.

● Makes 12 servings.

Helping family friend Peg Stonebreaker decorate our small farm church for Easter is easy, considering how many years she's been doing it. This photo was taken in March 2009.

Mom has special twin connection to Hagers

May 7, 2008

If you are a reader old enough to remember the country comedy variety show "Hee Haw," then you're old enough to remember Jim and Jon Hager, better known to most as the Hager Twins.

My family grew up watching shows like "Hee Haw" and "The Lawrence Welk Show."

Fun, clean, wholesome entertainment.

So what if it was a little corny?

Our house was and is surrounded by cornfields anyway, so the more the merrier.

I was surprised and saddened to find out Jim Hager, one of the famed Hager Twins who liked to parody country life with cornball one-liners on TV's "Hee Haw," died last Thursday; he was 66.

According to the report from the Associated Press, Hager was at a coffee shop when he collapsed Thursday in Nashville and was taken to Vanderbilt University Medical Center. It is believed he may have died of a heart attack.

The identical brothers, who originally were from Chicago, had just been together earlier that morning, planning and arranging plane tickets to visit their adoptive mom for Mother's Day.

My mom, who is also a twin, was especially a fan of the Hagers, who were discovered by Buck Owens while they were singing and playing their guitars while performing at Disneyland.

My mom is happily framed by the Hager Twins of "Hee Haw" fame in this 1992 photo at the Phillips Pro Classic Golf and Fishing Tournament in Bella Vista, Ark. Jim Hager, 66, died on May 1 from an undisclosed cause. Jon Hager died just eight months later in his sleep on Jan. 9, 2009. The inset photo is a publicity still from 1972. (Times Archive Photo)

Owens asked them to join his national tour as his opening act and then invited them to join the cast of "Hee Haw" when he was selected to become cohost with Roy Clark.

Sam Lovullo, the show's producer, told the Associated Press he was looking for attractive male talent to match the young, beautiful women on the show, when Owen suggested the then-23-year-old Hagers.

I got to know the Hagers, along with my parents, from our annual summer vacations in the late 1980s and early 1990s to Bella Vista, Ark., when we would attend a big celebrity golf and fishing charity tournament called The Phillips Pro Classic.

Clark and the Hagers always attended, and the brothers always liked to kid my mom about also being a twin.

In fact, the Hagers also became legendary at the tournaments for their fun, partying ways and staying out late. I'm sure some of the tales told by the other celebs, like Clark, Leslie Nielson, George Lindsey, Spanky McFarland and little Billy Barty, were exaggerated, since many of these names like to kid the Hagers about their playboy reputation, including posing nude as centerfolds in the very first issue of "Playgirl" magazine in 1973.

The last time we saw the Hagers was in 1996, when they performed in Valparaiso at the Porter County Fair with the late Eddie Rabbitt.

Today's recipe is a favorite from the Hager Twins' 1985 appearance on Florence Henderson's "Country Cooking" series on the cable network TNN and later, they whipped it up again on TNN on Lorianne Crook's show, "Crook & Chase."

Hager Twins' Poached Salmon in Orange Sauce

- Place fish in a frying pan.

- Pour orange juice over fish until it covers half the thickness of the filets.

- Place one slice (about 1/8 of an inch) of red onion on top of each serving of fish.

- Sprinkle with seasonings.

- Cook fish over medium heat, covered, until flaky (will depend on thickness of fish) about 5 to 10 minutes per inch of thickness.

- Remove fish to a warm plate, and allow onions to remain in pan and reduce orange sauce by simmering until it becomes thick, stirring and watching so it doesn't burn.

- Pour sauce over fish and top with the onions and serve warm.

- Makes 4 servings.

INGREDIENTS:

2-1/2 pounds salmon filets (skin removed)

2 cups orange juice

1 red onion, sliced

Salt and pepper to taste

Dash of seasoning salt

Small town roadhouse restaurant has history

June 11, 2008

This Sunday isn't just Father's Day weekend.

It's also the weekend of my town's 31st Annual Mint Festival in North Judson. Our small town has very few places to eat.

But among those few options, we have some out-of-this world old fashioned traditional favorite menu options.

One of my favorites is our little restaurant and pub Brantwood.

But while I was growing up, it was called Patterson's, because it was originally owned by brothers/husband and wife teams Jerry and Lois Patterson and Bobby Patterson and wife Barbara Gumz Patterson. Originally, the brothers had taken over ownership of the old Busy Bee Tavern before launching this new restaurant right on "busy" Highway 10 in 1973.

Along the paneled walls of the dining room, guests were welcomed by antique shipping crate lids displaying old advertisements for Nabisco Cream of Wheat, Coca-Cola, Post Grape Nuts and Ceresota Flour covered the walls, while on the walls of the tavern area just through the swinging doors, it was antique shipping crate lids for Schlitz Beer and Pabst Blue Ribbon. A few of these still even remain.

Reba Chronkite, Jerry and Bobby's mom, was the original cook who created the restaurant's famous signature Italian Beef Sandwich, which 35 years later, still attracts hungry appetites from counties near and far.

One of the favorite faces to see at Patterson's was Rosie Amidei, the longtime waitress who started at the eatery on its first day of business and remained until Jerry and Lois sold it in 1982. She was quick on her feet and always there with a coffee refill or to add extra ice or lemonade to a half-empty class.

As some readers might recall from earlier columns and recipes, Rosie, who is now 78 (and was a waitress on her feet for a total of 25 years!) and her husband Alfred, who turns 91 next month, also happen to be my older sister Carol's in-laws.

Today, Patterson's restaurant is called Brantwood, named for the early marketplace platted on Oct. 1, 1859 just a mile away from the restaurant and the 15 block area that was our town's original town square for business and the first post office location.

Today, Brantwood is more popular than ever.

It's been owned now, by Jerry and Sue Jonas, since 1983. (Sue's maiden name is Petry and her parents owned the old Petry's Pharmacy and Soda Shop in town.)

For anyone who visits our town this weekend for the Mint Festival, I recommend stopping in this favorite restaurant for one of their delicious Italian beef sandwich with one of Jerry's mint juleps or a great green grasshopper drink to wash it down.

In the meantime, printed today, is the recipe for an at-home version of the old fashioned Patterson's Italian Beef Sandwich, passed along from two late, great ladies (and sisters) from our little town, Emma Zimmerman and Betty Hoehn, and shared by Betty's daughter Joyce Hoehn-Parish, who says it came from Jerry's late mother Reba.

Patterson's Restaurant's Famous Italian Beef

- Rub roast on all sides with garlic powder. Slow roast meat "fat side up" at 325 degrees for a couple hours until a meat thermometer inserted reads "a medium-rare" level. Cool and slice VERY thin.

- Add water to drippings in pan, along with dry onion soup mix. Heat and add parsley, oregano, basil, thyme, garlic powder, rosemary and black pepper. Some beef base powder can also be added for taste, if desired.

- Add the sliced meat to the au jus and simmer for 1/2 hour. Allow to cool slightly and cover the meat and juice and refrigerate overnight. Reheat, simmering 2 hours, before serving.

- Serve on hard French bread or crusty rolls.

- Note: This freezes great.

- Makes 10-12 servings.

INGREDIENTS:

4-5 pounds rump or rib roast

1 heaping tablespoon garlic powder

3-4 cups water

1 (1.35-ounce) envelope of instant dry onion soup mix

1 tablespoon dried parsley flakes

1 heaping tablespoon oregano

1 tablespoon basil

2 heaping teaspoons thyme

1 teaspoon rosemary

Black pepper to taste

Hard French bread or crusty rolls

My older brother David and Auntie Lilly are all smiles in this 1978 photo taken at a Wedding in Chicago. Grandma Potempa is on the right

Mint Festival perfect for surprise reunion

July 2, 2008

It's always great to receive reader letters and requests.

After I wrote about my mom's good farm wife friend Marie Skuderna in a recent column, reader Denise Payne wrote asking me to retrieve one of Marie's favorite recipes that I had printed in this column a couple years ago.

Dear Phil:

I enjoy both of your columns in The Times. I am a little bit harried right now planning my son's graduation party.

I'm trying to remember where I put the recipe for a lime gelatin salad recipe from Mrs. Skuderna that I took out of the paper quite some time ago.

I even went on the Jell-O Web site. They need a recipe title to access and search recipes, and I don't remember the exact name.

Could you help? It was a recipe that did not even have to be put in the fridge for very long.

Thank you so much, if you can find the time to help. Denise Payne

The recipe from the late and great Marie Skuderna that Denise was searching for is an old favorite called "7-up Salad," which is included in my second cookbook

A surprise reunion with old friends is always nice. And these two rank as two of my oldest friends from my farm days youth. This was taken in our hometown at the 31st Annual Mint Festival in North Judson, Ind. on June 14, 2008. Tracy Skuderna (middle) and Ann Scamerhorn (right) were both longtime neighbors just down the road from the Potempa Farm. We all graduated two decades ago as the class of 1988 at North Judson-San Pierre High School.

"More From the Farm."

Because it's a green treat, it's also a favorite to serve at picnics and parties in our town during our Annual Mint Festival, which was held last month.

This week, I'm featuring another of the winning recipes that I judged in our annual "Cooking with Mint Contest" during the festival. This delicious pork chop recipe was created by our town butcher Carter Tucker and it scored a first place.

And while judging the contest, assisted by the farmer's daughter down the road, Ann Scamerhorn, I received a surprise of my own.

Tracy Skuderna, who was in my same graduating class of 1988, along with Ann, was sitting in the audience watching the judging.

Tracy, Marie's granddaughter, and the only other childhood friend who I've known even longer (not by too much) than Ann, now lives in Texas. But she came home for this year's festival. This summer also marks our 20th high school reunion, so it was also a mini private reunion of sorts.

Have a happy and safe Fourth of July holiday!

Boneless 'Hint of Mint' Pork Chops

- Spray the bottom of a shallow baking pan.

- For the best "cut of meat" pork chops, use a 5 pound string-tied "butterflied" boneless loan pork roast from the butcher shop.

- In a small bowl, combine the cheeses, pastrami and ham pieces and toss with spinach and spearmint to make mixture for inside.

- Spread mixture for the inside on one side of the roast and roll it and tie in five places.

- Cut between the strings to create the five thick chops, each still tied all around the outer edge.

- Lightly sprinkle the outer edges of chops with black pepper. Generously sprinkle top and bottom of chops with a seasoning salt, such as McCormick's All Season. Line chops in baking pan, adding just a little water in the bottom of pan.

INGREDIENTS:

5 pound boneless pork loin roast
5 slices mozzarella cheese, in small pieces
5 Provolone slices, in small pieces
5 turkey pastrami slices, in small pieces
5 slices boiled ham, in small pieces
3 cups uncooked spinach leaves
7 or 8 spearmint leaves
Butcher string
Black pepper
Seasoning salt
Cooking spray

- Cover pan with aluminum foil and bake at 350 degrees for 50 minutes or until chops test at an internal temperature of 165 degrees. Make certain thermometer is inserted in meat for reading and not in the filling mixture.

- Makes 5 servings.

Remembering friend Irene on her birthday

August 20, 2008

Time goes by so fast, and now the summer is ready to slip away.

It's this time of year that I always think about my friend Irene Jakubowski, who would have celebrated her 86th birthday this coming Monday, Aug. 25.

In fact, just a year ago, she spent the day with me for my birthday, surrounded by my family, friends and readers at the two birthday tea events held in Crete.

I remember Irene telling me not to drive down to her home in Monticello, Ind., to pick her up, because she didn't want me to have to spend part of my birthday in the car driving and that she would just stay home and be with us "in spirit."

But I told her the best birthday gift she could share would be the time spent together that day, including our visiting during the drive there and back.

It's always a wonderful feeling to not have regrets, and Irene would brighten any day with just her smile and sparkling personality.

So today's column is dedicated to Irene, who is still smiling, both in the photograph I have at my desk at work and up above, still enjoying each of these Wednesday farm columns, where her name and stories live on, as well as in my two cookbooks.

I know Irene would have loved this week's recipe, because she would always ask for fresh zucchini from our farm.

Today's recipe comes from my Times columnist colleague Marge Kullerstrand, who writes our Sunday society column.

I've worked with Marge for 15 years, and I like to call her "My Little Margie," and we both laugh that we are the only two people in the features department old enough to know that reference comes from the old 1950s television series starring Gale Storm.

I made this recipe for my mom's birthday breakfast on Sunday, and she loved both the taste and how elegantly it sliced for serving.

This February 2006 photo of me taken with my good friend Irene Jakubowski in Downtown Chicago at the Drury Lane Theatre at historic Water Tower Place, was the last traveling adventure Irene was able to take to the Windy City. We were in town to see a production of "Nunsense."

My Little Margie's Zucchini Tomato Bake

- Preheat oven to 350 degrees.

- Lightly spray a 9-by-9-inch square casserole dish.

- Spread a layer of grated zucchini along the bottom of the dish. Add enough sliced tomato to cover.

- Add fresh ribbons of Basil leaves or sprinkle dried Basil to taste.

- Sprinkle with grated Parmesan, and, if desired, chopped onion.

- In a large bowl, combine eggs and salt and pepper. Pour into dish and let settle throughout vegetables.

- Cover with the shredded mozzarella or provolone slices. Sprinkle generously with black pepper.

- Bake in preheated oven until eggs have set, about 30 minutes. Let cool for 10 minutes before serving.

- Note: If using a large zucchini, peel and de-seed it before grating. Also, recipe can be easily doubled for a 9-inch by 13-inch pan.

- Makes 6 servings.

INGREDIENTS:

1 small zucchini, grated

1 or 2 tomatoes, sliced

Fresh Basil leaves

1/4 cup Parmesan cheese, grated

6 eggs, beaten (or equivalent of egg substitute)

2 cups shredded mozzarella or provolone cheese

Salt and pepper

1 small onion, chopped (optional)

Cooking spray

Here I am arm-and-arm with our newspaper's two society columnists, Marge Kullerstrand (left) and Adele Mackanos at the October 2007 March of Dimes Signature Chef's Charity Dinner. Even though Adele retired in 2008 after helping write the column for a dozen years, this Sunday society features still lives on through Marge's pen and persistence.

Blue Chip anniversary dinner a special memory

September 10, 2008

It was five years ago this month in this Wednesday column that I wrote about my parents golden 50th wedding anniversary.

As I mentioned last week, my parents celebrated another five years of marriage vows last weekend.

When I wrote about my parents 1953 wedding Mass in the little neighboring town of Wheatfield, Ind., my mother's hometown, many readers told me how fascinated they were that my mom and dad returned to the family farm for their wedding reception. My two cookbooks share photographs from the event along with the story of my father's sister, Auntie Lottie, loaning my mother's twin sister, Aunt Patty, a bridesmaid gown that she had worn previously at Auntie Wanda's wedding. (They removed the hoop from the skirt to give the gown a new look.)

Auntie Lottie still remembers how many potatoes she and Grandma Potempa and Auntie Lill had to peel to feed the hungry guests. An even tougher job was assigned to Auntie Lottie's husband, Uncle Swede, who had to the kill and pluck the chickens that were featured as crisp and sizzling platters of fried chicken. I shared Grandma's recipe in that 2003 column.

Today's roast chicken recipe comes from Chef Eric Szczepanski of the wonderful William B's Steakhouse at Blue Chip Casino and Hotel, where my sister Pam joined me Friday treating my parents to a special anniversary dinner.

Pam had only been to the Blue Chip once before years ago, and was interested to see all of the changes happening with this Boyd Gaming property.

The new high-rise Blue Chip Hotel, soon to open in just a few months, boasts blue-tinted windows, 242-guestrooms, 60 suites, a new convention center, a 10,000 sq. ft. luxury spa and fitness center and 15,000 sq. ft. of ballroom space, in addition to new restaurants soon to be announced.

Blue Chip Community Relations Director "D" Alexander Scott and Patrick Cullars, the manager of William B's even surprised my parents by wheeling out an amazingly moist four-layer coconut cake. Chef Szczepanski of Chesterton is not only proud of his roast chicken recipe. He's also busting button about his new menu he's just unveiled to tempt guests.

Thank you to the many readers who expressed well-wishes to my parents last week and during the Popcorn Parade Saturday, as well to the kind folks at Blue Chip Casino who are sharing today's great recipe.

William B's Roasted Chicken

- Wash chicken inside and out.

- Season inside chicken with salt and pepper.

- Combine vegetables and herbs and stuff them inside chicken.

- Rub outside of chicken lightly with olive oil and season with salt and pepper. Tie legs together to keep vegetables inside.

- Roast for 45 minutes to an hour in a 300 degree oven.

- Remove chicken from oven and let cool. Once cool, cut chicken in half and remove vegetables and rib bones. Set roasted chicken aside.

- Place bones and vegetables on same roasting pan and place in 400 degree oven for 15 minutes.

- Remove pan from the oven and add white wine. Wait a minute then add water. Place back in oven for 10 minutes.

- Remove pan from oven and strain out solids.

- Season to taste with salt and pepper.

- Serve chicken over vegetables with the pan stock.

- Makes 6 servings.

INGREDIENTS:
1 (3-4 pound) whole chicken
1/4 cup chopped carrots
1/4 cup chopped celery
1/4 cup chopped onion
3 or 4 pieces of fresh garlic
1 fresh thyme sprig
1 fresh rosemary sprigs
Olive oil (as needed)
Salt and pepper, as needed
1/2 cup white wine
1 cup water
Cooking twine

This September 1953 photo has my mom and dad at the altar on their wedding day, as my mom's twin sister, Aunt Patty, keeps a close eye during the ceremony at Our Lady of Sorrows Church in tiny Wheatfield, Ind.

Class reunion a chance to reflect

October 8, 2008

Despite all the horrible moments associated with last month's excessive rain, at least something good (besides the team effort of neighbors helping neighbors) has developed from all of the water, along with this recent mild and warm weather.

While at the farm on Sunday, I enjoyed a bounty of fresh and delicious mushrooms, which my father has been finding all over in the woods and around the pond.

While enjoying our fungal feast, I filled my folks in about all the details of my much-anticipated 20-year high school reunion from the previous weekend, since I now had photos to share.

It makes me proud to see the accomplishments that our North Judson-San Pierre High School Class of 1988 has managed during the past two decades. We had 35 classmates from our graduation class of nearly 90 attend, along with spouses and guests.

Our class valedictorian Steve Tripenfeldas, is now the principal at Munster High School in Munster, Ind. Theresa Russell, who was the co-editor-in-chief with me for our senior yearbook, is now an elementary school teacher at the same school she once attended. Mike Reimbold, who was on the basketball team with me, now runs our

Former student council president meets former senior cabinet vice president, Pam Sturgell Eichelberger and the occasion is our 20th high school reunion held in October 2008.

town's newspaper, the same newspaper his father started. And the list goes on and on

Much of the night's conversation centered on stories like skinning deer and how Friday nights meant "cruising" downtown in our first cars.

Someone also reminded about our senior class prank, which had classmates gathering all the chalkboard erasers from the classrooms throughout the entire school and hiding them in an empty locker.

Our reunion was held at a little roadhouse restaurant in North Judson, Ind. called Route 10 (named for the highway it's located on, which runs right through town). It's owned and operated by the parents of another classmate of mine, Pam Sturgell, who was on our senior year homecoming court.

As student body president, it was my responsibility to crown the homecoming queen at the half-time of the big football game. I still remember the day of the school assembly, before the evening crowning, all five members of the homecoming court and their escorts had to wear their formals on stage in the school auditorium so they could randomly draw a question from the fishbowl, which I then would ask them to answer before the entire school before students voted.

I remember how nervous all the girls were, including Pam, about these impromptu questions. Just before the program, the five contestants tried to persuade me to allow them to answer prearranged "rigged" questions, so they would be assured to answer with ease. I refused to cave.

Pam and her parents also raised collies, which is where my parents found one of their most prized pets, our collie Laddy, who lived until 2002.

My parents are especially fans of the Sturgell's restaurant Route 10, because on Friday nights, they have an all-you-can eat Ocean Perch special, as well as specials on Bluegill and Lake Perch. On Saturdays, it's prime rib, steak and barbecue rib specials that are the most tempting.

Today's recipe is from Pam's file. It is for a delicious baked goulash. I've only ever published one other recipe for this one-dish favorite, and it was from the late great Eva Gabor for her "Hungarian Goulash" published in my "More From the Farm" (2007) second cookbook in 2007.

Easy Baked Goulash

INGREDIENTS:

1 pound ground beef

1 small onion, chopped

1/2 cup tomato juice

1/2 cup chopped stewed tomatoes

1 cup cooked noodles, thick but not wide variety

Dash of chili powder

1 cup Monterey-Colby Jack cheese

- Brown and cook ground beef with onion. Do not drain.

- Mix all ingredients together, EXCEPT CHEESE, and pour into a sprayed glass casserole.

- Sprinkle cheese on top of casserole and bake at 325 degrees for 30 minutes or until heated through.

- Serves 8

Your chance for a free Halloween party

October 15, 2008

In 2004, I hosted a popular sold-out Halloween party at Valparaiso Public Library that attracted nearly 200 guests both young and old.

The focal point of the party was something "above and beyond" created especially for the occasion.

Here's how I described my surprise for guests in an earlier column back in 2004:

"I'm fortunate I have parents who are very helpful and creative, even when my request for assistance is for something imaginative, that borders on the odd or unknown.

I decided months ago that the focal point for the Halloween party I'm hosting would be my own version of Dr. Frankenstein's famous monster.

Dracula 1931

For weeks, I've been planning with my parents on a design for a creation we could construct in my father's wood shop.

The Wolfman 1941

On Saturday, the plans on paper were transformed into a nearly 10-foot-tall grimacing creature with flashing eyes and a shoulder span stretching 5 feet wide. And by the way, my towering custom Frankenstein monster sports a size 70 black sportscoat from John Cicco's Menswear in Merrillville,

My father helped me with constructing the wood frame, while my mother did lots of sewing and padding. Fortunately, we built the brute in one of our largest garages with a huge suspended door to transport this wonder of the imagination.

If you can't be at this month's event, you can be sure, after all the hard work that went into our newest family edition, he'll be around to haunt future fall celebrations for years to come."

Well, true to my promise, my Frankenstein's Monster is making a return appearance with me at

Frankenstein 1931

a special FREE "Halloween From the Farm" party at the Crown Point Location of South Shore Arts, 138 S. Main St. which is the old, historic People's State Bank in Crown Point, right on the corner across from the courthouse. This event, from 6 to 9 p.m. Friday, Oct. 24 is sponsored by the Crown Point Mayor's Office as part of the 4th Friday Arts.

Today, I'm sharing a selection of spooky dinner favorites from the descendants of the famed actors who played the classic movie monsters made so legendary by Universal Pictures.

I had the pleasure of meeting and interviewing them at Hollywood Blvd. Cinema in Woodridge, Ill.

Bela Lugosi Jr. is a lawyer in Los Angeles and his father Bela Lugosi played Count Dracula. His recipe is for delicious Hungarian Stuffed Cabbage. Sara Karloff, is the daughter of Boris Karloff, who played Frankenstein's Monster. She admits her family was a "typical Hollywood movie star family" and therefore, she doesn't recall much cooking or family meals at home.

"We at most of our meals at the Hollywood Brown Derby restaurant," she recalls.

Her only recipe advice is for a mustard spread her father loved, as does she. To make it, just mix a little drink mustard powder with a few splashes of gin and then use the spread on sandwiches, especially corned beef or even as a salad dressing.

Ron Chaney, is the grandson of Lon Chaney Jr., who played The Wolfman, as well as the great grandson of Lon Chaney Sr., who played The Phantom of the Opera. He loves to brag about his recipe for The Chaney Family's Vegetable Stew, which is shared here for readers to also enjoy.

These are the descendants of the legendary actors who made Universal Picture's "classic movie monsters" so "classic." That's me with Sara Karloff, daughter of Boris Karloff and Ron Chaney, the grandson of Lon Chaney Jr. And doesn't Bela Lugosi Jr. look an awful lot like his father?

INGREDIENTS:

1 1/2 pounds lean ground pork

1/2 pound smoked ham, ground

1 medium onion, chopped

2 garlic cloves, minced

1/3 cup rice, cooked

2 eggs

1 1/2 teaspoons salt

1/2 teaspoon paprika

1/2 teaspoon black pepper

1/2 teaspoon seasoning salt

2 medium size cabbages

2 large (28 ounce) cans sauerkraut

1 medium (20 ounce) can solid pack tomatoes

2 tablespoons bacon drippings

2 tablespoons flour

1 small ham hock (optional)

Sour cream for garnish

Hungarian Stuffed Cabbage

● Saute onion and add to both meats in a large bowl, mixing well.

● Add garlic, eggs, rice and seasonings to meat mixture.

● Core and boil cabbage until leaves or soft and pliable. Remove cabbage from water and gently separate leaves.

● Place about 1/4 cup of the meat mixture on each cabbage leaf and roll up and tuck in at each end.

● Drain sauerkraut and pour into a large bowl. Mix with tomatoes.

● In a small frying pan, mix together bacon drippings and flour and heat on a low flame to make a roux.

● Mix roux with the tomatoes and sauerkraut.

● In a large Dutch oven, place ham hock on bottom (if desired), then a layer of the sauerkraut mixture, then all of the cabbage rolls layered on the bed of sauerkraut.

● Cover cabbage rolls with the remaining sauerkraut. Add enough water to cover all of the contents in pot.

● Bring pot contents to a boil, reduce heat, cover and then simmer for 2 and 1/2 hours. Serve with a dollop of sour cream on top of each cabbage roll.

● Makes 15 cabbage rolls.

Chaney Family Vegetable Stew

● Using a large soup pot or Dutch oven, brown meat in oil.

● Add 12 cups of water and all seasoning and bring to a boil, before reducing heat, simmering meat until tender.

● Add in all vegetables, cover and simmer until they test tender.

● Adjust seasonings as needed.

● Makes 15 servings.

INGREDIENTS:

4 pounds beef chuck roast, with bones

2 tablespoons oil

1 pound jar of white navy beans

8 potatoes, diced

4 small onions, chopped

1 large stalk of celery, chopped

2 (15 ounce) cans of corn

1 quart of stewed tomatoes

2 pounds of carrots, in slices

2 (15 ounce) cans of peas

1 head of cabbage, chopped

3 beef boullion cubes

1 teaspoon paprika

Salt and pepper

2 teaspoons minced garlic

2 teaspoons seasoning salt

Here's your chance to win Brooke Shields Tupperware

May 6, 2009

I've never had the chance (yet) to meet and interview actress Brooke Shields.

I almost interviewed her at a charity event at Marshall Field's in August 2001, but I had to go out of town.

So when the nice folks at Tupperware asked me if I'd like to share with my readers the chance to win their brand new line of sleek orange and white bowls called Radiance inspired by Brooke Shields, I couldn't resist offering a fun contest for early Mother's Day gifts. I have 40 bowls, in small, medium and large, valued at more than $1,000.

As for today's recipe, it's a celebrity recipe from Brooke Shields that my Auntie Lilly found more than 20 years ago. She loved watching her many times on Bob Hope's TV specials.

This recipe has been a family favorite of hers from more than 20 years ago and even at that time, she described herself as becoming "basically a vegetarian, but still liking pasta, chicken and fish, such as sole and Thai and Chinese food."

And though she said she loves Japanese food, she did NOT like the food she ate while filming "The Blue Lagoon" on location in 1979 in Fiji.

She says while on the set of television and film projects, she also insists that fresh fruit and granola be available.

Brooke Shields' Cabbage Smothered with Italian Sausage

- Spray the bottom of a deep Dutch oven.

- Remove sausage from casings and discard skins.

- Mash sausage meat with fork in the bottom of sprayed pot and add onion.

- Cook over a low heat until meat is cooked and onion has softened.

- Clean and cut cabbage into four wedges and place cabbage pieces on top of meat.

- Add the splash of water, salt and pepper and any other desired seasonings.

- Cook covered over low heat until cabbage is tender, about 20 minutes. Serve immediately.

- Makes 4 servings.

INGREDIENTS:
Cooking spray
1/2 pound Italian pork sausages
1 small onion, chopped
1 head of cabbage
2 tablespoons water
Salt and pepper

Reader looking for 'I Love Lucy' recipe help

May 20, 2009

I love helping readers out with requests.

And if I can't help, I at least try to find someone who can assist.

This week, I'm featuring a letter request from Barbara Musgrove of Munster, Ind.

"Hello Phil,

I thought I would ask you about Lucille Ball. I am having a small bridge group over and serving them lunch. We always have a theme to our luncheons and I have chosen Lucille Ball. I found aprons (like she used to wear) and a few other trinkets while taking my grandsons to Florida last October. My question is: Did her daughter, Lucie, have a favorite food? I am perplexed on what to serve for lunch. I do remember a couple of her 'I Love Lucy' episodes where Lucy served steak but had to eat salad because of dieting. Since I know she is one of your favorites, I thought maybe you might have a suggestion for me. Signed, Perplexed! Barbara Musgrove P.S. A Happy Mother's Day to your Mom!! Seems like we know her from seeing her at your affairs and such."

Thank you for your letter Barbara. Sounds like you have a fun event planned for your card group. I never had the honor and pleasure of meeting and interviewing the great Lucille Ball. However, I have met and interviewed Lucie Arnaz, the talented and gracious daughter of Lucy and Desi Arnaz. The last time I saw Lucie was in South Bend in 1997 to interview her while she was there to speak at the annual women's health expo event. However, I have e-mailed with her on occasion and she's helped me answer some reader questions related to her parents.

I've included one of her favorite recipes this week. She mentions "This chicken would taste best served with a wonderful dish called 'Arnaz Rice' which my father invented and used to serve to all the folks at the Desilu Studio company picnics. But, my Dad tried so hard to keep that recipe a secret, he even forgot to give it to me!"

Some other suggestions also come from other "I Love Lucy" episodes, one that has Lucy and Ethel making their own homemade salad dressing to sell or how about some chocolate candies (I have some great Bon-Bon recipes in both this book and my second cookbook, which look much like those Lucy

Lucille Ball with her children
Desi Arnaz Jr. and Lucie Arnaz

and Ethel had to wrap in tissue papers on the factory conveyor belt), like those from the famed "candy factory" episode or mini-hamburgers like the episode in which Lucy loses her wedding ring in a hamburger patty while helping Ethel build a brick BBQ pit.

From my own cookbooks, I would suggest some of funny lady Phyllis Diller's recipes as well, since she and Lucy were friends, along with their favorite mentor Bob Hope. Diller even shares the same birth date as Lucie Arnaz. I would suggest Phyllis' delicate Ice Box Lemon Drop Cookies and her Diller's Dynamite Honey Salad Dressing from the first "From the Farm" cookbook. And since there's a funny "I Love Lucy" episode with Lucy and Ethel eating watercress sandwiches while on a road trip to Florida, you might also try Lucy's friend and gossip columnist Hedda Hopper's favorite recipe for Watercress and Potato Soup featured in my second cookbook. In fact, Lucy was waiting by Hedda's hospital bed for her to recover from pneumonia when she died in 1966.

One of my personal all-time favorite "I Love Lucy" food related episodes actually comes from "The Lucy-Desi Comedy Hour" series the couple did in later years following the original series, but using their same popular characters.

In 1957, actress Tallulah Bankhead guest-starred as herself in an episode that had her moving to the country next door to Lucy and Ricky as a weekend home in Conneticut. After Lucy finds out Miss Bankhead has a live-in hired couple (maid and butler) working for her, she invites her new celebrity neighbor over for dinner, using friends Ethel and Fred (the wonderful Vivian Vance and William Frawley) pretending to be HER maid and butler to serve the dinner, which consisted of Southern fried chicken, mashed potatoes, gravy, buttermilk biscuits and fresh strawberry cake, the latter which Tallulah turns out to be very allergic to! ("Strawberries give me hives, dahling!" notes Bankhead.)

Good luck with your menu planning.

Lucie Arnaz's Sesame Chicken

- Blend eggs with milk.

- Combine flour, baking powder, salt, black pepper, paprika, almonds and sesame seeds in a paper bag.

- Dip chicken pieces in egg mixture, then place in bag and shake to coat thoroughly with dry mixture.

- Melt butter and spread in a shallow baking pan and place chicken evenly in single layers in pan.

- Bake in 400 degree oven for 20 minutes. Turn and bake for an additional 20 minutes.

- Makes 12 servings.

INGREDIENTS:
3 eggs, beaten
1-1/2 cups milk
2 cups all-purpose flour
2 teaspoons baking powder
2 teaspoons salt
1/2 teaspoon black pepper
1 tablespoon paprika
1/2 cup chopped almonds
1/2 cup sesame seeds
6 small broiler-fryers, cut in halves OR equivalent of boneless, skinless chicken tenderloins
1 cup butter, melted

Readers make Dad's 80th birthday all smiles

July 22, 2009

As promised last week, here are some of the details, including a photo, from my party at Avalon Manor in Merrillville, Ind. for my dad's 80th birthday on July 12.

On behalf of my parents, and me, thank you to all readers of The Times who attended, along with family and friends, to help with the hundreds of dollars raised for the Visiting Nurse Association of Porter County's Annual Christmas for the Elderly Fund.

Even though guests were asked not to bring gifts, a few presents slipped in along the way, including Polish beer, gift certificates for Ed's Barber Shop in our tiny town, homemade wine, fresh blueberry muffins and some other unique items.

The beautiful cake served was designed specifically with my dad in mind, including fresh flowers and real ivy in each of the corners and tiny green garden vegetables. It featured John Deere green and yellow icing colors, and a reproduced colored sugar-spun photo of my dad holding a crate of fresh picked mushrooms.

(How often do you ever get to see mushrooms on a birthday cake?)

Tiny garden gnomes were placed on the guest tables, along with flower vases using fresh asparagus fern from the farm and tiny bumblebees buzzing about the red carnation blooms.

When guests arrived, they were greeted by tiny jars of my mom's fresh, homemade wild black raspberry preserves at each place setting, made from berries my dad picked along the woods and old railroad track earlier this month.

Even my two older brothers and two older sisters were treated to a surprise gift. My dad's sister Auntie Lottie, 86, couldn't make it from Sarasota, Fla., to attend the party but she did send along potted sprouts from our late Grandma Potempa's 40-year-old Aloe Vera plant. She wanted each of us to have our own starts of this growing gift of ancient medical remedies.

Over the years, the soothing salve of this same plant has eased the pain from many a beesting and burns, among other ailments.

After a delicious and very generous dinner, prizes were given to every guest, from bags of fresh-picked green beans and children's books and toys to spices, cookbooks and other surprises.

On the subject of delicious dinner temptations, today's recipe is an old-fashioned Czechoslovakian favorite from the kitchen of our friend Marie Kozubik. I've had it in my file for 16 years, and today, finally it's being shared again.

Mrs. Kozubik's Liver Dumplings

- Put liver in a food processor or blender and chop.

- Add 1 onion, garlic, salt, pepper, egg, marjoram and parsley and chop or blend until well mixed.

- Pour cracker crumbs into a bowl and add the liver mixture and mix well.

- Allow mixture to stand in refrigerator for 20 minutes. If mixture seems too thin, add more crumbs to make mixture thick and workable.

- Bring broth to a boil in stock pot, then adding in the other chopped small onion.

- Shape liver mixture into walnut shape size dumplings. (Wet/flour hands to work with liver mixture and it won't stick to hands while forming shape.)

- Drop dumplings into boiling broth (salted if desired) and simmer covered for 10 minutes.

- Serves 6.

INGREDIENTS:

1/2 pound chicken or beef liver
2 small onions, chopped
1 clove garlic, crushed
1/2 teaspoon salt
1/8 teaspoon black pepper
1 egg
Pinch of marjoram
1 tablespoon minced parsley
1-1/2 cups finely ground cracker crumbs (or slightly more)
3 quarts beef or chicken both

When you turn 80, your cake can sometimes be so big, you need help holding it. That's where my mom comes in as we helped my dad display his birthday cake at his July 12, 2009 birthday party event celebrating his 80th birthday. The cake was designed and decorated specifically to include fresh flowers and real ivy in each of the corners and tiny green garden vegetables. It featured John Deere green and yellow icing.

Your chance to dine like John Dillinger or, if you prefer, actor Ernest Borgnine

July 29, 2009

I hope readers enjoyed all of The Times coverage and details of the June 18 world premiere red carpet event and screening of Universal Pictures summer blockbuster "Public Enemies" starring Johnny Depp, who plays John Dillinger, Oscar winner Marion Cotillard, who plays his moll, and Christian Bale, who plays FBI agent Melvin Purvis.

Even though the film didn't officially hit theaters nationwide until the beginning of this month on July, I was invited to walk the red carpet at the special invite-only star-studded June 18 opening at AMC River East 21 in downtown Chicago, with an afterparty across the street at River East Art Center, sponsored by Cartier.

And, of course, for our region, the equally fascinating stars are the local landscapes from the Sheriff's House in Crown Point, Ind. and scenes along the Dunes of Lake Michigan to Chicago's Union Station, the Biograph Theater, the Aragon Ballroom, the Auditorium Theatre, and all the way out west to the Paramount Arts Center in Aurora.

After many months of waiting, we finally have gotten to see what made the cut for this 2 hour and 23 minute film directed by Michael Mann.

And yes, it was exciting to be watching myself onscreen, wearing Walter Winchell's actual fedora hat as Reporter Number 3, while also scanning the screen for the who's who of others from our region who happened upon speaking roles and parts as extras, including Times Deputy Executive Editor Donald Asher who plays Reporter Number 1 and Post-Tribune Community Editor Andrew Steele, who plays Reporter Number 2, both who also attended the red carpet film opening, in addition to James Jackson, our Times automotive columnist, who also played a reporter.

Clip out this column for when you watch the film again when it arrives on DVD Dec. 1, 2009, because here are a few others to watch for from our readership: Robert Hollingsworth, Joe Carlson and Dave Innis, all playing Washington D.C. reporters swarming around J. Edgar Hoover's men. Watch for Times designer Katherine Higley as one of the period ladies in a nightclub scene, Times and Shore Magazine contributor Rob Earnshaw along with Yuri Victor and photographer Tony Arduino as background reporters. Jonathan Macchi plays the bank teller that Dillinger robs in one scene and Trent Steward, of Lowell,Ind. as a passer-by who encounters Dillinger. Karen Lubas, of Whiting, Ind. who plays an elegant woman with a chance meeting with Dillinger in a nightclub. David Standish of Highland, Ind. plays an Arizona law enforcement agent.

Hollywood worked its movie magic throughout Universal Studios' "Public Enemies," rebuilding walkways that have long since been torn down and turning one city into another. Here are a few things to look for when watching the movie.

Also, it's interesting to see how "Hollywood magic" involved using other shooting locations for some of the movie's most famous local landscapes.(Places like Wisconsin and Illinois are cheaper to film in than Indiana, because of tax breaks.)

So, for example:

● A car from the John Dillinger Museum in Hammond, Ind. was filmed for a scene that occurs in Indiana, although the scene was filmed in Wisconsin. Erika Scheeringa, the public and community relations manager of the South Shore Convention and Visitors Authority, traveled with the car to the set. She said the scene involves Dillinger and his gang going to meet Anna Sage. Scheeringa said in the scene Dillinger asks for two cars, a Plymouth and a Terra Plane and the Terra Plane that pulls up is from the John Dillinger Museum.

● The opening scene of the movie sets the scene at the Michigan City Penitentiary in 1933. However, that building is the old Statesville Prison in Joliet, Ill.

● The courthouse the movie depicts at the Lake County Courthouse, also know as the Grand Old Lady, located on the square in Crown Point, Ind. is actually the Lafayette County Courthouse in Wisconsin.

● Dan Rohaley, a member of the Old Sheriff's House Foundation Inc., the nonprofit that owns the Old Sheriff's House and Jail where portions of the movie were filmed, said originally a walkway connected the old jail to the criminal courts building next door. However that walkway has long since been knocked down. In the scene shot for the movie, Johnny Depp walks along the walkway, but when it was being filmed Depp walked toward a green screen.

● Rohaley also said a press conference where reporters, including myself, front and center, question Dillinger, WAS filmed in the Old Sheriff's Jail's actual booking room.

● Scenes that take place in Washington D.C. involving the FBI were shot at the Capital building in Madison, Wis.

● Back in the 1930s a mechanical system was used to open and close all of the doors to the cells in the jail. However, when Universal Studios fixed up the jail for filming, they tried to repair the original parts, but couldn't. In the movie, the doors are opened and closed by a pulley system.

● Meanwhile, Oshkosh, Wisconsin's Pioneer Field stood in for Chicago Midway Airport, while downtown Columbus, Wis., was transformed into Greencastle, Ind.

Author Bryan Burrough's book "Public Enemies, America's Greatest Crime Wave and the Birth of the FBI 1933-34" was used to help craft the screenplay for "Public Enemies."

Oh, while walking the red carpet, with my guest Amy Scamerhorn, I sported a fresh $9 haircut from our farm town barber Ed McDaniel, 28, who was very interested in how I was cast for my role.

I explained that this particular director likes to cast the parts of characters in certain occupations in his films, auditioning people who actually work in those fields to make the film more authentic, prompting Ed to tell me to ask director Mann tonight if he needs any barbers for his next movie project.

Today, I've included a photo from my original February 2008 audition in Chicago snapped by Times photographer Christopher Smith.

In "Public Enemies," Depp, in very little make-up and costume, had to tough-en up as Public Enemy No. 1 Dillinger. In one scene, he is shown dining on steak in some of Chicago's best restaurants of the day.

That's not unlike Depp himself, who loves to eat at Gibson's Steakhouse while in Chicago. He paid a late night visit to the celebrity favorite restaurant fol-lowing the June 18 Chicago premiere of "Public Enemies."

Depp even made headlines after he left his waiter a $4,000 tip for serving his party of 12.

But Dillinger wasn't always the biggest and the best for appeasing his appetite.

The farm boy raised outside Indianapolis in Mooresville preferred the "meat and potato basics," especially a good cut of beef and fresh fried chicken.

When on the run from the law, as shown in one of the earlier film scenes following his 1933 jailbreak at Michigan City Prison, even fried bacon sandwiches, wrapped in newspapers, were enough to satisfy his hunger while on the road flee-ing authorities.

Anna Sage, the Romanian madam who ran a brothel in East Chicago and became known as "the Lady in Red" after she helped FBI agents set up Dillinger to gun him down on July 22, 1934, even sometimes cooked for the most wanted man in America.

She told newspapers in 1935, just as she was being deported back to Europe, that Dillinger often dined with her, and his gal pal Polly Hamilton, at her North Side apartment in Chicago.

"He was fond of frog legs, chicken and steak," Sage wrote in one account.

"He used to go downtown to the big restaurants. And he'd buy these foods so I could cook them for him."

He also loved going to the horse track and to the movies, which is why he spent his final fateful evening in the comfort of the air-conditioned Biograph, watching Clark Gable as a mobster and Myrna Loy as his moll opposite good guy William Powell in the 1934 film "Manhattan Melodrama."

Since I just interviewed actor Ernest Borgine, while he was in Chicago this week, I secured a wonderful recipe from this 88-year-old Oscar winning legend. He played mobster thug Joe Castro in Columbia Pictures 1951 classic "The Mob."

Frank Sinatra, who also enjoyed this sausage and peppers recipe of Ernie's, once said of his pal Ernie, "I'm a cook who sings and Ernie is a cook who gets as many requests in the kitchen as I do on stage. I always enjoy eating a medley of his hits!"

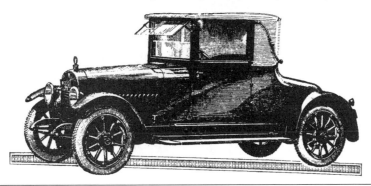

Pebronata a la Borgnine (aka Sausage and Peppers)

INGREDIENTS:

4 cloves garlic

Splash of olive oil

1 large onion, chopped

6 green bell peppers, diced

1 pound "sweet" Italian sausage, casing removed

1 to 1 1/2 pounds ground sirloin

Scattering of chopped parsley or dried parsley flakes

1/2 pound mushrooms, sliced

1 (16 ounce) jar/can Italian-seasoned tomato sauce

1 cup red wine

1 (16 ounce) package pasta of choice

- Saute garlic in oil in skillet.

- Add onion and cook until lightly browned.

- Stir in bell pepper and cook, turning frequently, until softened.

- In separate skillet, saute sausage and beef, stirring to crumble, until cooked and no longer red.

- Combine meat with the cooked vegetables.

- And parsley, mushrooms and tomato sauce to the meat and vegetable mixture.

- Stir in red wine and simmer for 20 minutes.

- While sauce is cooking, prepare pasta according to package instructions.

- Drain well and serve with sauce.

- Makes serves 6.

Looking great at age 88, I joined Oscar winning actor Ernest Borgnine when he was feted in Chicago in July 2009 to honor his career achievements and his Italian American roots.

Join me at Highland Public Library tomorrow for morning event

October 7, 2009

For anyone who's ever made homemade grape jelly, it's easy to really appreciate every bite of a classic peanut butter and jelly sandwich.

Ever since I was a young boy growing up on our farm, we've always treated our Concord grape vines as the means for a September "table treat."

And over the years, our town's postmaster, Tom Yost and his wife Carol, would sometimes come by to pick the grapes and make homemade wine, as years earlier, would my Uncle Swede and Auntie Lottie.

Other years, our farm friends down the road, Debbie and Larry Wappel, would come to gather grapes to make Larry's favorite homemade grape pie, which is pictured on the cover of my second cookbook "More From the Farm."

In fact, these traditional blue table grapes are very common in our area.

Other farm families like the Skudernas, the Lukacs and the Lakes all have/had even larger and more expansive grape trellis arbors than what we have in our farm yards.

But rarely, that I can recall, would we ever make jelly from our grapes.

With the help of my parents, we harvested all of our grapes last month and made four very large batches of pure, clear, strained grape jelly.

Compared to making the array of jams and preserves I'm more familiar with, grape jelly is far more messy and involved. But the taste and the final

This October 1978 photo shows just how much even a scaled down John Deer Tractor can haul, such as a 12-year-older sister trying to hitch a ride as part of the harvest.

results are beyond compare.

I've been asked to host this month's free "Morning Hour" presentation sponsored by the nice people at First Financial Bank's Crossroads Department for Programs.

I'll bring along some nice prizes, including some jars of this yummy homemade jelly for the free drawings.

This free event is 10:30 a.m. tomorrow at the Highland, Ind. Public Library, 2841 Jewett Ave., and I'll be talking about fall farm traditions and the importance of preserving both family and recipe memories and well as some stories of famed names featured in my books and columns. Since seating is limited, call to reserve your seat.

As for the rest of the grape jelly with my parents' blessing I'll be sharing 40 jars with guests on Monday night at this year's Taste of Home Cooking Show, which features me on stage for hosting duties at Star Plaza Theatre.

If you haven't purchased tickets, there's still time.

As for this week's featured recipe, after all of the steps involved with making homemade grape jelly, I decided to share something simply and equally satisfying for a fall comfort food favorite.

This is a recipe from reader Greg Quartucci, of Valparaiso, Ind. who recited it to me entirely from memory so you know it's an old, original family recipe that doesn't disappoint.

See you tomorrow and again Monday for all the fun and surprises that await readers!

Greg's Grandma Quartucci's Easy Spaghetti Sauce

INGREDIENTS:

2 tablespoons plus 2 tablespoons olive oil (cold hard-pressed variety) (divided use)

1/2 onion, chopped

1/2 garlic clove

1/2 pound ground (chuck) beef

1/2 pound ground pork sausage

1 tablespoon seasoned salt

3 (16-ounce) cans Italian tomato sauce

3 (8-ounce) cans Italian tomato paste

1 teaspoon basil

1 teaspoon marjoram

1 teaspoon oregano

1 bay leaf

3 tablespoons sugar

- Heat 2 tablespoons olive oil in a large skillet; add onion and garlic and sautÈ until browned.

- Mix ground chuck and ground sausage with seasoned salt; add to skillet and cook until browned. Drain grease from skillet and set aside.

- Mix all remaining sauce ingredients, in addition to the other 2 tablespoons olive oil in a large, non-aluminum pot.

- Add meat mixture and simmer for 4 hours.

- Best refrigerated overnight before sauce is served the next day over spaghetti noodles or pasta of choice.

- Makes 12 cups of sauce.

Time is right for leftover ham with scalloped potato recipe

December 30, 2009

Back in 2006, I featured my mom Peggy's recipe for homemade scalloped potatoes and ham.

After any family holiday featuring a spiral-sliced ham on the menu, it's always a guarantee my mom will save the ham bone and use any bits and scraps of ham for later menus during the week. She'll often whip up her ham and bean soup, in addition to a batch of her scalloped potatoes and ham.

Both of these recipe favorites are featured in my second cookbook "More From the Farm: Family Recipes and Memories of a Lifetime" (2007 Pediment Press $29.95).

Earlier this month, while chatting with one of my favorite smiling faces at The Times, Pamela Sutko, the executive assistant for our newspaper's publisher William Masterson, she told me about her recipe for Creamy Scalloped Potatoes and Ham.

Her family had "nibbled" on a ham during their Thanksgiving holiday, in addition to the traditional turkey and trimmings, and she decided to use the leftover ham to satisfy her longing for some "delicious homemade scalloped potatoes."

She even brought me a sample, and I've been singing the praises of her recipe ever since.

So, today, it's featured here for readers to also enjoy.

We always have ham and pork for our New Year's family dinner at the farm.

We never eat poultry or beef, only pork for good luck in the coming year.

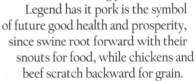

Legend has it pork is the symbol of future good health and prosperity, since swine root forward with their snouts for food, while chickens and beef scratch backward for grain.

And we always eat lots of cabbage, said to represent the green of future fortune to come in the new year.

Top all of that off with a heaping spoonful of herring (I like mine in sour cream while my parents like it soaked and pickled in vinegar), and in our family, you're sure to start off the year right (and with maybe a little gas, which always passes.)

Happy New Year and here's to a wonderful 2010!

Pamela Sutko's Creamy Scalloped Potatoes and Ham

- Preheat oven to 350 degrees.

- Butter the sides and bottom of a 9-inch-by 13-inch glass baking pan.

- Scrub potatoes and peel (if desired) and preferably use a mandolin slicer to slice uniform 1/8-inch thick slices of potatoes (Yield about 4 to 5 cups of potatoes.)

- Melt 3 tablespoons of butter in a large, deep skillet and cook onion until soft.

- Stir in flour and salt and pepper, cook until mixture is smooth and bubbly.

- Remove mixture from heat and stir in milk. Heat until boiling, stirring constantly.

- Boil, while stirring, for 1 minute.

- Layer bottom of prepared baking pan with a single layer of potatoes.

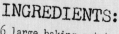

INGREDIENTS:
6 large baking potatoes
3 tablespoons plus 1 tablespoon butter (divided use)
1 large onion, chopped
3 tablespoons flour
1 teaspoon salt
1/4 teaspoon black pepper
2 1/2 cups whole milk
4 cups diced ham

- Add a layer of ham and then cover with a portion of the heated milk sauce mixture.

- Add another layer of potatoes and ham and add more sauce.

- Finish with a final layer of potatoes and remaining sauce and then dot with the 1 tablespoon of butter.

- Add a generous sprinkling of black pepper on top of casserole.

- Cover with foil and bake for 30 minutes.

- Uncover and bake another 1 hour or a little more until potatoes are tender.

- Allow to stand and cool just slightly to set up before serving.

- Makes 8 servings.

Pamela Sutko and Roy Evans share a moment with me at the Annual Meals on Wheels Dine with the Chefs event in March 2009. I was doing hosting duties that day, introducing each of the seven courses featured for the dinner menu.

Start off new year with Cubby's tasty, calorie conscious recipe

January 6, 2010

For readers who noticed the large spread in our Sunday newspaper, including a cover story in the Lifestyles features section, over the weekend, it won't be a surprise to find a healthy, calorie-counting recipe in my farm recipe column this week.

Yep, the time has come in my life when I can see my 40th birthday heading toward me just off in the horizon.

But before facing my big 4-0 in August, I've already been facing a big oh-no with a belly that might even rival that of Santa Claus.

Well Christmas is over and the new year is here.

And since my waistline has become a victim of my newspaper deadlines (which have prevented me from the kind of daily exercise needed to stay trim), it's time once again to slim down.

Readers might recall I did a similar effort in the summer of 2005, and shared weekly installments in the newspaper about the ups and downs of losing weight. My efforts resulted in a 30-pound loss in just two months.

This time, I'm facing 50 pounds to lose in three months.

Since I love adventure and new opportunities to learn from, I'm part of a new approach for this weighty effort.

I was selected by registered nurse turned diet guru Seattle Sutton to be part of a national weight-loss contest which began Monday with an official "weigh-in" at WGN television studios in Chicago. I'm competing against nine other participants selected from among thousands.

My mom enjoyed meeting weight-loss guru Seattle Sutton on Jan. 4, 2010 during a television taping in Chicago. That day just happened to be Seattle's 78th birthday.

For the next three months, I'm dining on only Seattle Sutton's Healthy Eating cuisine, fresh-prepared meals, which I pick up twice a week, Mondays and Thursdays. And just like my other nine counterparts, I'm limited to just 1,200 calories per day.

As for my starting weight, fully clothed, the "official scale" registered 230 pounds.

That number was the bad news.

The number that was the good news on Monday was 78, because Monday marked Seattle Sutton's 78th birthday and our very first meeting. We exchanged gift copies of one another's books and my mother Peggy came along with me, eager to also meet Sutton.

Today, I'm sharing Seattle's once carefully guarded "secret" recipe for her trademark Acapulco Taco Pie, which ranks as the favorite of Cubs baseball legend Ron Santo, an extreme diabetic and celebrity spokesman for Seattle's program. According to my first five-week menu plan, I get to enjoy this flavorful find for my dinner next Thursday.

However, you get to enjoy it right away, courtesy of Seattle and her dedicated staff.

Cub Ron Santo's Favorite Acapulco Taco Pie

- Brown ground turkey and onions and drain.

- Stir in chili powder and green chili peppers.

- Place this meat mixture into a sprayed 9-inch by 13-inch (or a slightly smaller pan, if desired) baking pan.

- Beat milk with biscuit mix and egg substitute, until smooth.

- Pour this mixture into the casserole pan directly over meat layer.

- In a small bowl, mix together shredded cheese and tomatoes and scatter over top of casserole as the final layer.

- Bake at 350 degrees uncovered for 40 to 45 minutes, but checking casserole after the first 30 minutes to prevent over browning.

- Remove from oven once an inserted knife comes out clean.

- Cut and serve with chips and salsa.

- Unused portions refrigerate well.

- Makes 15 servings.

- Note: a 5-ounce slice contains 184 calories, 14.9 grams protein, 14.8 grams carbs, 6.5 grams fat, 574 mgs sodium, 1.65 grams fiber and 3.95 grams sugar

- Recipe courtesy of Seattle Sutton and "The Seattle Sutton Solution: No Gimmicks" (2004 Amicus Creative Press $29.95)

INGREDIENTS:

2-1/2 pounds ground turkey

3/4 cup chopped white onions

2-1/2 tablespoons chili powder

1 cup diced green chili peppers, drained

1-3/4 cups skim milk

1 cup plus 2 tablespoons "quick" biscuit mix

3/4 cup egg substitute

1 cup diced tomatoes

6-1/4 ounces shredded Monterey Jack cheese

Further From the Farm

Mary Pickford 'buttered up' with tribute at Brown Derby event

February 10, 2010

At the time of the Great Depression, when my grandparents had just moved from Chicago a few years earlier to our family farm in Indiana, Hollywood seemed like another world.

Mary Pickford and her husband Douglas Fairbanks Sr. were among the movie stars who seemed to live a life of luxury. In fact, their estate, called Pickfair, was often featured in movie magazines and news film reels.

While hosting my "after Valentine's Day" luncheon later this month, I'll be including some mention of Pickford, who died in 1979 and during the days of the silent films, was dubbed "America's Sweetheart."

She, along with Will Rogers, Gloria Swanson and Rudolph Valentino, were among the very first patrons at The Brown Derby Restaurant, which is the theme for this year's luncheon. On display at the luncheon will be a silver butter plate and ivory handle butter knife from the Pickfair Estate auction which belonged to Pickford.

As for a reservation update, there are still 12 seats of the 200 still available, and here are the details.

I'll be hosting the full luncheon from noon to 3 p.m. in the large connected joining salon dining rooms at Teibel's restaurant in Schererville, Ind., which will be converted for that afternoon into a tribute to the famed Hollywood Brown Derby Restaurant, including real plates, menus, photos and rare displays from the legendary Tinseltown haunt that closed in 1980. And yes, lots of chances to win wonderful prizes. Each table seats eight.

Doors open at noon with lunch served at 1 p.m.

On the day of the luncheon, guests will be asked to pick from a choice of three main course entrees: Teibel's Fried Chicken or Beef Sirloin Tips or Teibel's Famous Boned and Buttered Lake Perch. Each will come with a dinner roll and cole slaw first course, and the entrees served with baby red potatoes, and a vegetable blend of young yellow summer squash, red peppers, onions and green zucchini. Each lunch also comes with choice of beverage, including coffee, hot tea, iced tea or milk.

For dessert, fresh vanilla ice cream will be served with a recipe featured in my second cookbook: Gossip Columnist Louella O' Parsons' Favorite Frosted Grapefruit Cake, which was a staple on the Brown Derby menu.

Luncheon tickets are once again $25 per person, which includes tax and tip. A portion of each ticket sold benefits one of my favorite nonprofit groups, The Caring Place, the Valparaiso shelter for victims of domestic violence.

Reservations are required by leaving name, contact telephone number and the number in your party attending.

As for today's featured recipe, it comes from Pickford's actress daughter-in-law Joan Crawford, who "America's Sweetheart" was not very fond of after she married her stepson Douglas Fairbanks Jr., who was several years younger than Joan.

According to Joan's accounts, during her few short years of marriage to Fairbanks, there weren't too many invites for her to visit her famous in-laws at Pickfair.

INGREDIENTS:

FOR SALMON:

3 pounds fresh salmon

3 lemons

6 cups water

10 peeled pearl onions

1/2 stalk celery, including leaves, chopped

2 sprigs fresh parsley

3 small bay leaves

12 crushed peppercorns

1 teaspoon salt

Cheesecloth

SAUCE:

2 cups mayonnaise

4 teaspoons prepared mustard

1/4 cup fresh lemon juice

GARNISH:

1 lemon, cut in wedges

Fresh cut parsley

Field lettuce leaves or watercress

Quartered hard-cooked eggs

Joan Crawford's Poached Salmon with Mayonnaise–Mustard Sauce

● To prepare salmon, place lemon slices around salmon and in cavity.

● Wrap fish in double layer of cheesecloth, secured with string. Set aside.

● Place water, onions, celery, parsley, bay leaves, peppercorns and salt in a large pot and bring to a simmer for 30 minutes.

● Place fish in water and simmer slowly for 40 minutes covered, using a rack or heat safe small bowl so fish is not entirely under water. Remove fish to cool slightly.

● Prepare sauce by combining all ingredients.

● Arrange salmon on a chilled platter on a bed of lettuce or watercress, surrounded by remaining garnishes if desired.

● Serve with sauce.

● Makes 8 servings.

Movie star Joan Crawford, still looking stunning in 1971 at her New York City apartment, with two poodles to keep her company.

Happy 8th Anniversary for this column with classic comfort food recipe

April 28, 2010

Yesterday, April 27 marks the 8th anniversary since this weekly farm recipe debuted on our newspaper food cover on April 27, 2002.

Many recipes and memories later, it's still going strong and more popular than ever, thanks to dedicated readers.

As I've mentioned before, I always thank and credit my very first newspaper food editor Sharon Rocchio and her husband Pat Rocchio, my first newspaper managing editor, for giving me my chance at writing about food, recipes and entertainment.

That was back in 1992, just after I had graduated from Valparaiso University when they gave me my first job at the daily newspaper in Valparaiso, Ind., The Vidette-Messenger, which was purchased by The Times in 1995.

The Rocchio Family now lives in Indianapolis, which is closer to the part

While in Indianapolis to attend the 91st Annual Indianapolis 500 Race in 2007, my former newspaper editors Pat and Sharon Rocchio attended a Saturday afternoon book signing for my second book. They seem amused to see themselves preserved on the pages in this May 27, 2007 photo. (Photo by Michael Berkos)

of the Hoosier state they originally called home before moving up north for their newspaper careers in 1900.

Whenever I'm in Indianapolis, we usually make time to get together.

And receiving Sharon's annual holiday Christmas newsletter is always a December highlight.

I always admired her breezy, entertaining "slice of life" newspaper column she wrote for The Vidette-Messenger, about parenting and just everyday life, called "Just A Moment."

Her's is a voice and writing style much like the late, great newspaper columnist and humorist Erma Bombeck, who unfortunately, I never had the chance to meet before she died at age 69 April 22, 1996 in San Francisco.

But I feel very fortunate I happen to meet and become friends with Pat and Sharon Rocchio, who pointed me in the right direction for my journalism career.

Pat and Sharon always loved the hear about what my mom or Auntie Lill would be cooking and baking at the farm.

And often time, I would bring in samples to share with them of "comfort food favorites."

One of my mom's specialties to make on Monday nights at the farm for my dad is her homemade fried liver and onions, shared here today.

My Grandma Potempa taught my mom the trick of soaking the beef liver in milk prior to breading it and pan frying it for extra added tenderness.

Our farm cats were always very thankful to get the leftover discarded "soaking milk," which my mom would usually tear up a slice of stale bread and add to it for her favorite feline friends.

Peggy's Fried Liver with Onions

● Soak liver in milk for 1 hour prior to preparing.

● Saute onions in cooking oil in skillet or electric frying pan, until soft and tender. Remove onions and retain oil.

● Cut up liver into serving sizes.

● In a small bowl, use a fork to mix flour with salt and pepper and any other desired seasonings.

● Dredge liver in flour mixture and add to hot frying pan oil and cook for 15 minutes on each side, until cooked tender.

● Return onions to frying pan, covering liver, and cook together covered for about another 5 minutes.

● Serve hot with boiled potatoes, cooked with butter and dill and a tossed salad.

● Makes 4 servings.

INGREDIENTS:
1 pound beef calf liver
1 cup whole milk
2 to 3 large onions, sliced
1/4 cup cooking oil
1 cup flour
1 teaspoon salt
1/2 teaspoon black pepper

Further From the Farm

Dad's surgery means late garden; lots of help

April 4, 2007

While sifting through old photographs for my second cookbook published in May 2007, one of my favorites I included is an old black-and-white shot from 1950 of my dad riding on (what he considered at the time) his "brand new" 1948 John Deere tractor.

He's right in the middle of his spring planting and you can see lots of dust billowing up behind him, as the angle of the photo makes it seem like he's headed right for the person behind the camera. I anchored this photo right on the introduction page of "More From the Farm: Family Recipes and Memories of a Lifetime" because I thought it would welcome and steer readers right into the first chapter of the new book.

You can see from the expression on his face, my dad is happiest when he's outside in his natural element.

And though my dad's been retired from farming large fields of crops for many years, he still looks forward to the end of winter and planting a huge garden big enough to feed our entire family, friends, neighbors, my co-workers in the newsroom

I couldn't have planned this farming family photo any more perfectly, had I wanted to. Here are the Wappels, Eric (left) and Larry Jr. with Debbie and Larry Wappel at a summer farm picnic in July 2008.

and, occasionally, even Times' readers (when we've brought fruits and vegetables to my events or for column giveaways).

In fact, every year for Good Friday during Holy Week, my dad reminds me how it's tradition to plant his potatoes and onion sets, just like Grandma and Grandpa used to every year while he was growing up.

This year, even though my dad has all of his seeds for tomatoes, carrots, leeks and peppers already started and sprouting in tiny cups on the windowsill of his heated shop, he is going to have a later garden this season.

Because of shortage of breath, he's had to stay inside and rest for the past three weeks as he prepares for a major surgery Monday at University of Chicago's special surgery center for cardiac cases.

With our family at his side, he will undergo six hours of surgery for repair (or replacement) of his mitral heart value, which is lodged open, and, at the same time, have bypass surgery to clear a 90-percent blockage of his main heart artery, and then, finally, have an additional procedure to correct an irregular heart beat.

At our meeting with the heart surgeon, my dad, who will be 78 in just a few months, was told his otherwise excellent health and strength will help him through this experience and within six to eight weeks, he can gradually work his way back to being in his garden (which it will be up to the rest of us to plant) and return to his other favorite hobby: mowing grass on the riding lawn mower.

In the meantime during this Easter week, please keep my father and mother, and our family in your prayers.

As for today's recipe, it is a favorite for Easter dinner and great as a side dish for your baked ham.

It is from our farm wife neighbor down the road, Debbie Wappel, who, like our other farm neighbors the Scamerhorns and the Lukacs, has been equally wonderful with helping my parents whenever they are in need.

INGREDIENTS:

1 small onion

1 small green pepper

1 tablespoon butter or margarine

2 (32-ounce) bags frozen Tater Tots, allowed to thaw for 15 minutes

1 pint mayonnaise

1 (16-ounce) jar processed cheese spread

Salt and pepper as desired

Cooking spray

Debbie's Easy Cheesy Potato Bake

● Heat oven to 350 degrees.

● SautÈ onion and green pepper in butter or margarine until soft.

● In a large bowl, mix Tater Tots, sautÈed onion and green pepper and all remaining ingredients until Tater Tots are well coated with cheese and mayonnaise. (A little milk or sour cream may be added to create desired consistency if needed for easier mixing.)

● Evenly spread mixture in a large, glass 9-inch-by-13-inch baking pan coated with cooking spray and bake for 50 minutes to 1 hour.

● Makes 10 servings.

Saturday is the big day for book party

May 9, 2007

The books have arrived and the party is all set for Saturday.

If you haven't already called in for a spot at the free Mother's Day weekend book-launch party from 1 to 3 p.m. May 12 at Borders Books and Music in Merrillville, this is the last reminder.

And if you're someone who already ordered and received your book, you're welcome to bring your own copy along to have it signed Saturday by me, my parents, siblings, aunts, friends, fellow readers and all the folks whose recipes and stories are included inside my second book.

My dad's been excited about two things all week: finally being able to pick morel mushrooms and attending this event, which will be his first official trip away from the farm since he returned from his surgery last month.

In fact, today's asparagus recipe is from Patrick and Jeannie Tuleja of Schererville, readers who are featured with recipes in the new cookbook.

And don't forget,you can watch me on TV this week on the PBS show "Just Around the Corner," chatting about this new second book and sharing a salute to "America's Mom," Ann Landers, whose famed recipe for meat loaf is included in my second cookbook.

Baked Asparagus Branches

● Heat oven to 350 degrees. Wash and cut asparagus spears and blanche in boiling water for about 4 minutes. Cool spears.

● Butter the bottom of a baking dish. Set aside.

● Wrap three asparagus spears in one slice of ham and place the wrapped spears on the bottom of the buttered baking dish. Continue until all of the asparagus has been wrapped and placed in the baking dish.

● In a small bowl, combine the bread crumbs with the Parmesan cheese, seasoning the mixture with a little salt and pepper. Sprinkle this lightly over the asparagus in the baking dish.

● Drizzle a little olive oil over all the coated asparagus and bake for 25 minutes. Serve warm as an appetizer or as a side dish.

● Makes 5 servings.

INGREDIENTS:

15 asparagus spears, 5 to 6 inches in length

1/2 teaspoon butter

1/4 pound ham, sliced thin

1/4 cup bread crumbs

1/4 cup grated Parmesan cheese

Salt and pepper to taste

Drizzle of olive oil

Dad's home, but Easter leftovers already gone

April 18, 2007

Just one week after my dad's open-heart surgery, and by yesterday, he was back at the farm for his first day home since Easter.

His visiting nurse marveled at her first time meeting my dad, because he's doing incredibly well.

His only disappointment after a week of hospital food was to find that all the leftovers from Easter dinner are now long gone.

(My brother Tom and his wife Linda even used up that last of the leftover roast lamb for stew last week.)

It's probably just as well, since my dad is still following a careful diet while he recuperates.

Even if he can't do much outside, other than a casual walk, my parents' home has a large picture window in their living room. This is the same window that also provides constant entertainment for their large Maine coon cat Tracker, who keeps a close watch on the birds and squirrels in the feeders in the front yard. (See my daily offbeat entertainment column today for more about my dad's surgery.)

My mom and dad's pet pride and joy: Tracker III, a pure-bred Maine coon cat with lots of personality.

Our good family friend Irene Jakubowski, who previously lived in Valparaiso for 30 years before retiring to Monticello, sent my dad a get-well card, along with a very old recipe for me that's ideal for any remaining Easter leftovers or extra ingredients from Easter dinner.

Her recipe for this clever and tasty sauerkraut ball appetizer is more than 40 years old.

What's even more interesting is everything that was once old seems to eventually become new again with later generations.

When I spent my 36th birthday last August at the Indiana State Fair in Indianapolis, the most popular "new" vendor food item being introduced to 2007 fair

---

goers in honor of its 150th birthday was, you guessed it, these same deep-fried sauerkraut balls. The line to purchase a $6 order of three of these breaded wonders was nearly an hour wait. Despite the line, I waited and even brought an order to Irene to sample as I drove home that Sunday, passing by Monticello on my way back to the farm.

We both agreed, Irene's are even better.

Irene's Sauerkraut Balls

● SautÈ onions in butter until yellow and soft, drain.

● Press sauerkraut through a colander until dry and chop it a little to make smaller pieces.

● Combine sauerkraut, cooked onions, ham (or bacon, if desired, cooked soft, but not crisp and drained), mustard, garlic powder, 1/4 cup bread crumbs and cream cheese. Mix well. Chill one hour.

● Shape mixture into balls, 1-1/4 inches in diameter

● Mix together eggs with milk and roll balls in flour, before dipping into egg-milk mixture. Roll in remaining 2 cups breadcrumbs.

● Heat vegetable oil to 350 degrees, and deep fry 2 to

INGREDIENTS:

3/4 cup chopped onion

2 tablespoons butter

1 (32-ounce) jar sauerkraut, well drained

1 pound finely diced ham or diced fried bacon

1 tablespoon dry mustard

1/2 teaspoon garlic powder

2 cups plus 1/4 cup bread crumbs (divided use)

1 (8-ounce) package cream cheese

4 eggs beaten

1/2 cup milk

1/2 cup flour

Vegetable oil for frying

3 minutes until brown. Drain on paper towel. Serve warm.

● If fried in advance and reheating to serve later following refrigeration, reheat in 350-degree oven 15 to 20 minutes until heated through. These also can be made well in advance, since they freeze well. If frozen, re-heat at 375 degrees by baking on a cookie sheet for 35 minutes or until heated through.

● If desired, serve with a ranch dressing or mustard dipping sauce.

● Makes 6 dozen.

This photo was snapped of good friend Irene Jakubowski meeting "the Polish Prince" Bobby Vinton in 1998, backstage, after his concert at Drury Lane Theatre in Evergreen Park, Ill.

Join me for free recipe sampling party

May 16, 2007

Thank you to the many people who have purchased my second cookbook "More From the Farm: Family Recipes and Memories of a Lifetime" (2007 Pediment Press $29.95) and shared so many kind words of praise for the book and my family.

We had more than 150 guests attend the Mother's Day weekend book launch event and party at Borders Books & Music in Hobart.

If you missed that event because of travel or Saturday chores, here's a second invite I think you'll enjoy.

Two months ago, the Griffith Lutheran Church Women Group asked to host a free party event for Times readers not only to "officially unveil the new cookbook," but also offer a chance for you, the reader, to sample more than half-dozen of the recipes showcased in the new book.

So at 7 p.m. Tuesday, May 22, 2007, I'll be featured with my parents at "An Evening From the Farm" at the large gathering hall attached to Griffith Lutheran Church, 1000 N. Broad St. in Griffith.

I'll host a program with some fun games and lots and lots of giveaways. I'll sign books. There will be plenty of decorations and displays from the farm and best of all, plenty of tables and seating for everyone, so you can relax as you sample some of the great dessert, salad and appetizer recipes featured in my new book.

I'm grateful to The Rev. Andrew Bailey and his wife Rebecca and the entire ladies group for hosting this wonderful event.

Please make sure to call the RSVP line so the ladies will know how many people they will be preparing food for to serve that evening.

I hope to see you next Tuesday for all the food, fun and prizes.

This week's recipe, ideal for a party, once again is from dedicated readers Patrick and Jeannie Tuleja of Schererville.

Patrick's Quick Fix Cheesy Rye Appetizers

- In a bowl, mix together all topping ingredients.

- Foil line a cookie sheet and spread slices of rye evenly spaced.

- Top each cocktail rye with some of the cheese topping mixture.

- Either bake in a 350 degree oven for 8 to 10 minutes or until bubbly or place in oven broiler for just a couple minutes until bubbly. Serve immediately.

- Makes 25 pizzas.

INGREDIENTS:

1 cup grated Swiss cheese

1/4 cup crumbled real bacon bits

1/2 cup mayonnaise

1/4 cup diced black olives

1 loaf mini cocktail rye bread

Once again time for Taste of Chicago

June 27, 2007

It's hard to believe Summer 2007 marks the 27th annual Taste of Chicago.

Once again, for my third consecutive year, at the invitation of Chicago Mayor Daley and his special events committee, I'll be on stage at 11 a.m. Sunday, July 1, 2007 cooking and creating in front of thousands of people gathered together to share in the food, music and fun.

Taste of Chicago officially kicks off this year on Friday, June 29, 2007.

When I look through the roster of names also appearing this year on stage at the Dominick's Cooking Corner Pavilion during the 10 days of Taste, it makes me feel proud and honored that I'm the only person without the title of chef in front of my name.

I'm always grateful to be included. This year, I've decided to make the delicious and unusual recipe for "Mrs. Wappel's Old-fashioned Grape Pie," which is also pictured right on the cover of my second cookbook.

It's always an honor to be onstage and overlooking Lake Shore Drive in Chicago while performing each year at Taste of Chicago.

Remember, if you can't make it down to Grant Park by Buckingham Fountain to watch me on stage at Taste this year, you can still enjoy the remaining three TV segments I've been hosting for our PBS station on Lakeshore News Tonight at 9 p.m. every Wednesday and Friday this month, with the final segment airing on Wednesday, July 4, 2007.

Despite last week's broadcast outage because of the storms, I'm told the station is back up to nearly all viewers.

Tonight, I'll be joined by my personal trainer Erik Carpenter sharing his delicious recipe for Grilled Tilapia with Black Bean and Fruit Salsa featured in my second cookbook. If you've ever wondered what I looked like fat, the segment includes some shots of me two years ago when I ballooned to 215 pounds and then worked with Erik to lose 30 pounds in two months.

And on Friday and next Wednesday, I'll be joined by Ken Blaney Jr., owner of Kelsey's Steakhouse in Valparaiso, sharing some great grilling do's and don'ts.

As for today's recipe, it's a great addition to any picnic or barbecue. It comes compliments of my friends Patrick and Jeannie Tuleja of Schererville.

INGREDIENTS:

1/4 cup sun-dried tomatoes in oil (about 8 tomatoes), drained and chopped

8 ounces cream cheese, softened at room temperature

1/2 cup sour cream

1/2 cup mayonnaise

10 dashes hot pepper sauce

1 teaspoon salt

3/4 teaspoon ground black pepper

2 scallions, thinly sliced (use both white and green stems)

Basic Sun-Dried Tomato Dip

● PurÈe tomatoes, cream cheese, sour cream, mayonnaise, hot pepper sauce, and salt and pepper in a blender or, preferably, food processor.

● Lastly, add the scallions and quickly pulse twice.

● Serve gently chilled with assorted fresh vegetables and crisp crackers.

● Makes 3 cups.

Win 'favorite' waitress-inspired gift basket

August 22, 2007

I admire anyone who works as a waiter or waitress, because I know it's not easy work.

Our small town only has one tiny restaurant and, while growing up, I can remember my sister Pam trying her hand as a waitress during the summer of her sophomore year in high school.

After just one summer, she decided to return to working in the farm fields with me rather than do waitress work.

On Monday, I wrote in my daily offBeat entertainment column about "Waitress," the great film that brought Andy Griffith out of retirement.

It's a smaller film from 20th Century Fox's independent film division, written and directed by the late Adrienne Shelly, who also stars in it. Griffith's role is definitely more than just a cameo.

The movie is the story of a waitress named Jenna, played by Keri Russell, who is unhappily married and busy squirreling away money. She has a wonderful hidden talent for baking pie, and she's been socking away her tips and pie contest prize money to start a new life so she can leave her husband Earl, played by Jeremy Sisto. But her life at Joe's Diner takes a few sudden and interesting turns.

Still need some convincing about why you should see this film?

Not only is this one worth the price of admission but, coming up, The Times has teamed up with The Caring Place, the shelter for victims of domestic violence, for a charity benefit using a pie theme and a special screening of this great new movie.

It's at 7 p.m. Aug. 30, 2007 at the classic The Art Theatre in Hobart. I'll be there serving up food and pie from the one-and-only Marilyn's Bakery at the 5:30 p.m. reception before the film.

And, following the film, Times movie columnist Jim Gordon will lead the audience in a short film discussion.

Now, on to today's fun "Waitress"-inspired contest.

I've assembled an amazing gift basket (actually, a large waitress tray), brimming with fun items in homage to the "on your feet" art of waitressing.

Valued at $200, the basket includes coffee, coffee cups, a $50 pie gift certificate, a collector's DVD featuring episodes of one of my favorite TV shows "Alice," starring Linda Lavin as Alice and Polly Walker as Flo, a Times apron, straw and napkin holders, a "Mel's Diner Home of Mel's Famous Chili" T-shirt, a DVD of the 1945 Joan Crawford movie "Mildred Pierce" (Joan worked as a waitress famous for baking great pies), and assorted other goodies.

NOW ... for the contest question to be entered in the free drawing for the gift basket:

Name one of Flo the waitress' favorite catch phrases that she used to verbally sling at her boss Mel, while he was slinging hash at Mel's Diner?

Salads, Side Dishes & Appetizers   *225*

To try your chance and be entered in the free drawing for this fun gift basket, simply call my voicemail before **midnight tonight** and leave your name and the correct answer, and I'll print the lucky winner's name in my Saturday morning column.

Speaking of waitresses and restaurants, today's featured recipe is one I've been trying to get for more than a year.

It's the signature salad dressing recipe served at Annie's Cafe in Crete, Ill. and the one that was enjoyed by so many at my birthday tea earlier this month. Make sure to clip and save this one.

Annie's Cafe Old-Fashioned Celery Seed Salad Dressing

- Whisk all ingredients together in a bowl and chill for a few minutes before serving on your favorite green salad.

- Makes 2 cups.

INGREDIENTS:
1/2 cup sugar
1/3 cup vinegar
3 tablespoons grated onion
2 teaspoons celery seed
1 teaspoon salt
Dash black pepper
1 teaspoon dry mustard
1 cup vegetable oil

Grandma Potempa's flower gardens were some of the biggest and most beautiful blooming wonders I've ever seen.

BLT side salad an easy hit

September 12, 2007

Now that the gardens at the farm are starting to fade, it's a great time to try new recipes using any remaining vegetables that remain plentiful.

Like zucchini, when it comes to picking cucumbers, it's easy for one or two to blend in with the leaves and vines so perfectly, they get skipped over until they are so large, you nearly trip over them.

Today's recipe puts those larger cucumbers to good use, as well as all of those tiny cherry tomatoes that seem to ripen overnight.

I love a good bacon, lettuce and tomato club on toast, with lots of sandwich spread.

I've always thought the BLT concept would lend itself to a yummy side salad, except I hate the idea of soggy, slimy lettuce.

That's where the cucumbers come in. Peeled, sliced thin and sans seeds, they stay just firm enough in this salad to pass off as the all-important "L."

This BLT Side Salad is not only really delicious, it also really does taste like a BLT.

And sprinkled with a few bread crumbs to provide a hint of "toasted goodness," it also looks so appealing I couldn't resist sacrificing some column space to include a photo.

Phil's BLT Side Salad

● Peel cucumber and then slice into small pieces, making sure there are no seeds.

● In a medium bowl, toss cucumber with cherry tomato halves. Set aside.

● Cut bacon into 1-inch pieces and place in frying pan, sprinkled with Mrs. Dash. Fry until crisp, but not over-cooked. Drain bacon pieces and blot on paper towel. Allow to cool slightly.

● Toss cucumbers and tomatoes with salad dressing spread to coat. Add in crumbled bacon pieces and a sprinkle of black pepper and mix well.

● Serve sprinkled with bread crumbs.

● Makes 6 servings.

INGREDIENTS:

1 large salad cucumber or 2 cups sliced cucumber

16-20 cherry tomatoes, halved

1/2 pound bacon

1 heaping teaspoon of Mrs. Dash Original Seasoning

3/4 cup whipped salad dressing spread (like Miracle Whip)

Black pepper

Bread crumbs

Family's friend will be missed

October 10, 2007

One of the annual holiday traditions I enjoy with my parents is when we share a dinner get-together with our friends the Scamerhorns and the Russells before all of the holiday demands start to build.

The Scamerhorns always have all of us over before Christmas, and then my parents annually plan a New Year's Eve party. And in between, we all look forward to seeing our friends Joe and Debbie Russell of Kouts, Ind. at other get-togethers, fish fries or barbecues during the rest of the year.

On Friday, we received the sad news that our friend Joe passed away all-too-soon at age 64.

We knew he had just returned home from the hospital and my parents had talked with him on the phone less than a week earlier.

My parents have a special connection to Joe and Debbie, who I featured with a great photo in my second cookbook.

Joe's late uncle, Joe Ruszczyk, whose farm is across from the Scamerhorns' farm, was not only a good friend of my dad's, but also the best man at my parents' wedding. The wedding photo of my parents with Joe, who passed away in 1991, and my mom's twin sister, my Aunt Patty, as her maid of honor, is one of my favorite photos featured in my first cookbook.

Like his uncle, Joe Russell also passed away from heart problems.

Many readers who receive our Porter County editions are probably also familiar with Debbie, since she served as a longtime community columnist with a photo byline covering local events in Kouts.

I'm glad we still have so many wonderful memories and photographs to remember Joe and all of our great times together.

When selecting a recipe today, I decided to use Joann Scamerhorn's old-fashioned recipe for Picklelilly Relish, since I know it's something we've enjoyed, along with the Russells, at so many of our party get-togethers.

Joe Russell is seen with my parents at their house celebrating New Year's Eve 2000 and the arrival of a new decade.

Further From the Farm

INGREDIENTS:

RELISH:

10 green peppers, cored and cut into strips

2 red peppers (for color), cored and cut into strips

24 medium-sized onions, peeled

24 medium-sized green tomatoes, cored and cut into small chunks

24 medium-sized pickles, unpeeled and cut into strips

BRINE:

10 cups sugar

3 pints white vinegar (5 percent acidity)

4 tablespoons canning salt

1 cup pickling spice, tied in a cheesecloth

Mrs. Scamerhorn's Picklelilly Relish

- Wash all vegetables before prepping.

- Using a coarse blade, grind all vegetables with a hand grinder or grinder attachment of a mixer. (Do not use a food processor, as the vegetables will be mushy.)

- Place ground vegetables in a colander and drain off excess liquid for at least one hour.

- To make brine, bring all ingredients to a boil.

- Once brine has reached a boil, add drained vegetables and simmer for about 20 minutes or until vegetables change color.

- Pack relish into sterilized pint jars, seal, and process in a boiling water bath for 10 minutes.

- Makes 10 pints.

Joann Scamerhorn is ready to embrace summer with a tray of her delicious mini vegetable pizza, a prized recipe that can be found in my second cookbook.

Betsy Palmer sad about Phil Smidt's

October 31, 2007

Readers have written me about Phil Smidt's Restaurant in Whiting, Ind. closing earlier this month.

With a 97-year history, it's no wonder it attracted so many famous and everyday faces who enjoyed the food and atmosphere.

Since it opened in 1910, everyone from Jimmy Cagney, Bob Hope and Frank Sinatra to Babe Ruth, Jack Benny and the Prince of Wales pulled up a chair and picked up a menu.

My own parents, Chester and Peggy, have been eating at Phil Smidt's since they first got married in 1953.

Sue Harrison of Chesterton wrote me the following letter this week:

"I thought you might be able to help me if you'd be so kind. As you know, with the recent closure of Phil Smidt's, we've lost a restaurant legend. Our next-door neighbor was a devotee of their tartar sauce (!!!) which she believed to be homemade. I wondered if you might by chance have the recipe. I'd love to surprise my neighbor."

I called owners David and Barbara Welch and they are still confident the eatery will resurrect in a new location at some point in the future.

In addition to their famous frog legs, lake perch, gooseberry pie and side salads, their lightly tinted green homemade tartar sauce was another trademark favorite. During our chat, David was kind enough to give me the scoop on their tartar sauce recipe, or at least enough for me to share his close version.

Someone else who is sad about this restaurant's closing is actress Betsy Palmer, who originally hailed from East Chicago, Ind. and who celebrates her 81st birthday Thursday, Nov. 1, 2007.

INGREDIENTS:

1/2 cup mayonnaise (do NOT use Miracle Whip)

4 or 5 sweet pickle chips, patted dry and finely diced

1 heaping tablespoon finely minced fresh onion

Hint of garlic powder (optional)

Sprinkle of salt and black pepper

1 drop green food coloring

Phil Smidt's Tribute Tartar Sauce

- Mix all ingredients together and chill 4 to 5 hours before serving.

- Makes 1 cup.

Eckert Family part of town's legacy

January 16, 2008

As I've written in the past, the Eckert Family stands out as a founding family in our tiny farm town.

When I reached my teens and worked as a stock boy at the local grocery store, I spent many afternoons carrying out groceries for sisters Clara and Emma Eckert, who married brothers Ernie and Hank Zimmerman, as well as Erna Eckert, my stern third-grade teacher with a heart of gold, who married one of the middle brothers, Bob Eckert.

For years, all of the Eckert women would do their grocery shopping after their weekly wash and set at Sandy's Beauty Shop, run by our local beauty operator Sandra Eberhart.

After she retired and closed her shop a few years ago, Erna began going to Becky's Beauty Shop, run by another of her former students, a young beautician who was just a few years older than me in school.

I still smile when I think of the first time Erna came in for an appointment to the new shop and she asked for her usual "finger wave" (which I since have found out, is how ladies used to wear their hair in the 1940s ala Betty Grable), much to the confusion of poor Becky, who is much more familiar with styling mousse than setting gel.

I've been thinking a lot about the Eckert Family lately after they were kind enough to give me a copy of their family cookbook for Christmas called "August & Amelia Eckert Family Favorites: 100th Anniversary Collection."

Since Ash Wednesday is just three weeks away, I've included two of the family's meatless salad favorites, which are especially great served to compliment a lenten fish dinner.

Erna's Snow Pea Salad

- Quickly rinse peas in colander to remove any ice and drain well.

- In a medium bowl, whisk together mayonnaise and sour cream and add salt and pepper to taste.

- Add peas and all remaining ingredients to bowl with dressing and toss to coat. Serve chilled.

- Makes 8 servings.

SNOW PEA SALAD INGREDIENTS:

1 (16 ounce) package frozen snow peas

Salt and pepper

3/4 cup mayonnaise

1/4 cup sour cream

1 tablespoon basil

3 hard-boiled eggs, diced

1/2 cup celery, finely diced

1/4 cup onions, diced

3/4 cup nut meats of choice

1/4 cup sweet pickles, chopped

6 slices bacon, cooked crisp and crumbled

3/4 cup finely cubed American cheese

Clara's Potato Salad

- In a medium bowl, whisk together salad dressing, pickle relish, mustard, vinegar and salt and black pepper.

- Add all remaining ingredients and combine, mixing well.

- Note: Clara always reminded that potatoes should be boiled with a little salt and black pepper and that the dressing for this potato salad should sweet, while also a little sour.

- Makes 12 servings.

POTATO SALAD INGREDIENTS:

3 cups whipped salad dressing

1 heaping tablespoon pickle relish

1 tablespoon table mustard

1/2 to 3/4 cup sugar, depending on taste

3 tablespoons vinegar

Salt and pepper

8 cups potatoes, cooked and diced

1 cup celery, chopped

3/4 cup onions, diced

6 eggs, boiled and mashed

1/2 cup carrots, shredded

1/2 cup green pepper, diced

Friends Clara and Ernie Zimmerman were always a hard working, fun and generous couple in our small town. And her potato salad recipe is out of this world!

Casserole recipe reminds of past Easter memories

April 2, 2008

It wouldn't be Easter at the farm without delicious smoked Polish sausage.

If you're a familiar reader of this column, you've probably already guessed from reading previous columns that my mom is busy making her recipe for split green pea soup, the very recipe I published last month, using the leftover Easter ham bone.

As for our Polish sausage, these days, I usually buy in from one of the Polish meat markets on Archer Avenue on Chicago's South Side.

But every year, I still find myself missing the homemade Polish sausage we would get from our good farmer friends the Scamerhorn Family.

Of course, years ago, Grandma and Grandpa Potempa would make their own homemade sausage. But, after they were gone, our family became grateful for Joann Scamerhorn's late father, who I also liked to call "Grandpa Wojdula," who continued to make homemade Polish sausage and even had his own little smokehouse.

It's hard to believe he's been gone for five years. He died at age 94 on Feb. 1, 2003, just a few years after "Granny Wojdula," who died at age 80 on Jan. 1, 1999.

I've been thinking about them both a lot this week, after my friend Ann Scamerhorn, Steve and Joann's oldest daughter, gave me a recipe from her Aunt Mary Okeley,

who is now age 93, and is Granny Wojdula's surviving sister.

On Easter Sunday, Mrs. Okeley, made this old, old noodle casserole dish for their Easter family get-together, and it was a huge hit. She was so happy that everyone wanted the recipe, so I've decided to share it with readers this week.

If you visit the online computer version of this column, you can see a great photograph of Joann Scamerhorn and her sister Alice, with their Aunt Mary, on Easter Sunday.

This is a wonderful family photo I took in the late 1990s of the entire Scamerhorn Family, including Granny and Grandpa Wojdula and Grandma Scamerhorn, along with Ann and Amy's Aunt Alice and Uncle Byron.

Mrs. Okeley's Easy Noodle Casserole

- Preheat oven to 350 degrees.

- Dissolve bouillon cubes in water in a large bowl.

- Add canned soup, onion, Worcestershire sauce and garlic powder and mix well.

- Stir in cottage cheese, sour cream and noodles; mix well.

- Pour mixture into a greased 2-1/2-quart baking dish.

- Sprinkle with the Parmesan cheese and desired amount of paprika.

- Cover baking dish with foil and bake for 45 minutes or until heated thoroughly.

- Makes 8 to 10 servings.

- Note: Casserole may be assembled the night before, covered, and refrigerated, but allow to stand at room temperature for at least 30 minutes before baking.

INGREDIENTS:

3 chicken-flavored bouillon cubes

1/4 cup boiling water

1 (10-3/4-ounce) can cream of mushroom soup, undiluted

1/2 cup chopped onion

2 tablespoons Worcestershire sauce

1/8 teaspoon garlic powder

2 cups (16 ounces) cottage cheese

2 cups (16 ounces) sour cream

1 (16-ounce) package medium noodles, cooked and drained

1/4 cup shredded Parmesan cheese

Paprika to taste

Alice Bailey (left) and Joann Scamerhorn (far right) are shown with their aunt, Mary Okeley, 93, (center) at the family's 2008 Easter gathering.

South Bend gal off to Pillsbury Bake-Off

April 9, 2008

It's hard to believe, but it's time once again for the annual Pillsbury Bake-Off.

In 2006, it was Mary Beth Schultz of Valparaiso, Ind. and her award-winning Chicken Fajita Quiche in the spotlight competing in Orlando, Fla.

This weekend, it's Sherry Klinedinst, 44, of South Bend, Ind. who's our local creative cook we'll all be cheering for to win the big $1 million dollar check, which will be announced live from the 2008 43rd Annual Pillsbury Bake-Off on Tuesday on location at The Fairmont Hotel in Dallas, Texas.

And, just as with the previous two Pillsbury Bake-Offs, in 2004 in Hollywood, Calif., and 2006 in Orlando, Fla., I'll shadow our local contestant's every step and spoon stir with daily updates in my offBeat column on the lookListen page of The Times.

Klinedinst's winning recipe for Creamy Smoked Salmon Cups is shared in my column this week for readers to sample. It is one of 100 winning recipes all competing for the grand prize. The entire collection of this year's contest recipes are available in the new "43rd Annual Pillsbury Bake-Off Cookbook" ($3.99), which went on sale this week at the check-out magazine racks in major supermarkets.

Popular Food Network television host and lifestyle expert Sandra Lee has been selected to announce the next million-dollar recipe during the April 15 awards ceremony and the official announcement, scheduled for 8:30 a.m. Central Time Tuesday morning. This 43rd contest brings eight men and 92 women competing with a diverse range of original recipes from pizzas and appetizers to sweet treats, breakfasts and brunches, and Mexican-inspired dishes.

From the tens of thousands of recipe entries, contest officials used rigorous screening, taste panels and kitchen testing to select the final 100 recipes. The recipe creators-amateur cooks from across the country will now prepare their recipes in the contest finals on April 14, in Dallas competing for the really serious dough

---

that's at stake.

Seven of the contest prizes will be determined by a panel of judges working in jury-room secrecy. One award, "the America's Favorite Recipe Award," will be determined by consumers across America.

For more information, visit the Bake-Off Contest Web site at www.bakeoff. com and watch my daily column beginning Saturday for all the best on-location behind-the-scenes "dish."

Creamy Smoked Salmon Cups

- Heat oven to 375 degrees.

- Spray 48 minimuffin cups with Crisco Original No-Stick Cooking Spray.

- In medium bowl, mix cream cheese and sour cream until well blended. Stir in lemon-pepper seasoning, chives, capers and salt. Stir in corn until well mixed.

- Fold in salmon.

- Separate dough from both cans into 8 rectangles; press perforations to seal.

- Cut each rectangle into 6 (2-inch) squares. Press one square in bottom and up side of each mini muffin cup. Spoon slightly less than 1 tablespoon salmon filling into each cup.

- Bake 10 to 18 minutes or until light golden brown. Cool 2 minutes; remove from pan to serving platter. Serve warm.

- Makes 48 appetizers.

INGREDIENTS:

4 ounces cream cheese, softened

1/2 cup sour cream

1 teaspoon lemon-pepper seasoning

2 tablespoons chopped fresh chives

2 teaspoons small capers, drained

1/4 teaspoon salt

1 (10 ounce) box Green Giant Niblets frozen corn & butter sauce, thawed

4 ounces smoked salmon, flaked

2 (8 ounce) cans Pillsbury refrigerated crescent dinner rolls

Sherry Klinedinst of South Bend, takes a break from her contest cooking in Dallas, Texas, as one of the national finalist for the 43rd Annual Pillsbury Bake-Off to snap a photo with Food Network's cooking personality Sandra Lee, who was serving as the celebrity host for the 2008 competition.

Names and phrases passed on and on

April 30, 2008

It's surprising how often we use catchphrases, names and words in our everyday conversation without really knowing how they originated.

This occurred to me earlier this month after I saw the Associated Press obituary for one of the two Swiss ice skaters who were part of the original Ice Follies show as comedy ice skaters: Werner Groebli and Hansruedi (Hans) R. Mauch.

You might recognize them more easily by their performing names, Frick and Frack.

Always together and known for their silly stunts on ice, Frick died on April 14, 2008 in Zurich at age 92.

According to David Thomas, one of his skating partners after Mauch retired, Frick died from complications after breaking a leg at a nursing home outside Zurich.

Mauch, aka Frack, died in 1979, and once described the origin of their show biz names as a result of Frick's taking his name from a small village in Switzerland and Frack's coming from the Swiss-German word for a frock coat.

For years, while growing up, I have always heard the names "Frick" and "Frack" used to describe any two people so closely associated, they seem indistinguishable. In fact, I've used the expression many times while teaching my university classes when referring to students who fit the description.

And it never fails; after hearing me make the reference, my students give me a quizzical look.

Now, I can finally tell them the origin of this expression.

My own family, my mom especially, uses similar expressions for the same "joined at the hip" types, especially for people dressed alike.

Most often, names like "The Bobbsey Twins," taken from characters from the popular series of books, and "The Gold Dust Twins," inspired by the logo used for a line of soap powder manufactured years ago by Lever Brothers, conveyed the same meaning.

While growing up, I also remember these same references used on popular television shows from the past, such as episodes of "I Love Lucy" and "The Honeymooners."

Today's recipe comes from one of my Valparaiso University students who has, at times, given me a quizzical look over some of the dated expressions I've used.

Kyle Carlson of Fort Wayne is a freshman at VU, and he made this delicious recipe for his favorite taco salad for his demonstrative speech in my public-speaking class.

INGREDIENTS:

1 pound ground hamburger

1 small onion, chopped

1 envelope taco seasoning

2 (10 ounce) bags of chopped salad lettuce

1 quart red cherry tomatoes, rinsed

1 (12 ounce) bag nacho-flavored corn chips

1 (16 ounce) package Mexican-style shredded cheese

1 (14 ounce) bottle of Western salad dressing

Kyle's Favorite Taco Salad

● In a skillet heated over medium heat, brown ground beef with chopped onion. Drain. Sprinkle in seasoning and mix with meat to combine.

● In a large bowl, gently chop or break apart lettuce into bite-size pieces. After rinsing tomatoes, slice each one in half and add to lettuce.

● Add meat to lettuce and tomatoes in bowl and toss.

● Lightly crush flavored corn chips and add to salad, along with shredded cheese.

● Lastly, add enough salad dressing to create desired consistency.

● Salad is best when prepared fresh just before serving.

● Makes 8 servings.

"Frick without Frack"

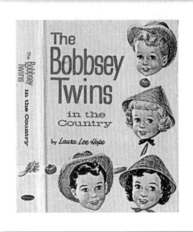

From "Frick and Frack" to "The Gold Dust Twins" and "The Bobbsey Twins," names and expressions go hand-in-hand from generation to generation.

Egg nests surprise both Mom and Aunt Ruby

May 28, 2008

Everyone needs and deserves a smile.

And some stories can work that magic.

As I've mentioned in previous columns, my dad keeps busy in his spare time making birdhouses from dried gourds from the garden and hollow tree logs from our woods.

His specialty is bluebird houses, topped with a neat little cedar shingle. I like to tell co-workers these birdhouse will attract not just any bluebirds to their homes, but "the bluebird of happiness."

Earlier this month, while my mom was working in the backyard, she discovered a lone, completely intact Robin's blue-speckled egg under one of our apple trees.

Remembering that my dad mentioned one of his bluebird houses near the garden had a fresh nest filled with five new eggs (unusual, since bluebirds only usually lay three eggs), my mom's idea was to simply slip on her garden gloves and the slip the orphaned

This February 2006 photo of my mom, her twin sister, my Aunt Patty (middle) and their older sister, my Aunt Ruby, is shot in Downtown Chicago at the Drury Lane Theatre at historic Water Tower Place. I took the trio, and my friend Irene Jakubowski out for lunch in the city and then to see a production of "Nunsense.".

robin's egg into the tiny nest in tiny bluebird house.

Fortunately, she mentioned her motherly plan to my father, who was working nearby, and he explained the shock and confusion of the mother bluebird to find yet ANOTHER egg added to her nest.

My dad then explained there would be even more confusion for this family of bluebirds if, by some extreme act of nature, the robin egg DID hatch inside with the little bluebirds, resulting in a giant, beaked "black sheep" trying to blend in with this unsuspecting bluebird family.

My mom's older sister, my Aunt Ruby, has also been facing her own egg-ceptional situation this month.

While working around some low-growing ground-cover shrubs near the outer wall of her house, she discovered a mama duck sitting on a nest with 10 eggs!

And since Aunt Ruby lives right in the middle of a house-to-house neighborhood in Highland, her home for more than 47 years, there aren't any ponds in sight. (Even the Calumet River is quite a distance away from her address.)

It will be interesting to see what happens once Aunt Ruby's new quacking lawn ornaments hatch.

Anytime we visit Aunt Ruby, we usually have fruits and vegetables to share, starting with fresh-picked asparagus this time of year and by July, assorted peppers, onions and tomatoes.

Today's recipe is not only easy, but also very healthy. It was shared during my Valparaiso University public speaking class, which I teach every semester. Student Kristin Buch of Chicago shared this unique salsa recipe as her demonstrative speech assignment.

INGREDIENTS:

1 large onion, peeled and chopped

2 heaping teaspoons fresh minced garlic

1 red pepper, diced

1 yellow pepper, diced

1 green pepper, diced

1 small jalepeno pepper, diced (optional)

Juice of 1 small lime

Salt and pepper to taste

Easy Tomato-less Salsa

● Prepare and mix all ingredients, except lime, in a mixing bowl.

● Roll the lime on a hard surface, like countertop or table, to open up juice glands, before slice in half.

● Squeeze lime juice over ingredients in bowl and mix well to combine.

● *Adjust seasoning to taste and serve with warm tortilla chips.

● Makes 4 1/2 cups of salsa.

Farm gathering features Polish favorites

July 16, 2008

My dad celebrated his 79th birthday on Saturday surrounded by family, friends and all of his favorite Polish foods.

Over the weekend, we were guests at a large barbecue and corn boil at a neighboring "retired" dairy farm.

Harry and Sandy Maranowicz are a terrific couple and part of a large Polish family who keep the traditions started by Harry's father Bruno, who died in 1989.

It was Bruno's parents who came from Poland and purchased the tiny 80-acre dairy farm near our farm. Today, Harry and Sandy come down from "the city" aka Downers Grove, Ill. and spend their weekends at the farm, including their 10-year tradition of hosting this large July gathering, which features favorite Polish meats and recipes from both the city and farm.

Harry and four of his siblings attended Saturday's party, along with our neighboring farm friends the Wappels and the Scamerhorns.

Clara Mae Rucka, Harry's youngest sister who now lives in Hoffman Estates, Ill., made her mother's favorite recipe for tiny Polish dumplings called "Kopytka."

And since the Whiting Pierogi Festival is just a week away, I managed to convince her to share this recipe, which she has "tweaked" in recent years to make it even more simple and convenient.

She included a nice note, along with her recipe, explaining: "A writer I am not, but boy can I make dumplings."

You can see photos from this farm gathering, including one of Clara Mae with me in the potato patch, with today's column.

"These potato dumplings have been part of our family gatherings, celebrations, and yes, often our

Here's Clara Mae Rucka, sister to Harry Maranowicz, as we stand in her brother's potato patch for the sake of quick photo op. Her recipe for tiny potato dumplings are delicious and an annual staple at Harry's summer picnics.

shared meals during a busy work week. Over the years, I have made these dumplings with my family and my heart, Clara Mae wrote.

"This recipe is not mine, but that of a Mrs. Emily Rogowski. Mrs. Rogowski and my mother, Celia, were friends. No, I correct that, they were good 'girlfriends.' When they were together, what big fun and laughs they shared.

Mrs. Rogowski owned and operated a small grocery store on the Southwest Side of Chicago. Located in the middle of the block, it almost looked like the other homes. Often after entering the store, you needed to ring a bell at the counter for her to come and add up your groceries. This was often done with a pen and paper. Mrs. Rogowski was also an amazing baker and cook. Besides the grocery store, she also ran a catering business consisting of salad, roasted chicken, beef, Polish sausage, sauerkraut, dumplings, coleslaw, vegetables , and pastries of cookies, kolachky, and cheese cake...all home made.

As a young girl (I'm now 51), I would help with this catering business. This was where the dumplings come in. Her dumplings were made fresh daily and on the site of where the celebration was being held. Which means, dumplings were made for 50-350 people depending on the celebration. A lot of memorable conversations happened while making this many dumplings. Although she originally used real mashed potatoes, instant works well.

This tradition continues in my home with my husband Bob, and my two children, Angela and Brian. Again, there is always conversation and laughs while making dumplings as a family. As Mom always said, 'Family and girlfriends are two of life's blessings.'

Kopytka (Polish Fingerling Potato Dumplings)

● In a large bowl, use a whisk to combine potato flakes with melted butter and just enough hot water until mixture begins to look like thin mashed potatoes. Allow to set for 5 minutes.

● Add eggs and baking powder and then begin adding flour, a little at a time, just enough flour until a heavy dough is formed. Allow dough to rest in bowl for 20 minutes, covered with a cloth or towel.

● On a floured surface, roll a handful of dough into a snake-like shape, approximately 1/2-inch in diameter.

● Cut the piece of dough into 1/2-inch to 3/4-inch pieces and roll pieces in hand to make tiny, individual dumplings.

● Drop finished dumplings into pot of boiling salted water for 6 minutes. Stir gently. After boiling, immerse in cold water. Drain.

INGREDIENTS:
1 1/2 cups dry instant potatoes
2 sticks butter, melted
6 eggs, beaten
1 teaspoon baking powder
2-3 cups flour
1 medium onion, chopped
3/4 cup bread crumbs (garnish)

● Boiled dumplings may be frozen or refrigerated until ready to serve.

● To serve, fry dumplings in butter and chopped onion, sprinkling with bread crumbs for garnish during final minutes of frying.

● Makes 6 dozen.

Further From the Farm

Pets are friends missed and remembered

July 30, 2008

My family has enjoyed the companionship of a long list of wonderful pets through the years.

And it's always sad when a pet dies.

During the past six years I've written this "From the Farm" column, I've written about the passing of some of our beloved pets, like our first Maine coon cat Tracker II and even our farm rooster Oscar.

Recently, we lost two other favorite pets.

On May 23, my Dad lost his favorite farm dog Lucky, who was seven-years-old.

And on July 20, my little yellow canary bird Rudy sang his final song.

Rudy was 8-years-old and he had a lot of personality.

His favorite treat in the morning was to have a Cheerio, which he would hold and eat like a tiny donut.

I even brought Rudy to one of my book events in 2003 at Barnes & Noble, in Merrillville, and readers had a chance, in person, to hear a sample of his warbling.

One of the questions I would often be asked about is why I chose the name "Rudy."

My family liked to kid me that he was named after one of the cast members from the original season of the reality show "Survivor," Rudy Boesch, the 72-year-old tough-as-nails retired Navy Seal. They figured any little canary brave enough to live with a 40-pound Maine coon cat was a true survivor.

Actually, he was named after singer Rudy Vallee and the canary that was a pet of newspaper gossip columnist Dorothy Kilgallen, who was a regular panelist on the old panel game show "What's My Line?"

Kilgallen and her husband Richard Kollmar were also the stars of their own popular morning radio show called "Breakfast with Dick and Dorothy," which featured banter about the New York plays and parties they had attended the night before. The radio show was done live at their spacious 16-room Park Avenue apartment and part of the charm was the sound of their pet canary chirping in the background.

Photos and columns about Lucky, Tracker and Rudy have been featured in both of my previous books.

My parents still have the company of their prized indoor Maine coon cat, Tracker III, a half

Rudy

brother to our first feline of the same name,

And they also enjoy daily walks with their collie dog Laddie, 6, who definitely has a mind of his own.

Earlier this month, while Dad was walking Laddie in the early morning hours, he stopped along the woods line to pick black raspberries so we could make jam. Seeing dad carefully pick the ripe berries one by one, Laddie followed his lead, carefully picking only ripened berries off the thorn vines and swallowing them whole.

As for today's recipe, it is a definite crowd-pleaser and it contains a fun and very retro ingredient: Green Goddess Salad Dressing.

Green Goddess Dip

- Combine all ingredients in a large bowl; mix well.

- Spread ingredients in a 9-inch by 13-inch glass pan.

- Chill spread for at least an hour.

- Serve with tortilla chips.

- Makes 8-10 servings.

INGREDIENTS:

2 green peppers, finely diced

4 tomatoes, finely diced

2 bunches green onions, sliced

4 cups shredded mozzarella cheese

4 cups shredded sharp cheddar cheese

1 (16-ounce) bottle Green Goddess Salad Dressing

1 to 5 dashes hot sauce

Tortilla chips

Hearst Gossip Columnist Dorothy Kilgallen not only hosted a popular morning radio show from the dining room of her New York apartment, but she was also a powerful journalist, in addition to her game show panelist identity on CBS's "What's My Line?".

Field work and weeding go with dreaming

August 6, 2008

Even though it's been two decades since I worked summers as part of field weeding crews. I still dream about it.

From cutting corn out of the soybean fields and weeding peppermint to spading up the dirt around new rows of strawberry plants and "hilling" up the sand around other plants like tomatoes, peppers and potatoes, it was hard work and long days, usually 7 a.m. to 4 p.m. But the money earned always meant so much more than "an easy reward."

Because this was the money I, as well as my older brothers and sisters, used for new school clothes and spending money for going to Indiana Beach.

And of all the things to weed, the most tedious assignment was always carrots.

Lately, I've been snacking on carrots at work in hopes of dropping a couple of extra pounds since this is the summer of my 20-year high school reunion.

For the past week, my dad has been picking carrots and beets from the garden and my mom has been busy canning large quarts of Grandma Potempa's pickled beets recipe.

Whenever I think of my mom and carrots, I'm reminded of her own dreaming experience of weeding while growing up and a story that she and her twin sister, my Aunt Patty and their older sister, my Aunt Ruby, still laugh about today.

While weeding the large, vast carrot fields at the Gehring Family Farms, during the summers of their youth, my mom and her sisters would also be very "over-tired" and weary by bedtime. On one particular night, my mom's sisters discovered my mom out of bed busily picking at the large floral print rug in the middle of the hallway, while still sound asleep, believing she was still weeding carrots.

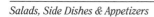

On the subject of losing some weight, I've also been using the healthy low-calorie recipe for grilled tilapia with a fruit salsa topping, as featured in my latest "More From the Farm" cookbook. A number of readers say they have trouble finding jars of fruit salsa, which I've always found at Wiseway or health food stores.

Today's recipe solves that problem and it is from Glenn Thompson of Valparaiso. Because he doesn't particularly like the cilantro/vinegar taste of most salsas, he makes his salsa with peaches and pineapple for a more "tangy" flavor.

Salads, Side Dishes & Appetizers

INGREDIENTS:

3 pounds tomatoes, seeded and chopped

1 bunch celery, tops removed and chopped

2 green peppers, seeded and chopped

6 to 8 Jalapeno peppers, seeded and chopped

1 or 2 hot banana peppers, seeded and chopped

1 or 2 cubanelle peppers, seeded and chopped

Half of a red onion, finely chopped

4 peaches, peeled, pitted and chopped

2 tablespoons lime juice

1 (6-ounce) can tomato paste

1 (20-ounce) can crushed pineapple in 100 percent juice (not syrup)

1 (28-ounce) can crushed tomatoes

Glenn's Tangy Peach-Pineapple Salsa

- Mix above ingredients in a large bowl or container.

- Depending on the size of your electric blender's pitcher, blend mixture in several batches.

- Place blended ingredients in a non-aluminum pot and bring to a slow boil for 15 to 20 minutes, stirring often. Lower heat and simmer, uncovered, for about one hour.

- Refrigerate salsa overnight; mix well before serving with tortilla chips.

- Stores well refrigerated.

- Makes about 1/2 gallon salsa.

Auntie Judy, my dad's sister, is shown here with Uncle Joey and my cousins Elaine and Bobby. Growing up, fair-skinned Auntie Judy never did field and garden work like her siblings, preferring to stay inside for cooking and cleaning duties.

Say hello during 30th Annual Popcorn Parade

September 3, 2008

I credit the first story of my journalism career to be when I interviewed the late and great Orville Redenbacher in September 1988 for my first story assignment as a freshman at Valparaiso University working for the college newspaper The Torch.

I drove out to the Porter County Airport in Valparaiso, Ind. to meet Redenbacher for my interview, just as he arrived in town early in the week on Wednesday before the big 10th Annual Popcorn Festival weekend that year.

Both he and his grandson Gary Redenbacher were extremely nice. When the story published that Friday carrying my byline, I was hooked on both settling on a career in journalism and my love of interviewing people: both famous and everyday great personalities.

It's hard to believe that first interview was two decades ago and just two weeks after my 18th birthday.

This weekend marks two special occasions.

It's the 30th anniversary of the annual Popcorn Festival in Valparaiso and it's also my parents' 55th wedding anniversary.

Orville Redenbacher

I asked them what they wanted to do to celebrate their special day and they've decided they want to attend the Popcorn Festival for the first time. They're especially excited about watching the famous and fabled Popcorn Parade on Saturday, which I'll be marching in along with my friends from The Times.

I've marched in many parades over the years, from Peirogi Parade to The Wizard of Oz Parade, but never the Popcorn Parade.

I hope if you're a faithful reader and you're watching from the sidelines, that you'll shout out my name so I can toss you (or hand you) something special from the basket of great candies and toys I'll be carrying with me. If you've ever seen me in any of our region parades before, you already know I'll be wearing my German lederhosen and green checkered shirt (even though I'm Polish), with a small stuffed goat perched on my shoulder.

Redenbacher and this festival, which attracts more than 75,000 visitors every year, features a 100-unit parade with floats constructed entirely of popcorn, hot air balloons, music, crafts, have inspired many traditions over the years.

But one of my favorite keepsakes, given to me years ago by former Popcorn Festival Executive Director Glennas Kueck, remains a rare treasure among my kitchen collection.

For one year only, a special festival cookbook compiled in 1990 was published following the first -- and only -- popcorn recipe contest.

The contest was sponsored by a local company, Okaya Electric America, according to Kueck.

The recipe that won top prize for the 1990 contest was created by then-Morgan Township High School senior Rick Steur for his recipe for "popcorn pizza."

All things unusual and attention-getting have long been a festival trademark, a trend started by the late Orville Redenbacher, who inspired the first festival with his Valparaiso factory and farming roots to the area.

"When you think about that cooking contest, it's a lot like Orville's ambitions," Kueck said.

"You can do anything you want with popcorn if you put your mind to it. I was recently talking with Orville's longtime business partner, Charlie Bowman, who still lives in Valparaiso. He was explaining just how amazing Orville's experimentation and accomplishments with popcorn were over the years. Charlie said if someone is lucky enough to be able to develop a hybrid of popcorn in a lifetime, it's truly a fantastic feat. Orville was able to create two hybrids in his lifetime. What does that tell you about this man and his spirit of accomplishment?"

When Orville died at age 88 in 1995.

Popcorn Pizza

- Preheat oven to 425 degrees.

- Grease a 12-inch pizza pan.

- Spread dough on pan. Add sauce provided with mix kit. Spread on evenly.

- Brown meat in skillet and drain off excess grease.

- Sprinkle meat over sauce.

- Spread mozzarella cheese over meat.

- Bake in oven on 425 degrees for 15 minutes.

- Remove from oven and immediately add popcorn, cheese and sprinkle with garlic salt.

- Return to oven for three minutes.

- Allow to cool for 10 minutes before serving.

- Serves: 6

INGREDIENTS:

1 commercial boxed (12-1/2 ounce) pizza mix
1 pound ground hamburger
1 cup shredded mozzarella cheese
1 cup shredded colby cheese
1/2 cup chopped onions
5 cups popped popcorn
Garlic salt (added to taste)

Anyone have Goldblatt's Cheesecake recipe?

November 19, 2008

I know it's not even Thanksgiving yet, but all minds are on Christmas, in our region, because of Saturday's big festival in Hammond, Ind. celebrating the 25th anniversary of the classic 1983 movie "A Christmas Story."

The film is region claim-to-fame author and radio personality Jean Shepherd's homage to his childhood in Hammond during the holidays.

I'll be judging the first-ever "Christmas Story Festival Fudge Recipe Contest" on Saturday, so I wanted to share a reminder about the details.

But first, thank you to the more than 160 people who attended my Thanksgiving program with my parents at Hammond Public Library last Sunday.

And as promised, I want to ask for readers' help with a recipe request I have been asked about for the past 8 years I've been writing this column.

Since the Hammond Public Library's lobby features the original "grand clock" from the old Goldblatt's Department Store from Downtown Hammond featured in "A Christmas Story" (although, in the scene where Ralphie visits with Santa and the mean elf, the store is called Higby's Department Store), a number of guests mentioned they would love to have the recipe for "Goldblatt's Department Store's Cheesecake." It was made and sold there for decades. If anyone has this, please let me know.

I'm in good company, framed by two elves as I prepare to serve as judge for a fudge recipe contest in Hammond, Ind. in 2008 honoring Northwest Indiana's holiday movie claim-to-fame "A Christmas Story."

My recipe today is as different from visions of cheesecake and fudge as possible. But it's a special one.

It's the original exact recipe for the cooked red cabbage scene in "A Christmas Story," which Ralphie and his little brother Randy hated so much (it was served with meatloaf).

However, despite what kids might think, this is delicious!!!

Ralphie's Mom's
Braised Red Cabbage

- Toss together cabbage, red wine vinegar, salt and pepper in a large bowl.

- Cook bacon in a large Dutch oven over medium high flame for 10 minutes or until just crisp.

- Add onion to bacon and saute another 5 minutes or until tender.

- Stir in cabbage mixture, apples, red wine, sugar and garlic to onion and bacon mixture in the pot. Cover and reduce heat to medium and simmer 30 to 35 minutes, adding a splash of water, if necessary.

- Makes 6 servings.

- Recipe courtesy of Warner Bros. Studios

INGREDIENTS:

1 medium-size red cabbage, thinly sliced
1/4 cup red wine vinegar
1 teaspoon salt
1/2 teaspoon black pepper
4 bacon slices, diced
1 large onion, thinly sliced
2 apples, peeled and diced
3/4 cup red wine
1/4 cup sugar
1/4 teaspoon minced garlic

Christine Griggs, of Hammond, one of the winners in Downtown Hammond Council's 2009 A Christmas Story Fudge Recipe Contest held Nov. 21, 2009 displays her winning fudge, while flanked by "Little Ralphie" look-a-like Zane Rayson, 6, of Hammond and Karen Maravilla as the movie's "Grouchy Elf."

Florida visit includes jam-packed week

March 11, 2009

DATELINE: Tampa -- Philip Potempa is reporting from Florida while traveling.

Thank you to all the readers who said hello at last weekend's charity events. The winning recipes from Saturday's NWI Lupus Foundation Chili cook-off will appear next week after I've returned with my parents from visiting my dad's sisters, Auntie Lottie and Auntie Loretta, at their homes near Sarasota, Fla.

Sunday's 8th Annual Meals on Wheels Dine with the Chefs event at Avalon Manor in Hobart was also a great success.

The silent auction, featuring a bottle of Uncle Swede's and Auntie Lottie's Dandelion Wine was a bit hit and helped raise some of the money toward the day's $50,000 goal.

In fact, despite the tough security regulations, my parents and I managed to pack some of last spring's bottled Dandelion Wine, plus some wild black raspberry jam, red raspberry jam and apricot preserves to share with both aunts.

Today's recipe was one of the delicious featured hot appetizers served as part of the first course of Sunday's Meals on Wheels feast, for which I served as master of ceremonies for the afternoon, introducing each course.

The "meat-free" tart filling makes this an ideal menu item for our meatless Fridays during Lent.

Rustiç Onion Tart Appetizer

- Prepare pie dough and keep chilled in refrigerator while preparing onion filling.

- Peel and slice onions.

- Heat olive oil and butter in a large heavy-bottomed saute pan on medium heat. Once butter is melted, add onions and salt and pepper. Cook, stirring occasionally for 10 minutes, until onions have softened and are translucent. Reduce heat to low and cook for an additional 40 minutes, stirring constantly to caramelize onions, but watching so they don't burn or stick, adding a splash of water if needed.

- Add Balsamic vinegar and cook another 10 minutes until onions are entirely caramelized. Remove from heat.

INGREDIENTS:

1 bottom pie crust (your favorite)
3 medium red onions
2 tablespoons olive oil
1 tablespoon butter
Salt and Pepper, dash of each
1 teaspoon Balsamic vinegar
3/4 cup grated Gruyere cheese, divided use

- Preheat oven to 450 degrees. Remove dough from chilling and let stand 5 minutes before rolling out.

- Roll dough on lightly floured surface to make a 10-inch diameter. Remove dough circle to a cookie sheet lined with parchment paper.

- Place all but a couple tablespoons of cheese in the center of the dough, spreading cheese within 1 and 1/2 inch away from edge of crust.

- Add onions to cover cheese. Fold in the edges of crust towards center, allowing just a small circle of exposed onions in the center and sprinkling onion center with remaining cheese in center of tart.

- Place tart on cookie sheet in middle rack of oven and bake 10 minutes at 450 degrees, reducing heat to 350 and baking for another 20-25 minutes, until crust is golden brown.

- Remove from oven and allow to set 10 minutes before serving in slices.

- Makes 6 servings.

I seem right at home with Ann Scamerhorn standing in the tomato patch and enjoying the inviting sun's rays, while she prefers to shield her eyes and skin to make sure not to become "over-ripe" and red!

Columbia's Spanish Yellow Rice a family favorite

March 25, 2009

My Grandma Potempa always loved rice, as does my dad and my aunts, while my mom prefers potatoes for her usual side.

In fact, one of our favorite family recipes is for my dad's sister's, my late Auntie Judy's, recipe for her Baked Chicken and Rice, featured long ago in this column and now preserved in my original "From the Farm" cookbook published in 2004.

When I traveled with my parents earlier this month to Florida to visit my dad's sisters, my Auntie Lottie and Auntie Loretta, one of the restaurants we wanted to experience ranks as the oldest restaurant in all of Florida and holds the title of "the world's largest Spanish restaurant."

And as you might imagine, it is famous for its rice recipes as well as the beautiful dining room murals paying tribute to Christopher Columbus.

The Columbia, tagged "the Gem of Spanish Restaurants," opened in 1905, is celebrating more than a century of success in historic downtown Ybor City, near Tampa. It now is run by the fourth and fifth generation of Cuban immigrant and founder Casimiro Hernandez Sr.

In addition to its rice claim-to-fame, we were eager to toast a glass of its delicious sangria fruit wine around the Columbia's indoor courtyard fountain to experience the same atmosphere enjoyed by so many famous names of the past.

President John F. Kennedy, actress Esther Williams, actor Cesar Romero, television legends Garry Moore and Carol Burnett, Marilyn Monroe and Joe DiMaggio all dined at the Columbia.

Even Auntie Lottie agreed the Columbia's Spanish Yellow Rice is the best she's ever tasted, and when made with vegetable broth, it's ideal for Lenten menus.

My dad with his sisters Lottie and Loretta during a September 2003 Florida visit.

Columbia Restaurant's
Spanish Yellow Rice

- In a large skillet or cooking pot over low flame, heat olive oil and saute onion, green pepper, garlic tomatoes and bay leaves until onion and pepper begin to turn soft.

- Add rice, saffron or food coloring, and broth and bring mixture to a boil, lower heat, cover and cook for 18 minutes, either on top of stove or in a 400 degree oven.

- Add peas and other garnishes as desired.

- Makes 4 servings.

INGREDIENTS:

1/2 cup extra-virgin olive oil
1 large Spanish onion, chopped
1 medium-size green pepper, cut in strips
4 garlic cloves, minced
2 bay leaves
2 tomatoes, seeded, peeled and chopped
2 cups long-grain rice, uncooked
1/2 teaspoon saffron or yellow food coloring
2 teaspoons salt
4 cups chicken (or vegetable) broth
3/4 cup cooked green peas
Pimento pieces, red pepper pieces and parsley for color and garnish as desired

What a great meal, while soaking up historical surroundings, as I join my parents at the landmark Columbia Restaurant just outside Tampa, Fla., where a delicious pitcher of Sangria fruit wine always awaits.

Reader proud of potato salad legacy

April 1, 2009

I had a wonderful visit last week with reader Janet Bremer of Crete, Ill.

She first contacted me earlier in the year to tell me about a family cookbook she was working on for her children, sharing many of her relatives' delicious Dutch recipes and traditions.

Designing it in the style of a scrapbook, she recently completed her project and called it "A Treasury of Table and Traditions."

What especially fascinated me about this masterpiece was a particular section with heirloom recipes from her grandmother who, alone used to cook for weddings of up to 250 guests, and also a few famous recipes from her own mother, Jennie Hoeksema, who appeared as a featured "Cook of the Week" in the old Hammond Times in 1955.

Hoeksema, who died 10 years ago today, April 1, 1999, is a region culinary claim to fame, since it was she who started the deli at the old Burger's Super Market in 1959, the same chain of stores that are now called Strack & Van Til.

Today, this chain still makes her Mom's original potato salad recipe at their Munster store and other locations.

"I know of people that come from out east and bring a cooler so they can take home some of that potato salad," Janet said.

"I also have a picture of Mom with an old cart filled with groceries that was used in store advertisement in the 1950s. As for sharing the recipe, since Strack & Van Til still makes it, and my mom signed off on her recipes to Mr. Burger way back when, I feel I should check with Dave Wilkinson, CEO of Strack before I give it out, as well as check with my brother about this. It would be so fitting on the 10th anniversary of her death to talk about her salad. One problem might be that the stores use a product called Ivory Jell, which is a stabilizer for use in commercial salads and products. It does nothing to the flavor, so I imagine it can be made without it."

After speaking with the good people at Stracks, Janet decided it might be better to share a great alternate recipe for me to showcase for Times readers.

She included a large recipe portion since it is ideal to serve for Easter dinner with all the menu usuals, like ham, baked beans, sauerkraut and sausage. Janet was kind enough to drop off a sample for me at the newspaper office and it's not only delicious, but the recipe is also sold at Stracks and also includes her Mom's famed potato salad recipe as the ingredient base.

Jennie Hoeksema's Potato-Macaroni and Spaghetti Salad

- Mix all ingredients together.

- Add mayonnaise slowly, one tablespoon at a time, blending ingredients and adding more mayonnaise a little at a time to create desired consistency.

- Makes 15 to 20 servings or roughly 6 pounds.

INGREDIENTS:

8 cups of your favorite deli potato salad

3 cups cooked elbow macaroni

3 cups cooked spaghetti, broken into 1-inch pieces

1 green pepper, chopped

1/8 cup chopped onion or more to taste

1/2 cup diced sweet pickles

2 pimentos, diced or more to taste

1 tablespoon sugar

1/4 teaspoon black pepper

1/2 (scant) teaspoon salt

Mayonnaise to taste

Jennie Hoeksema featured in 1955 grocery advertisement.

Fred Waring and famed blender still in demand

July 15, 2009

Sunday's 80th birthday party for my dad at the Avalon Manor in Merrillville, Ind. was a great day shared by Times readers, which includes both family and friends. I'll have more details and photos to share next week. The fun was for a good cause, benefiting the Visiting Nurse Association of Porter County.

This week, we salute inventor Fred Waring, whose musical claim to fame was leading his orchestra -- The Pennsylvanians -- and recording such popular radio hits as "Dancing in the Dark," also a hit for fellow bandleader Artie Shaw.

Waring, who would have been 109 last month, died July 24, 1984 at age 84.

His second claim to fame lives on in kitchens everywhere.

In 1937, Waring introduced the first working electric blender -- the "Miracle Mixer" -- at the National Restaurant Show in Chicago. The blender is more popular than ever, instantly recognizable with its cloverleaf glass carafe.

One of my favorite Fred Waring moments is an old black-and-white clip from the early days of television, which I show to students in my Introduction to Mass Media classes at Valparaiso University and Purdue.

Waring was a guest on TV personality Faye Emerson's 1949 show "The Faye Emerson Show," also called "Fifteen with Faye," since most TV shows then were only 15 minutes long. Sponsored by Pepsi Cola, Faye, then famous/infamous for her plunging necklines and divorce from FDR's son Elliott (and remarriage to bandleader Skitch Henderson), convinces Fred to use his blender to mix up a drink concoction featuring Pepsi, ice cream and bananas. While I can't detect any beverage passing through her brightly painted lips, Faye gushes about how good it is, shilling: "And remember friends, Pepsi has more bounce to the ounce than other sodas."

I may not sound as bubbly as Faye, but I guarantee that today's featured recipes, courtesy of Waring, are both easy and delicious.

Bandleader-turned-inventor was never very far from his multi-blade claim-to-fame patented electric blender.

ARTICHOKE HEARTS SPREAD

INGREDIENTS:

1 small can artichoke hearts (not marinated)

1 cup mayonnaise

1 cup Parmesan cheese, grated

1/2 teaspoon onion powder

1/2 teaspoon salt

1-1/2 teaspoon Worcestershire sauce

1 (16-ounce) jar marinated artichoke hearts, drained very well

Fred Waring's Favorite Artichoke Hearts Spread

- Blend first six ingredients together.

- Transfer to a bowl. Chop marinated artichokes. Stir in to first mixture.

- Place in refrigerator for 2-3 hours to let the flavors develop.

- Spread on Melba toast and serve, or, if desired, put toast with spread under the broiler until golden brown.

- Makes 5 cups of spread.

"Dancing in the Dark" Stuffed Mushroom Caps

- Place a few mushrooms at a time in blender to chop.

- Put in a bowl and continue until all mushrooms are chopped. Stop and scrape down sides occasionally.

- Next, place parsley, thyme, shallots and garlic in blender and run for 30 seconds.

- In a saute pan, melt the butter. Add mushrooms and parsley/thyme mixture to pan. Saute for 3-4 minutes.

- Add spinach and cook for 2 minutes more.

- Remove from heat and fold in Parmesan, bread crumbs, salt and pepper.

- Remove stems from large mushroom caps and throw away.

- Fill caps with stuffing and drizzle with olive oil.

- Sprinkle with Parmesan cheese, and bake in 350 degree oven for 20 minutes. Serve warm.

- Filling can be made a day ahead.

- Makes 24 mushroom caps.

STUFFED MUSHROOM CAPS INGREDIENTS:

15 mushrooms

1/4 cup parsley (no stems)

1 teaspoon fresh thyme

1 shallot

1 clove garlic

2 tablespoons butter

1/2 cup frozen spinach, thawed and drained

2 tablespoons Parmesan

2 tablespoons breadcrumbs

Salt to taste

Pepper to taste

Olive oil

24 large mushroom caps, for stuffing

Neighboring egg farmer Mr. Dolezal will be missed

August 5, 2009

Readers will recognize the Dolezal Family name from my columns and cookbooks throughout the years.

In addition to the small grocery store in our town run by Otto Dolezal, and years later, his son Duane Dolezal, my parents were always good friends with the Dolezal egg farmers just a few roads/country miles away from our own family farm.

Art Sr. and Jeanne Dolezal, both graduates of the Class of 1945 at our San Pierre High School, were close to my parents not only because we bought our eggs from them, but also their children were close in age to my own older brothers and sisters.

On June 15, 1989, we lost Jeanne.

And last week, Art Sr. died at age 82.

I joined my parents to attend the visitation and they also attended the funeral the following day, which was last Friday.

Jeanne's pie crust recipe is one of the "old stand-by" recipes from my column and cookbooks, that readers so often mention to me.

Art Dolezal is at the far right with his class of 1945, including Bud Royce, Peg Daly and Dorothy Hewitt (seated in middle).

A farmer all his life, he farmed corn and soybeans, and as the owner of Dolezal Farm Fresh Eggs, he had 19,000 chickens under his charge.

Even after Jeanne passed away, Art Sr. (and his cigars) would still usually attend my mom and dad's annual New Year's Eve Party at their home, along with all the other farmers and friends, like Ed and Lorraine Wappel, Pat and Bud Royce, Bill and Marie Skuderna and the Scamerhorns.

He was one of nine children (Frank, Mary, George, Rudy, Norbert, Benjamin, Arthur, Ann, and Joseph). Joe, the youngest, is now the only remaining member of Frank and Bessie's large farm family. In fact, Joe and wife Donna, who are featured in photos in my second cookbook, along with Donna's Mile-High Cocoa Chiffon Cake, still reside on the original family farm near our farm.

Art Sr. was a great basketball player while growing up. He was captain of the team and they won what was then called the Kankakee Valley Tournament in 1945.

Art and Jeanne's six children, Pat, Kay, Betty, Art Jr., Ruthie and Eddie, continue to carry on the strong faith and traditions of their parents.

The couple was very proud of all their children's accomplishments, including Dr. Betty Curtis' physician practice. She graduated from the University of Notre Dame and the Chicago College of Osteopathic Medicine.

Art also loved hearty farm meals, topped by his favorite dessert: blueberry or apple pie.

His favorite meal was roasted pork with dumplings and sauerkraut.

The Dolezal Family was kind enough to share Jeanne's easy dumpling recipe, created with her older sister Vivian) to feature this week.

Jeanne Dolezal's Potato Dumplings

- Add eggs to potatoes.

- Slowly add flour, while combining with potatoes to create a stiff, but not sticky, dough.

- Turn out dough onto a floured board. Knead the dough so it is completely firm, as if making bread dough.

- Divide the dough and roll into a log, approximately 2 inches in diameter.

- Cut into 1-1/2 inch slices and place in a large pot of boiling, salted water. Cook for about 20 minutes.

- Makes 3 dozen dumplings.

INGREDIENTS:

9 cups mashed potatoes or 3 cups of instant potato flakes with 2 cups of boiling water to make a stiff consistency

2 eggs, beaten

2 to 3 cups flour, approximately

1 teaspoon salt

Aunt Rose always favored dill's flavor

August 19, 2009

It's not often you find many full vegetable gardens in the hustle and bustle of a big city like Chicago.

Yard space, if any, is as my mom likes to describe it "the size of a postage stamp."

But my Aunt Rose and Uncle Joe always designated a portion of their "Tornado Fenced" backyard near their garage for a good-sized vegetable garden.

Uncle Joe, my dad's oldest brother in the large Polish family of nine Potempa children, realized the worth in being able to pick a ripe tomato from the vine or pull some green onions to have for cooking.

And even though all of my dad's siblings left the farm (except him, since he was the youngest and had to stay and help run the family farm) to find work in the city, they each took turns coming back to the farm to spend the weekends.

For Aunt Rose, that often meant taking additional vegetables, and sometimes,

Aunt Rose, shown visiting with my brother Tom's wife Linda in this July 1995 photo, always enjoyed her visits to the farm, for a chance to have a change of scenery and a slower country pace compared to the hustle-and-bustle of Chicago.

even seeds and herb plants, back to the city for their own garden.

One of Aunt Rose's favorite flavorings was dill.

She liked it on boiled and buttered steaming tiny new potatoes and with the ever-familiar cans of pink salmon she would buy and store on the wooden storage shelves in her basement pantry.

Today, even though Uncle Joe died in 1995 and Aunt Rose died in 2000, behind their raised ranch-style brick bungalow in the Polish neighborhood near Midway Airport on the southside of Chicago, there's still plenty of fresh dill weed (and it does really spread like a weed) and spearmint growing each year.

When I tried today's delicious recipe, given to me by my former food columnist friend Nora Rinehammer Edinger from my old stomping grounds - "The Vidette-Messenger," Valparaiso's newspaper until the early 1990s - I included some fresh dill as a flavor enhancer.

When Nora, who now lives in West Virginia, shared the recipe with me via our friend Ann Scamerhorn, here's what she had to say about this great salmon spread.

"Summer may be on the wane, but it's not too late for a beach picnic. Here's one recipe that can get you out to the lakeshore with a minimum of delay. It's easy summer fare as the spread begins with canned salmon, which is fully cooked. If it's used as a topping or with salad vegetables, there's no need to heat up one's kitchen. It also travels well a spread or pasta salad with a minimum of cooling. I served this flavorful mix with pasta during a recent visit with family to the Indiana Dunes. Add some other basic foods like bottled drinks (no glass on the beach, please), fresh fruit and a bare-bones dessert like brownies or chocolate chip cookies, and you have a light meal that is simple to pack up yet is a bit more elegant than sandwiches and chips," Nora said.

Nora includes the tiny bones in the salmon. However, I, following my own mother's lead, have always removed these bones, along with any skin when preparing my canned salmon for a recipe.

Nora's Lemony Salmon Spread

● Mix all ingredients together to form a smooth spread.

● NOTE: According to Nora, this means crushing the tiny salmon bones into the mix, a step best done with the fingers. "Icky," as Nora describes it, but she says "they provide a calcium boost in addition to salmon's overall heart healthiness." I see Nora's point, but personally, I prefer to remove any bones/skin. Serve mixed into cooked pasta, as a topping for baguette slices or other special breads or crackers, or stirred into a variety of salad ingredients.

● Makes 2 cups of spread.

INGREDIENTS:

1 (16 ounce) can red salmon, drained

1/4 cup olive oil

2 tablespoons apple cider vinegar

1 tablespoon lemon juice

1/2 teaspoon lemon zest (just the yellow part), minced

1 tablespoon chopped fresh parsley

1 tablespoon chopped fresh dill (optional)

1/8 teaspoon freshly ground black pepper

Saturday's salsa contest in Lowell is 'spice of life'

September 2, 2009

In a column a few years ago, I wrote about all the extra apples at our farm and how we shared them with Sister Shawn Mitchell and the nuns of St. Michael's Convent of Franciscan Sisters of the Sacred Heart in Schererville, Ind.

This year, my dad has been sharing an extra large bounty of tomatoes and squash with friends, neighbors and my co-workers, in addition to another convent of nuns in Gary, Ind. who enjoy the squash for soup and the tomatoes for stew, sauces, salsa and other dishes.

This weekend, I'll be in Lowell for part of the Labor Day weekend festivities. Tomatoes will be in the spotlight during a taste test of many different flavors of salsa and "chip dip" contest.

Last summer, I was in Crete, Ill., for a big salsa contest at Balmoral Horse Race Track , a competition which was only for restaurants.

But this Saturday, everybody has a chance to enter this free contest. There are two categories - the salsa group and the basic "chip dip" group. Entries can be dropped off anytime between 3 p.m. and 4:45 p.m. Saturday at "the big tent" in downtown Lowell, Ind. at the American Legion yard. Please remember, since many chip dips include sour cream or mayo, please properly chill and maintain the proper temperature of the salsa and dip until the judging, which is promptly at 5 p.m.

As for the rest of the Labor Day Weekend Festival activities, it all starts 4 p.m. to midnight Friday and then

When I think of classic entertainers, Steve Lawrence is always on my list of great talents. Here we are (sans Eydie) in October 2007 following the couple's performance in Aurora, Ill.

(Photo by Michael Berkos)

2 p.m. to midnight Saturday, followed by noon to 8 p.m. Sunday and then finishing Monday from 11 a.m. to 5 p.m.

Most of the events and activities will be based in the area of the tent and the Lowell American Legion, 108 1/2 E. Commercial Ave. There will be Texas Hold 'em, bingo and a fish fry on Friday evening. Saturday the American Veterans Motorcycle Riders Association will be on the grounds from 2 to 5 p.m. and this first salsa and dips recipe contest at 5 p.m. There will also be food, a beer tent, entertainment and a general "family day atmosphere" with old-time games and contests, tug of war, hula hoop and potato sack contests. The 56th annual kiddie parade is at 1 p.m. Sunday with fireworks on Sunday evening. And on Monday, celebrate and enjoy the oldest and longest running parade in our state at 10 a.m. with more than 100 units featured.

The Lowell folks tell me the first Labor Day celebration dates back to 1919, the year Lowell and area communities shared a parade to welcome home the WWI soldiers. This year, marks my first year attending and it also marks the 90th anniversary of this amazing parade.

This week, I'm sharing my own mother's delicious homemade salsa recipe, which has helped use up some of our sea of red ripening tomatoes at the farm. You can check some of our farm shots of the tomatoes ripening "here and there" with the online version of this week's column at nwi.com.

Peggy's Super Salsa

● Sterilize 9 pint canning jars, rings, lids and allow to dry.

● In a large stock pot, combine all ingredients and cook over a medium flame until mixture comes to a boil.

● Simmer 1/2 hour to 1 hour, until mixture begins to slightly thicken.

● Pour into jars and carefully seal and place in a boiling water bath for 8 to 10 minutes and then remove to clean towel to dry and for lids to seal.

● Store any remaining salsa in a air-tight container and refrigerate for table use.

● Makes 9 to 12 pints.

INGREDIENTS:

3 quarts chopped tomatoes, plum or Roma preferred

3 cups chopped onion

1 to 2 tablespoons fresh minced garlic (to taste)

4 hot jalapeño peppers, diced with seeds removed

1 small (3-1/2 ounce) can green chili peppers, diced

2 large (12 ounce) cans tomato paste

1-1/2 cups lemon juice

1 tablespoon salt

1 tablespoon sugar

1 rounded teaspoon black pepper

1 tablespoon cumin

2 teaspoons dried parsley

1 teaspoon chili powder (to taste)

1 teaspoon dried oregano

1 bunch fresh cilantro leaves, finely chopped

Like JoAnne Worley, Lowell's salsa contest is both sweet and spicy

September 9, 2009

If you happened to see Sunday's news story covering the Lowell, Ind. Labor Day Weekend Festival, you probably spotted some photos from my judging of the 90th annual event's first homemade salsa contest.

I was pleased there were 18 entries to judge for the competition, organized by Sue Peterson and the LowellChamber of Commerce.

Joining me on the judging panel was a "real" judge, as in Lowell Town Judge Thomas Vanes. The third evaluating palate for the event was Lowell Town Council President Phillip Kuiper.

Lowell's Laura Baiel came in first place with her Salsa del Norte, which includes peppers and tomatoes she fire-roasts. She describes her recipe as "the champagne of salsas."

Second place went to Lowell's Norb Shebish for his "Fiery Fruit Salsa." Terry Killem, of Lowell, earned third place with a traditional salsa and Lori Eenigenburg, of Cedar Lake, was fourth place with a delicious cherry-infused salsa.

I had never been to Lowell's annual Labor Day Weekend Festival, but felt very at home with the quaint small-town feel and plenty of food, music and neighborly chit-chat, much like my own farm town's community gatherings.

These scenes and the landscapes always remind me of the 1957 movie "Peyton Place," starring Lana Tuner, Hope Lange and Terry Moore, during the town's big Founder's Day Park Picnic and Parade, when folks are shown enjoying ice-cold watermelon, listening to barbershop quartets and sharing a feast of hot dogs and homemade pies served from checkered tablecloths.

And to make things even more special, this Labor Day weekend, on Sunday specifically, it was Lowell's show biz funny claim-to-fame JoAnne Worley's 72nd birthday. Comedienne Worley, usually draped in a boa with a scarf in her hair and best known as a regular on "Rowan and Martin's Laugh-In," was born and raised in Lowell.

I remember chatting with her a few years ago about her hometown.

"So have you been to Lowell lately?" Worley warbled during the telephone interview.

"You have?! Why on earth did you go there for?"

She was only joking and really loves Lowell, but said she doesn't "really have any close family left in that area."

"But I do still keep in touch with friends," she said.

"I almost came back there a couple of years ago for my high school reunion. But I had to go on tour with a new show I was signed on for. But Lowell is where I first became interested in acting and making people laugh."

Worley told me it was participating in the church choir with her sister in Lowell and starring in the annual Lowell High School talent show that gave her an early start at developing her voice.

"I used to pantomime a lot and sing along with songs while growing up," she said.

"I'll never forget the place I'd work every summer while in high school. It was called Robert's Hotel, Gas and Cafe and it was at the intersection of U.S. 41 and Hwy. 2. They had an old jukebox in the cafe where I worked and I'd sing and joke around whenever business was slow, which seemed like most of the time."

Laura's Salsa del Norte

- Grill the tomatoes and jalapeño directly over coals for 20 minutes, turning every five minutes.

- The skins will split and turn dark in spots. Cool slightly.

- Remove only the stem from the pepper.

- In a blender, purée the tomatoes and pepper with the rest of the ingredients.

- You can serve the salsa warm or cold. Many prefer it at room temperature.

- This salsa is best made a day before serving to allow flavors to meld.

- Refrigerate unused portions.

- Makes 8 cups.

SALSA DEL NORTE INGREDIENTS:

1-3/4 pounds Roma tomatoes, unpeeled

1/2 medium yellow onion, chopped

1/3 cup chopped fresh cilantro

1 large fresh jalapeño pepper

4 cloves fresh garlic

1-1/2 teaspoon salt

2 tablespoons white vinegar

Lori's Cherry Salsa

- Sterilize and prepare 10 pint jars with rings and lids.

- Mix and combine above mixture in a large saucepan.

- Bring to a boil for 20 minutes, stirring occasionally.

- Add cherry pie filling and continue boiling for another 10 minutes.

- Pour hot salsa into prepared jars and seal.

- Process in boiling water bath for 10 to 15 minutes.

- Makes 10 pints.

CHERRY SALSA INGREDIENTS:

2 quarts tomatoes, peeled and chopped

4 large jalapeño peppers, peeled and chopped

3 medium onions, peeled and chopped

2 large bell peppers, peeled and chopped

1 cup vinegar

2 tablespoons salt

1 teaspoon garlic salt

1 cup brown sugar

3 (6 ounce) cans tomato paste

1 (14 ounce) can diced tomatoes with mild green chilies

1 (15.5 ounce) can cherry pie filling

This weekend's holiday party includes a special recipe to Cher

December 16, 2009

A chance to get away from the holiday hustle and bustle of the season, even for just a couple hours, is a gift to cherish while enjoying a change of scenery.

Last week's Wednesday column, both my From the Farm recipe column and my daily Off Beat entertainment column gave some of the details for this weekend's holiday recipe sampling party I'm hosting at Lowell Public Library, in Lowell, Ind. on Saturday.

For any readers looking for a few hours of fun, this terrific holiday party celebrates "a salute to Christmases Past." As mentioned last week, one of the highlights I've managed to stumble upon to share is a true classic clip of the late Sonny Bono and then-wife Cher on their popular 1972 CBS variety show, featuring the couple talking and joking about the holidays, including Cher cracking a few jokes about having to cook for and entertain her hard-to-please mother-in-law, Sonny's traditional Italian mother.

Both of today's recipes are retro favorites and both will be served to guests on Saturday.

If you've ever wondered how the talented Cher stays so thin and still full of energy (besides the fact she's getting $60 million for her current three-year engagement deal at Caesar's Palace in Las Vegas), her recipe for "Cher's Tuna Pasta Salad" might be part of her secret. This recipe, which my late Auntie Lilly saved in her recipe file box years ago, has what she thought was an exotic seasoning ingredient called Beau Monde, which is really just a spice blend of celery seed, nutmeg, mace, bay leaf, cloves, cinnamon and ground pepper. But it really does add a nice zip.

As for Saturday's party, only 14 seats still remain.

Cher's Tuna Pasta Salad

- Prepare pasta according to package directions. Drain and set aside to cool.

- Stem tomatoes and turn over and cut an "X" in the skin.

- Blanch tomatoes in boiling water for 1 minute and rinse with cold water before peeling and dicing.

- In the bottom of a large bowl, mix drained tuna with mayonnaise.

- Add in diced tomatoes and pasta, along with diced celery and olives and toss.

- Add in seasonings and stir to blend and combine, adjusting seasonings as necessary according to taste.

- Makes 6 servings.

Salads, Side Dishes & Appetizers

INGREDIENTS:

1 (8-ounce) package pasta shells

2 medium tomatoes

1 (12-ounce) can white tuna, drained

1/4 cup mayonnaise

2 ribs of celery, finely chopped, including leaves

1 (4-ounce) can black olives, drained and diced

3 tablespoons minced parsley

3 tablespoons minced dill

Sprinkle of Beau Monde seasoning, to taste

Additional salt and pepper, to taste

You're invited to belated Valentine's salute to Brown Derby

January 13, 2010

As many readers have been asking, it's time for this year's Valentine's Day luncheon party at Teibel's restaurant in Schererville, Ind.

This was a very popular event that sold out quickly last year.

Next month's event will be a "belated Valentine's Day" gathering, on Sunday, Feb. 21, so mark your calendars.

I'll be hosting the full luncheon from noon to 3 p.m. in the large connected joining salon dining rooms at Teibel's, which will be converted for that afternoon into a tribute to the famed Hollywood Brown Derby Restaurant, including real plates, menus, photos and rare displays from the legendary Tinsletown haunt that closed in 1980. And yes, lots of chances to win wonderful prizes.

Seating is limited to 200 guests, with reserved seating at each of the 25 tables, which will seat eight.

Bob and Dolores Hope dining at the Brown Derby in 1957

Doors open at noon with lunch served at 1 p.m.

On the day of the luncheon, guests will be asked to pick from a choice of three main course entrees: Teibel's Fried Chicken or Beef Sirloin Tips or Teibel's Famous Boned and Buttered Lake Perch. Each will come with a dinner roll and cole slaw first course, and the entrees served with baby red potatoes, and a vegetable blend of young yellow summer squash, red peppers, onions and green zucchini. Each lunch also comes with choice of beverage, including coffee, hot tea, iced tea or milk.

For dessert, fresh vanilla ice cream will be served with the showcased recipe featured in my second cookbook: Gossip Columnist Louella O' Parson's Favorite Frosted Grapefruit Cake, which was a staple on the Brown Derby menu.

Luncheon tickets are once again $25 per person, which includes tax and tip. A portion of each ticket sold benefits one of my favorite nonprofit groups, The Caring Place, the Valparaiso shelter for victims of domestic violence.

Reservations are required by leaving name, contact telephone number and the number in your party attending.

Since I'm still in the midst of my Seattle Sutton diet plan, I'm featuring a very famous salad recipe for today's column.

It was in 1937 that Robert H. Cobb, the owner of Hollywood's Brown Derby restaurant, dreamed up his great menu idea.

Cobb went into the restaurant's kitchen to fix a late-night snack for Sid Grauman, a Hoosier claim-to-fame and the man who created Grauman's Chinese Theater.

He combed the refrigerator for what ingredients he could find and chopped them up finely, because Grauman was suffering from a terrible toothache.

Thus, the Cobb salad was born.

Brown Derby's Famed Cobb Salad

- To make dressing (makes a total of 1-1/2 quarts, great for marinades), blend together all ingredients, except the 2 types of oil.

- Using a whisk, add oils in a fine stream and blend. Set aside to chill.

- To prepare salad, cook bacon until crisp, drain and chop.

- Halve, peel and dice the avocados and sprinkle with salt and fresh lemon juice.

- Combine the greens and chop finely.

- Toss all ingredients together in a large bowl.

- Add 2 cups of Brown Derby French Dressing and toss.

- Makes 8 to 10 servings.

INGREDIENTS:

SALAD:

2 cooked chicken breasts, chopped

1 head iceberg lettuce

1 head Romaine lettuce

1 bunch of watercress

1 bunch of chicory leaves

4 tablespoons chopped chives

4 medium tomatoes, diced

2 ripe avocados

1 pound bacon

6 hard-boiled eggs, chopped

Finely grated Roquefort cheese, to taste

2 cups Cobb's Dressing (see recipe)

DRESSING:

1 cup water

1 cup red wine vinegar

1 teaspoon sugar

Juice of 1 lemon

1 tablespoon salt

1 tablespoon black pepper

1 tablespoon Worcestershire sauce

1 tablespoon dry English mustard

1 clove garlic, minced

1 cup olive oil

3 cups salad oil

Cheesy-Shrimp Puffs an easy, delicious quick fix appetizer

February 17, 2010

I'm always grateful to readers for their willingness to share favorite recipes to showcase to our Times readership.

And since today is Ash Wednesday, and for many folks, many meatless Fridays are in our future, I'm happy to share today's special treat, a recipe that is both delicious and easy.

If entertaining guests on a Friday evening, these golden wonders, served with a marble slab with your favorite cheeses, some assorted crackers and a nice, cold wine are sure to be a satisfying hit, without any worries of guilt.

I had the great fortune to sample these early last month at the 80th birthday party celebration in St. John, Ind. for a former editor's mother-in-law, Shirley Porch, who is the mother of one of our Times correspondents, Sue Bero.

Shirley's daughter, Mary Anne Caudle, of Dyer, Ind. who is Sue's sister, made her famous Cheesy-Shrimp Puffs, which are always out-of-this-world!

Here's the note from Mary Anne she included while sharing the recipe, which took a little pleading from me! Since we have plenty of fresh chives and dill at the farm, this recipe was made to order for my family's tastes.

"I would like to thank you again for taking the time to surprise my Mom, Shirley, at her birthday party! It was so great to see how shocked she was when you walked through the door with flowers. She is your biggest fan and sure does enjoy reading your columns! She will never forget her 80th birthday party, that's for sure!! Well, thank you again, and below is the recipe for the shrimp appetizer you enjoyed so much, in all its simplicity! I believe this recipe is all about the presentation, flaky phyllo, and the great 'hinted at' taste of a zesty shrimp cocktail, not to mention it is so easy to do. Again, our thanks, Mary Anne Caudle, Dyer, Ind."

Shirley Porch of St. John received a selection of surprises for her 80th birthday celebration.

Mary Anne's Easy Cheesy-Shrimp Puffs

- Bake phyllo cups per package directions for a bit of added crispness.

- In a medium bowl, whip cream cheese with enough cocktail sauce to make a good consistency.

- Add about 1-1/2 cups chopped mini shrimp.

- Drop by dollops into phyllo cups.

- Top with one full-size salad shrimp in arched fashion.

- Garnish with three spikes of chive in front of the shrimp.

- And sprinkle with small amount of dill weed or add a tiny sprig of fresh dill if desired.

- Makes 40 appetizers.

INGREDIENTS:

40 mini phyllo dough cups (available in any store)

1 (8-ounce) package cream cheese

2 cups tiny salad shrimp

1 (8-ounce) jar cocktail sauce

1 bunch of chives, cut into 1/2 inch spikes

Sprinkle of dry dill weed, or fresh sprigs, if preferred

Here's a great March 2010 meeting of two like minds, both who enjoy cooking. I exchanged cookbooks with actress Dawn Wells, who played Kansas farm girl Mary Ann Summers on "Gilligan's Island," and she added one of her custom Mary Ann dolls just for fun.

Birthday celebrations always a great event for Cubs baseball legends

March 10, 2010

Dutchie Caray, widow of the late, great Cubs announcer Harry Caray, knows how to celebrate a birthday in style.

If you read my Wednesday "From the Farm" column in our food section, then you know the name Ann Scamerhorn, the farmer's daughter down the road that I've known since diaper days.

On Monday, March 1, Dutchie and a roster of famous friends gathered at Chicago's Navy Pier for the opening of another new Harry Caray's restaurant and toast what would have been Harry's 96th birthday.

The last time I attended such an event, it was in late August 2007, when I surprised Ann with an invitation to Dutchie's 78th birthday party, a private event hosted in Lombard, Ill., at the newly opened "Harry Caray's Restaurant" location.

If you're keeping score, that time marked the third Harry Caray's Restaurant in the Chicago area, with the flagship restaurant still based downtown on Kinzie Street, just a baseball's throw from State Street.

These steakhouse restaurants, which boast unbelievably good food and reasonable prices, were the dream of late Chicago Cubs announcing legend Harry Caray, and his widow is not only keeping that dream alive, but she's also helping them to thrive.

Harry, who died at age 83 suddenly just days after suffering a massive heart attack on Valentine's Day 1998

It was loads of fun to be part of Dutchie Caray's August 2007 birthday bash, while also spending some time chatting with legendary Cubs announcer Steve Stone. However, there's no denying how much we all miss the late, great Cubs microphone legend Harry Caray!

(Photo by Michael Berkos)

at a restaurant near his Palm Springs home, opened the first restaurant in 1987.

The last time before Dutchie's big birthday event that Ann and I spent some time with the always-smiling and ever-gracious Dutchie was in March 2003, in the greenroom of Michael Essany's show, when she was a guest on the interview couch.

At her birthday event, Dutchie was feted by famous and everyday friends from near and far at her party, which included a custom-made 30-pound towering birthday cheesecake from Eli's, that served 150 people.

In addition to singing "Happy Birthday," guests, including Harry's longtime announcing partner Steve Stone, also joined Dutchie to sing "Take Me Out to the Ballgame," along with Harry's voice piped over audio speakers.

Dutchie has a wonderful recipe for a salad which features all of her favorite ingredients and it's even served in some of the Harry Caray restaurants.

In 2003, she even shared it with Jane and Michael Stern to include in their book "Recipes from The Harry Caray's Restaurant Cookbook (2003 Rutledge Hill Press).

INGREDIENTS:

CANDIED WALNUTS:

1 tablespoon butter

1 cup walnuts

1/4 cup brown sugar

1 tablespoon molasses

SALAD:

1 pound mesclun (mixed) greens

2 Granny Smith apples, cored and sliced

2 DíAnjou or Bartlett pears, cored and sliced

1 cup crumbled Gorgonzola cheese

3/4 cup raspberry vinaigrette

RASPBERRY VINAIGRETTE:

1/2 cup canola oil

1/2 cup raspberry wine vinegar

1/2 cup white sugar

1 tablespoon Dijon mustard

1/2 cup raspberries

3 tablespoons honey

3 tablespoons red wine vinegar

1/4 teaspoon dried oregano

Dutchie Caray's Favorite Raspberry Vinaigrette Salad

- To candy-glaze the walnuts, preheat the oven to 350 degrees.

- Melt butter in a saute pan over medium heat.

- Stir in the walnuts, brown sugar and molasses until the walnuts are thoroughly coated.

- Spread the sugar-coated walnuts on a cookie sheet.

- Bake for 10 minutes; set aside to cool.

- For the salad, mound the mixed greens in the center of six individual plates.

- Alternate sliced apples and sliced pears around the greens.

- Top the greens with the candied walnuts and Gorgonzola cheese.

- To make dressing, combine all ingredients in a food processor or blender and puree; refrigerate before using. (Makes 3 cups total).

- Drizzle prepared salads with raspberry vinaigrette.

- Serve immediately.

- Makes 6 servings.

St. Patrick's Day puts cabbage and other favorite Irish symbols in the spotlight

March 17, 2010

When I think of St. Patrick's Day, I always think of the big birthday party given for my columnist colleague Marge Kullerstrand that I attended when I first started working for The Times.

It was held in an Irish pub, and Marge, who writes our weekly society column, was all smiles about the surprise gathering.

Like Marge, I also share a love for St. Patrick's Day.

And since we're both Catholic, it's only natural, even though we're not technically Irish.

I think the symbolism of the day is one of the reasons it's so special.

Consider these origins:

• The harp - This stringed musical instrument is considered to be a genuine Irish emblem. It is represented on Irish coins, called doubloons, and on the green flag that preceded the present day tricolor.

• Shamrock - considered to be the religious symbol of the Holy Trinity (Father, Son and Holy Trinity), shamrock clover is valued on the Island of Ireland as the grazing resource that makes mutton fat.

• Four-leafed shamrock - Irish folklore says anyone who is fortunate to have "a four-leafed shamrock within his or her grasp will be graced with good luck and enchantment."

• Leprechaun - This name literally means "wee body" or "small one." According to Irish fables, leprechauns served as shoemakers to Ireland's fairies. Like many of the overworked shoemakers in Ireland centuries ago, leprechauns were said to be irascible and stingy. Always very wealthy, leprechauns are fabled to buy their freedom if captured by telling their captor where they have hidden their crock of gold.

• Banshee - This is the name given to the witches of Ireland, and a nemesis to leprechauns. Also called "the Irish mourner," she is said to stroll near homes and cottages wailing and lamenting while pulling at her hair (a sign of someone in grief.) Banshee are said to only pester those whose last name has a prefix of "O," "Mc" or "Mac."

• Saint Patrick - An Irish bishop and missionary who founded the first cathedral in Ireland in 444 A.D. He used a shamrock to explain The Holy Trinity while on missions. He died in 461 A.D..

And of course, there's all the wonderful food.

If a 2-pound brisket of corned beef boiling in the kitchen on St. Patrick's Day is enough to fill your home with an unmistakable aroma, imagine how far the drifting smell of 2,000 pounds of boiling corned beef will carry?

I remember my surprise while doing a favorite St. Patrick's Day interview in 1997.

Cooking 1 ton of corned beef was the norm each year for the kitchen staff at Finn McCool's Pub and Grill in Porter, Ind.

Owner Christopher May, who opened the pub in 1993, said he wanted to create a place with an Irish atmosphere of which his great grandmother would be proud.

"Finn McCool was a mythical character of fables," May told me, explaining how he settled upong that name.

"He was very similar to America's Paul Bunyan. He supposedly lived around 500 A.D. and protected the first king of Ireland."

May said he made it his mission to make the pub's surroundings as "authentically Irish" as possible, even using the pub fireplace to burn the official fuel of Ireland."

Rather than clearing trees from the island's rocky terrain, May said the Irish

Marge and Doug Kullerstrand love to cook. And during the past 10 years, they've also learned a few handy, healthy tricks for their menus without sacrificing flavor.

(Photo by Michael Berkos)

Salads, Side Dishes & Appetizers   275

burn "bricks" of peat moss.

He told me in 1997, that the last time friends of his made the trip overseas to "the country of green," they brought him back peat bricks for the pub's fireplace.

May said one of the things patrons enjoy the most about Ireland's offerings is the taste of the country's stout ales.

"We probably go through a couple barrels of Ireland's Guiness Stout beer every week," he said during that interview more than a decade ago.

"We sell even more of that than Killian's Red Beer. We're very particular about how we serve up our Guiness too. It's kept at a special temperature so it's served slightly warmer than most beers. And some special gases are also added."

And of course, there's always cabbage, which like potatoes, carrots and turnips, is a stable of Irish meals since these crops grow easily in the rocky soil.

Marge makes some of the most delicious cabbage and noodles I've ever tasted.

And when she adds some of my dad's fresh-picked mushrooms from his annual fall and spring mushroom hunts, this simple meal is a feast.

"When my husband, Doug, had a five-way bypass a few years ago, I had to learn to make some of our favorite foods healther," Marge said.

"Of course, you can also do the old-fashioned way with butter and bacon drippings as well. But with this healthier version, minus the bacon crumbles, but with mushrooms, makes it a Lenten favorite."

Happy St. Patrick's Day!

Marge's Basic Healthy Cabbage and Noodles

- Bring a large pot of lightly salted water to a boil.

- Cook the egg noodles in the boiling water until the pasta is tender yet firm to the bite, about 8 minutes. Drain.

- While the noodles cook, melt the margarine and olive oil in a large skillet over low heat.

- Add the onions, garlic and cabbage and, if desired, mushroms; season.

- Cover and cook until the cabbage wilts, 7 to 10 minutes.

- Stir the drained noodles into the cabbage.

- Serve warm with fresh crusty bread.

- Makes 8 servings

INGREDIENTS:

1 medium head of cabbage, shredded

1 large or 2 medium sweet onions, cut into strips

2 garlic cloves crushed or 2 teaspoons garlic powder

2 tablespoons of fat-free soft margarine (or butter equivalent)

2 tablespoons of olive oil (or bacon drippings, after frying 8 pieces of bacon to crumble later and add in if desired)

1 (16 ounce) package wide no yoke noodles (or your favorite wide noodle variety)

1 cup cleaned and rinsed sliced mushrooms (optional)

Mrs. Dash to taste

Fresh ground black pepper to taste

Easter bread and Polish eggs a blessed tradition

April 8, 2009

Like so many other families in our readership region, tonight begins my family's church schedule of services leading up to Easter weekend.

As a little boy, I always remember going to mass on the Wednesday before Easter and our priest referring to today as "Spy Wednesday," noted as such, because it marks the day before Christ's Last Supper (Thursday) when disciple Judas Iscariot made his deal with the chief priests and Pharisees to sell Jesus for 30 pieces of silver.

Legend had it when Judas took his life, he hung himself on a tree that is the spring flowering ornamental tree we refer to as a Redbud Tree, with blossoms that sprang forth from the barren tree following this final act of Judas.

For readers that faithfully read this column, most know that on Saturday, my family follows the Polish tradition of bringing our "swieconka" (Polish for Easter basket) filled with Easter foods and necessary ingredients to our church altar for our priest to bless.

Of course, always included in the contents are bread and eggs.

Reader Angie Cichon wrote me a letter last month requesting a recipe for the special twist bread with golden raisins so popular, especially this time of season:

Thank you for your letter and kind words Angie. I am familiar with your recipe request. I published the varied recipe for this bread, which we call Koloc, in this column April 7, 2004. You can find it in my original "From the Farm" cookbook that published in 2004. After many requests, I also published a second more traditional variation of the recipe in February 2005, which includes the addition of the sweet farmer's cheese topping, which can be found in my second "More From the Farm" cookbook from 2007.

For today's recipe, family farm friend Ann Scamerhorn was kind enough to invite me, along with Serbian friend Sanjin Bosnjak to attend a class for decorating old fashioned European Easter eggs, called Pisanki in Polish. The class, held at Nativity of Our Savior Catholic Church in Portage, was taught by the wonderful Theresa Child, of Valparaiso, who not only supplied all of the dyes and melted beeswax, but also her creativity and knowledge for this ages old art.

She was also kind enough to share her delicious recipe for egg salad, which will be even more valuable next week for any cracked eggs.

Theresa Child's Easter Egg Salad

- In a medium bowl, blend together mayonnaise, mustard and sour cream; mix in remaining ingredients.

- Serve chilled on warm, crisp toast.

- Makes 6 cups.

INGREDIENTS:

1/2 cup mayonnaise

1 teaspoon yellow mustard

1/4 cup sour cream

6 to 8 hard-boiled eggs, peeled and chopped

8 slim green onions, finely diced

1 rib of celery, finely diced

Salt and pepper, to taste

Game Show Great is also a great friend to many

April 28, 2010

Betsy Palmer's broad smile is as much of a television trademark as her girl-next-door charming personality.

The first time I met and interviewed Betsy was while we were both in Hollywood in July 2004.

When my interview with her ran the next weekend, it reported that the last time this television and movie star claim-to-fame from Northwest Indiana had returned to our region, it was in 1994 for an East Chicago Roosevelt High School 50-year class reunion.

This is a woman noted for many show biz accomplishments, including her long-standing role as a game show panelist on CBS' "I've Got A Secret" from 1957 to 1967.

Within five months, Betsy returned to Indiana to headline a production of the play "Love Letters" as an April 2005 local charity fundraiser.

Despite the name of the game show she made famous, she has no secrets of her own.

- About her age: "I'm really 83 years old. I was born Nov. 1, 1926. Many of the reference books say I was born in 1929, because when I was signed for my first movie studio contract with Columbia, I was 25, which they thought was too old."

- About her childhood home: "If you really want me to be perfectly honest, I grew up in a house in Hessville (section of Hammond, Ind.). I was right across the street from Harding Elementary School and I was friends

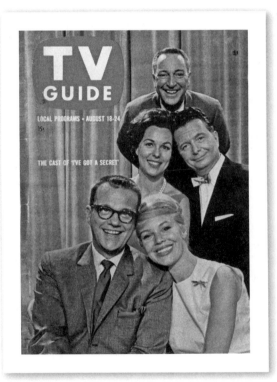

Betsy Palmer is shown with Bill Cullen, and Bess Myerson and Henry Morgan (middle) and Garry Moore (top).

with Jean Shepherd, who wrote 'A Christmas Story.' We both had the same teacher featured in the film, Miss Shields. When she was in the fourth grade, Palmer's family moved to East Chicago, Ind..

● About her real name: "The folks back home in East Chicago probably remember me by my real name: Patricia Betsy Hrunek. It doesn't just roll off the tongue like 'Betsy Palmer,' does it?"

Betsy, who had lived in Los Angeles for 20 years, moved back to New York City in the late 1990s.

Like fellow Hollywood Hoosier Karl Malden, who hailed from Gary, Ind., before stardom, Betsy also lined up a "Plan B" career. While Malden toiled in the Gary Steel Mills, Betsy attended East Chicago Business College.

"We called it ECBC and my mother was the woman who actually ran it for a number of years," she said.

But of all her unusual career stories, it was in 1979, while appearing in a Broadway play, when her career entered its newest and strangest chapter, a page on her resumé audiences might never have expected.

"My car was about on its last legs," Palmer said. "I had my eye on a Volkswagen that cost $9,999, but I wasn't ready to plop down that kind of cash for a car at that moment. Like fate would have it, I got a call from my agent asking if I wanted to do a new movie. As soon as he said it was a horror flick, I said 'no way.' I was already known for game shows. So I didn't want to also become typecast for scary movies, too."

The movie was about a murderous rampage at a summer camp carried out by a man wearing a hockey mask. Palmer was cast as the equally bloodthirsty mother of "Jason." The film was "Friday the 13th."

"It was 10 days of shooting in New Jersey, with me getting $1,000 a day," she said. "I said 'yes' to the project because it would get me the new car and I figured this was just some piece of junk film that no one else would ever see."

During the shooting of one particularly gory scene, Palmer asked her director about what has become a much-repeated part of Hollywood history: "Are you sure Bette Davis and Joan Crawford made their comebacks this way?"

For 20 years, Betsy was married to Dr. Vincent J. Marandino, a pediatrician and they have a daughter, Melissa, who is 47. And though a vegetarian, it doesn't mean she doesn't sometime prepare meat courses for her family and friends, including her mother's traditional German ham and noodle casserole.

She told me she got her famous gig on "I've Got A Secret" because the producers and the sponsor Winston Cigarettes wanted her to replace Faye Emerson, who they thought was "too political."

"I guess they thought I was just the opposite of her," Betsy said.

"And they figured I'd be a wholesome contrast for sophisticated Jayne Meadows and urbane Bess Myerson, who was a former Miss America, while being a balance to comedian Henry Morgan's dry humor and Bill Cullen's quick wit."

And a few times, she also filled-in for fellow "good girl" Arlene Francis on the equally popular CBS panel game show "What's My Line?."

I asked her what it was like working with New York City newspaper gossip columnist Dorothy Kilgallen, who was a regular on "What's My Line?" and died under mysterious circumstances in 1965.

"I didn't know Dorothy as well, and she was rather aloof," Betsy said.

As for Joan Crawford, who was also a close New York friend of Kilgallen's, with both sharing legendary P.J. Clark's as a favorite haunt, Betsy first met Joan while starring opposite her in the 1955 Columbia film "Queen Bee."

keyed to Curiosity

Since it was Betsy's recipe printed first at the front chapter of this book, it's seems made-to-order that her recipes be the lead for the last final chapter, including a parade of selections from famous friends.

Betsy's Shank and Flanken (Ham and Noodle Casserole)

- Cook noodles in boiling water following package directions.

- Butter the bottom and sides of a 9-inch by 13-inch baking pan and set aside.

- Place on tablespoon butter in a large skillet and add anchovy filets, cooking until dissolved. Add the cooked noodles to the skillet and toss for a minute or two, just to coat.

- Pour noodles into a large mixing bowl and add in cubed ham and beaten eggs and mix to coat. Pour mixture into prepared casserole and bake in a 350 degree oven for 30 minutes or until golden brown. Remove from oven and allow to cool slighting and serve by slicing into squares.

- Makes 12 servings.

BETSY'S SHANK & FLANKEN INGREDIENTS:

1 pound flat egg noodles

1 tablespoon butter

1 or 2 anchovy filets

3 eggs, beaten

3 cups "sweet meat," or any unsmoked ham/pork, preferably pork butt roast, cubed

Karl Malden's Sarma Recipe
(Serbian Stuffed Cabbage)

- In a large bowl, make filling by combining both ground meats with garlic, onion, bullion, black pepper, paprika and rice. Add just a little of the chili sauce to filling, to make it moist and a little sticky.

- Prepare cabbage by coring centers of each head and removing and separating leaves, also removing the hard vein from back of larger leaves. Cook in simmer water, with the vinegar added, until leaves are soft and pliable, but not soggy. Cool slightly, enough to handle.

- If desired, line the bottom of a large Dutch oven with a layer of sauerkraut. Place 2 tablespoons of filling into each cooked leaf and roll up and fold in ends, so tightly wrapped. Line pot with cabbage rolls and if desired, use remaining sauerkraut to cushion between rolls.

KARL MALDEN'S SARMA INGREDIENTS:

1-1/2 pounds ground chuck

1/2 pound ground pork

2 cloves garlic, crushed

1 large onion, chopped fine

1 beef bullion cubed, dissolved in 1/4 cup warm water

Black pepper to taste

1-1/2 teaspoons paprika

1-1/2 cups uncooked rice

2 heads cabbage

1/4 cup vinegar

1 large (16 ounce) jar sauerkraut, rinsed (optional)

1 large (20-ounce) can tomato soup

1(12-ounce) bottle chili sauce

1 teaspoon sugar

Sour cream garnish

- Combine tomato soup with remaining chili sauce and sugar to make a sauce and pour over cabbage rolls.

- Cook covered on stove over low flame for 45 minutes or bake covered in 350 degree oven for 45 minutes.

- Serve each roll, coated with some sauce and with a dollop of sour cream.

- Makes 20 cabbage rolls.

Joan Crawford's Flavorful Boiled Chicken Breast

BOILED CHICKEN BREAST INGREDIENTS:

1 skinless chicken breast

1 medium onion, sliced

2 large carrots, sliced

2 stalks celery, sliced

1/2 teaspoon kosher salt

1/4 teaspoon black pepper

1 bay leaf

● In a medium sauce pan add whole chicken breast and all prepared vegetables and seasonings to pot, adding enough water to cover contents.

● Bring contents to a boil and then simmer for 10 minutes or until chicken breast is cooked through and vegetables are tender.

● Remove chicken and allow to cool slightly, before serving on the bed of drained vegetables, with a little cottage cheese as preferred side.

● Makes 1 serving.

Joan with Colonel Sanders in 1968, while she served on the board of directors for Pepsi Cola Co.

Bill Cullen's Cheese Souffle

● Butter a 1 1/2 quart souffle dish and set aside.

● Using a double boiler, melt butter. Blend in flour and then stir in milk and seasonings. Remove from heat.

● Immediately beat in the egg yolks, one at a time, alternating with adding in cheeses, a little at a time.

● Return to double boiler and stir until cheese is melted and mixture is smooth. Remove from heat and allow to cool slightly.

● Beat egg whites until stiff and fold into cheese mixture.

● Pour into a prepared souffle dish, leaving about 2-inch of space from the top for baking.

● Served topped with favorite basic white sauce recipe (simply, a little milk with butter, heated to bubbling in saucepan, with a sprinkling of flour to thicken), that's been flavored with a little Dijon mustard.

● Makes 4 servings.

CHEESE SOUFFLE INGREDIENTS:

3 tablespoons butter

3 tablespoons flour

1 cup milk

1/2 teaspoon salt

4 egg yolks

1/2 cup Swiss cheese, crumbled

1/2 cup Sharp Cheddar, crumbled

5 egg whites

Pinch of cayenne pepper

Further From the Farm

Jayne Meadows' Gingered Beef

- Cut flank steak diagonally against the grain into thin 3-inch by 1-1/2 inch strips.

- Combine salt, egg white and 1 tablespoon cornstarch.

- Heat peanut oil in wok or skillet until very hot.

- Dip beef strips in the egg coating and deep fry beef half very quickly in hot oil for barely 1 minute. Remove beef strips.

- Drain off all but 2 tablespoons oil from wok. Reheat the 2 tablespoons peanut oil and deep fry ginger, red pepper and green onion for 1 minute.

- Combine soy sauce, Hoisin sauce, chicken stock and remaining 1 teaspoon cornstarch in small bowl; pour into wok along with the cooked vegetables and return the cooked beef as well. Stir fry 30 seconds, adding sesame seed oil and heating through quickly, stirring.

- Serve at once over hot cooked rice or Chinese noodles.

- Makes 4 servings.

GINGERED BEEF INGREDIENTS:

1 pound flank steak, trimmed

1 teaspoon salt

1 egg white

1 tablespoon plus 1 teaspoon cornstarch (divided use)

2 to 4 cups peanut oil

1/3 cup julienned strips of preserved ginger

1/4 cup julienned red pepper

1 green onion, sliced diagonally

1 tablespoon dark soy sauce

2 tablespoons Hoisin sauce

1/4 cup chicken broth

1 tablespoon sesame seed oil

Hot cooked rice or Chinese noodles

Jayne and Steve Allen Wedding Day 1954.

Phil with Jayne and her son Bill Allen in L.A. in March 2005.

Henry Morgan's Blueberry Buttermilk Pancakes

● In a small mixing bowl, combine flour, baking soda and salt.

● In a slightly large mixing bowl, whisk together the eggs with buttermilk and melted butter. Gradually stir in the dry ingredients until blended.

● Heat a little oil in a large skillet or use a greased griddle and ladle 1/4 cup of batter per pancake. Immediately drop several berries on eat pancake as it cooks. When bubbles begin to form around berries, flip pancake and cook until both sides are golden, about 2 to 3 minutes per side. Serve immediately with warm maple syrup.

● Any remaining batter can be refrigerated for up to three days.

● Makes 24 pancakes.

BLUEBERRY PANCAKES INGREDIENTS:

3 cups flour

1 tablespoon plus 1/4 teaspoon baking soda

1/2 teaspoon salt

4 eggs

2 cups buttermilk

6 ounces butter, melted

1 pint blueberries

Warm maple syrup

LIVER PATE SPREAD INGREDIENTS:

1 pound chicken livers

4 tablespoons chopped onions

3 tablespoons vegetable oil

2 hard-boiled eggs, mashed

Salt and pepper to taste

Pinch of cinnamon

Pinch of poultry seasoning

Bess Myerson's Liver Pate Spread

● Saute onions in oil until soft and add liver, cooking gently until done.

● Combine liver and onion mixture with eggs in a food processor, along with seasonings and process until smooth, adding a little more oil if needed if additional moisture is needed.

● Served chilled as a spread on club-style crackers or if used as an appetizer, serve small amounts on lettuce leaves.

● Makes 4 servings.

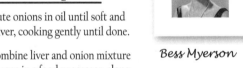

Bess Myerson

Miss Kilgallen's Favorite Vodka Tonic

● Fill highball glass with ice.

● Pour in vodka over ice.

● Add tonic water and garnish with lime.

● Cheers!

VODKA TONIC INGREDIENTS:

3 ice cubes

2 ounces premium imported vodka

4 ounces tonic water

1 lime wedge

DATE DROP COOKIES
INGREDIENTS:

1/2 cup shortening

3/4 cup brown sugar

1 egg

1 teaspoon vanilla

2 cups sifted enriched flour

2 teaspoons baking powder

1/2 teaspoon salt

1 cup sliced dates

1/4 cup milk

Arlene Francis' Date Drop Cookies

- Preheat oven to 350 degrees.

- In a mixing bowl, blend shortening sugar, egg and vanilla.

- In another bowl, combine flour, baking powder and salt and stir in dates.

- Add the date mixture, alternately, with milk, to the shortening mixture.

- Drop cookie batter by the teaspoon onto greased cookie sheet and bake for 12 minutes or until done.

- Makes 2 dozen cookies.

Fellow "What's My Line?" game show panelist Faye Emerson looks amused in this 1958 photo with fellow celebrity panelist Arlene Francis sporting an eye patch featuring the CBS network "eye" logo.

Recipe Index

NOTE: Roman numeral page numbers indicate the color insert in the middle of the book.

People Index